Byculla to Bangkok

S. Hussain Zaidi is a veteran of investigative, crime and terror reporting. He has worked for *The Asian Age*, *Mumbai Mirror*, *Mid-Day* and *The Indian Express*. His previous books include bestsellers like *Black Friday*, *Mafia Queens of Mumbai* and the more recent *Dongri to Dubai: Six Decades of the Mumbai Mafia*, and *Headley and I*. Zaidi is also associate producer for the HBO movie, *Terror in Mumbai*, based on the 26/11 terror strikes. He lives with his family in Mumbai.

Byculla to Bangkok

S Hussain Zaidi is a veteran of investigative, crime and terror reporting. He has worked for The Asian Age, Mumbai Mirror, Mid-Day and The Indian Express. His previous books include bestsellers like Black Friday, Mafia Queens of Mumbai and the more recent Dongri to Dubai: Six Decades of the Mumbai Mafia, and Headley and I. Zaidi is also associate producer for the HBO movie, Terror in Mumbai, based on the 26/11 terror strikes. He lives with his family in Mumbai.

Byculla to Bangkok

S. HUSSAIN ZAIDI

HarperCollins *Publishers* India

First published in 2014 by
HarperCollins *Publishers* India

Copyright © S. Hussain Zaidi 2014

ISBN: 978-93-5136-225-8

2 4 6 8 10 9 7 5 3 1

S. Hussain Zaidi asserts the moral right
to be identified as the author of this work.

The views and opinions expressed in this book are the author's own and
the facts are as reported by him, and the publishers are not in
any way liable for the same.

HarperCollins *Publishers*
A-53, Sector 57, Noida, Uttar Pradesh 201301, India
77-85 Fulham Palace Road, London W6 8JB, United Kingdom
Hazelton Lanes, 55 Avenue Road, Suite 2900, Toronto, Ontario M5R 3L2
and 1995 Markham Road, Scarborough, Ontario M1B 5M8, Canada
25 Ryde Road, Pymble, Sydney, NSW 2073, Australia
31 View Road, Glenfield, Auckland 10, New Zealand
10 East 53rd Street, New York NY 10022, USA

Typeset in 11/14 Adobe Caslon Pro
by Jojy Philip, New Delhi 110 015

Printed and bound in India by Thomson Press India Ltd.

For Velly
and
my sons Ammar and Zain,
the centre of my universe

Author's Note

Byculla to Bangkok completes my previous book, *Dongri to Dubai* (D2D), which chronicled the Mumbai mafia and its tryst with the city in the last six decades. D2D concentrated on Dawood Ibrahim's exponential rise from a street thug to a global ganglord and the people around him who contributed to his growth, including Haji Mastan, Karim Lala, Bashu Dada, Varadarajan Mudaliar and other criminals of the era.

While writing *Black Friday*, my first book, I had keenly felt the absence of any literature on the Mumbai mafia. When D2D finally emerged in 2012 after seven years of gruelling and intensive research, I found that much had been left unsaid. While D2D spoke of Dawood and his predecessors, I had left out the sons-of-the-soil (if I may borrow the late Bal Thackeray's favourite buzzword). The Mumbai mafia lore is incomplete without the inclusion of the local lads – those from the mill heartlands who were born in Byculla, Parel, Lalbaug and got sucked into the vortex of the socio-economic quagmire that kept the poor in a circle of poverty for generations. As we remodel south-central Mumbai into a Manhattan, we have to remember that we have failed to redress the issues that once drew promising young men to a life of crime. No city can grow unless there is a concomitant growth of its denizens. The transformation of the mill lands into a swank upper-crust module has left thousands of young men from these areas in the red. The malls are no compensation, as they are filled with restless young men who work twelve hours a day with hardly any job security or personal growth. Thus the stories of the first batch of wayward youth who became gangsters are relevant even today and are also inextricably linked to the social history and map of the city.

Chhota Rajan, Arun Gawli, Amar Naik, Ashwin Naik, Suresh Manchekar, Sunil Sawant, D. K. Rao and so many other boys grew up at a time when money was scarce and opportunities limited. Save for a handful of survivors, all the rest were killed in police encounters. Their story runs parallel with that of the degradation of the Mumbai police force. Until the early nineties, the Mumbai police by and large had some credibility. But with the onset of 'encounters', they became pawns in the hands of politicians. Political parties that had initially patronized the mafia marked them out in a use-and-throw policy.

The only redeeming aspect of these encounters was that fewer local boys dared to step out of line.

In this book, I have not dealt with several events already elaborated upon in D2D, for example the J.J. Hospital shootout or Chhota Rajan's assassination attempt in Bangkok. Those and other incidents have been comprehensively covered in the earlier book. It is also not possible to chronicle the entire history of Mumbai's Maharashtrian mafia in a few hundred pages. However, I have chosen those stories and narratives that form the crux of their rise and decline to provide a perspective to readers who want to know more about the mafia landscape of Mumbai.

Prologue

The police cruiser was racing along at breakneck speed. The plainclothes men from crime branch unit VII were anxious, uncertain as they were about this operation.

They were chasing three occupants of a Neptune-blue Maruti-Suzuki 800, the car of choice for most Indians from the moment it hit the roads in 1983. The Mumbai mafia loved the little car; it was easy to manoeuvre when the police were hot on their heels.

In the back was a man called Chandrakant Talwalekar. The two men in the front seat were considered to be Mumbai's most ferocious hitmen: Subhash and Ganesh Kunchikurve. Together, they were known as the Makadwala brothers. Their community is known for broom- and basket-making and training monkeys for roadside shows, hence the moniker Makadwala. The Makadwala compound in Dharavi, in south-central Mumbai, is inhabited by the Kunchikurves, a simple community considered incapable of doing what these renegades were about to do. The notorious Subhash Kunchikurve wielded not a broom but an AK-56. This at a time when Mumbai had not even heard of automatic machine guns; the Mumbai police were still struggling with their outdated self-loading rifles (SLRs) from the 1940s.

The Makadwala brothers were part of the hunter-gatherer Yerukala community, which had been forced out of the caste system after it lost the right to a livelihood; the hunting and gathering of forest produce had been banned in 1878. They were from Andhra Pradesh, Karnataka and Tamil Nadu, and in the north, they were related to the Bhils and the Kiratas. The British had declared them a criminal tribe in 1935. They were among fifteen communities branded in this manner, with the result that they had to report to the police station every time their settlements moved from one place to another. They spoke two languages – one within the community, which had secret codes, and another with outsiders.

In the 1930s, the community migrated to Mumbai and several of them settled in Dharavi, in what is now called the Makadwala compound. The women of the community were said to be good at fortune-telling. But fortune-telling in Mumbai did not take off as they had expected, and they took their place at the margins again, making brooms, weaving baskets and training monkeys. The Yerukalas were such precise, expert hunters that they could easily nail a running animal or a flying bird; the Makadwala brothers' skill as sharpshooters was taken for granted.

Subhash Makadwala was part of the group led by Anil Parab, who was Dawood Ibrahim's trusted aide. Subhash had a record of more than twenty-five murders, most of them executed with a ruthless spray of AK-56 bullets. Mumbai was used to high-profile killings, daylight murders, executions by the mafia. But the use of the Russian-made Kalashnikov assault gun in a civilian killing chilled the blood of even the most hardened police officers.

Subhash walked around with his AK-56 just as people walk around with their umbrellas during the monsoon. He carried it with him everywhere. When he went to a beer bar, he kept the gun on the table. His close aides were terrified of both the gun and its owner: Subhash was known to open fire indiscriminately, at the slightest provocation.

The terror the Makadwala brothers evoked had spread amongst Mumbai's business community. Builders, hoteliers, share brokers, film producers, distributors and even actors were threatened, tortured and exploited by them. Subhash was especially notorious. A buxom Pakistani actress who sang with a nasal twang was the hapless recipient of his attentions – and the victim of his baser instincts. The gangster sexually exploited the Bollywood diva for a considerable period, and it is said that he made her sing each time before raping her. She was so terrified that she could not even muster up the courage to lodge a formal police complaint against him.

The Mumbai police were reduced to mere spectators in the face of Makadwala's terror spree. The impotence of the police and their adherence to the basic police credo of 'qayeda mein fayeda' (the benefits of following the law) had so emboldened Subhash Makadwala that he boasted that no one but the Special Operations Squad (SOS) could touch him, let alone arrest or kill him.

And this was one such attempt. The Bandra unit of the crime branch had received information that Subhash and his men were about to exit a flat at Amrut Nagar in Ghatkopar, in the north-eastern suburbs of Mumbai – and had sprung into action.

Within seconds, Inspector Shankar Kamble was on the phone with Additional Commissioner of Police (ACP) Hasan Ghafoor, who was with the crime branch, for consent to raid the flat. Ghafoor's response, full of grit and purpose, was: 'Get Makadwala, dead or alive'. It was 6 May 1993, the city was still reeling from the serial blasts of 12 March and Ghafoor had sworn to uproot the mafia menace from the city. The directive was to cost him dearly.

But the order was a shot in the arm for the disparate group of seasoned plainclothes officers who immediately left for Amrut Nagar. Kamble had shown great presence of mind by assembling a rag-tag team of officers who were willing to take risks. Eventually, this team went on to become Mumbai's top encounter specialists.

Sub-inspectors Vijay Salaskar and Pradeep Sharma were part of the team. Salaskar took the wheel and Sharma cradled a .9 mm carbine on his lap as he took the seat next to Salaskar.

Bravado aside, they were unsure whether they would come back on their feet or on a stretcher. Before leaving their offices, they all called home nervously and spoke to their wives and children, without letting on anything about their destination or explaining the sudden burst of affection.

As the police cruiser arrived at the building, they saw the blue Maruti leaving the building premises. Caught at last!

Salaskar recognized Subhash immediately and tried to block his exit, though wary of Subhash's infamous AK-56. The driver of the Maruti 800 gave the police the dipper. Salaskar ignored it.

The driver immediately reversed the car, turned and straightened it with amazing dexterity, wheels screeching loudly in protest, and began to climb the steep slope of Amrut Nagar, in the opposite direction.

It was Salaskar's turn to display his skill as a driver. He revved the engine, almost standing on the accelerator, and jumped ahead of the other car. Both vehicles were now racing, sides bumping against each other in the dark night. Amrut Nagar was yet to be developed at the time, and the infrastructure was still in a shambles. The roads did not even have streetlights, so both vehicles kept grinding up against each other.

Salaskar shouted to Pradeep Sharma to shoot through the windscreen, instructing him not to lean out of the window as he did so. Sometimes a delay of nanoseconds at a time like this could drastically influence the outcome of an operation.

Suddenly, the wheels of the Maruti 800 screeched loudly and the vehicle crashed into a tree. Subhash grabbed his AK-56 and his bullets shattered the windscreen of the police jeep. This was the decisive moment.

The night was rent with the sound of incessant gunfire as Sharma acted swiftly and fired his carbine. It was a do-or-die moment for the police team.

Salaskar and Kamble drew their .38 weapons and fired round upon round on the sharpshooters, praying that they would find their mark before the gangsters did. Soon, silence reigned in the other camp. At long last, victory! The crime branch cops had managed to eliminate Mumbai's most wanted gangsters.

Though the skirmish was over in a matter of seconds, it seemed like an eternity for the police party. Two AK-56 guns and an abundance of magazines, pistols and grenades were found in the boot of the car.

The police department heaved a collective sigh of relief. The worst was over. Or, was it?

The killing of the Makadwalas had drawn the curtains on another chapter in the history of the mafia in Mumbai. Members of the business community burst crackers and organized a feast. The newspapers were full of panegyric reports the next day and the media hailed Sharma and Salaskar as heroes.

Hasan Ghafoor was elated at the success of his men and wanted to felicitate the bravehearts who had risked their lives in such a fashion. The next day, he summoned them to the police headquarters so that he could present them to the police commissioner for due praise.

For the officers of sub-inspector rank, appreciation and encouraging words from the police commissioner are no less than a gold medal in the Olympics. So, when Ghafoor called to say he wanted them to meet Police Commissioner Amarjeet Singh Samra, the police party was charged with anticipation.

Samra was an upright cop and his tenure in the IPS had witnessed zero controversy. During the communal riots of 1992-93, when the whole country burnt and blood was spilt on the streets, Thane had remained peaceful and registered no incidents of communal discontent. It was this sterling track record that had earned him the job of Mumbai police chief. Within days of taking charge, however, he had come up against the enemy force in an unprecedented manner: the city suffered one of the most horrific attacks on it, on 12 March.

Muslim police officers in the force, regardless of their rank, were demoralized by the blasts. They were embarrassed and ashamed of the handiwork of the terrorists who masqueraded as good Muslims. Ghafoor, a Muslim himself, had gone through personal hell and was at a loss to explain the heinous acts that stigmatized a whole community.

Ghafoor hoped the Makadwala encounter would bolster the

sagging confidence of the police force. But he did not know what lay in store for him when he led the police team to the commissioner's office on the first floor of the main building.

He knocked and entered the cabin, followed by his team of police officers, who formed a row and gave Samra a stiff salute. The turbaned Sikh cop looked up at Ghafoor curiously, asking who the men were and what had brought them there. Ghafoor said, with a mixture of pride and diffidence, 'Sir, these officers were successful in getting Makadwala. I thought you would want to see them and commend them on their good work.'

What happened next had Ghafoor reeling. The usually cool-headed Samra sprang to his feet and shouted, 'What the hell! Why have you brought them here? I don't want to meet these killers. Ask them to get out of here. Out!'

Kamble, Salaskar, Sharma and the others looked at each other and rushed to the door. They stopped only at the reception, where they waited for Ghafoor to join them. None of them uttered a word until they saw a flustered Ghafoor emerging from the office of the police commissioner, beads of sweat and worry lines on his face.

'The commissioner said one of the three men killed in the encounter had no criminal record. He is upset about his death,' Ghafoor tried to explain his boss's fury.

Kamble, considered to be one of the most blunt and outspoken officers of the Mumbai police force, showed remarkable patience when he told Ghafoor, 'Sir, when someone opens fire at us and we are in danger of being killed, we cannot wait to check the person's criminal record. We retaliate to save our lives. And these men were with Makadwala. For us, each of them was as dangerous as Makadwala was.'

Ghafoor nodded. But as he turned to leave, he said, 'He does not want any more encounters.'

He walked away. The much anticipated success party had ended in an anticlimax, throwing another pall of gloom over the crime branch.

Soon, Hasan Ghafoor was shunted out of the crime branch, apparently for administrative reasons, and posted at the nondescript Anti-Corruption Bureau.

Two police officers, though, were unperturbed by these developments: Vijay Salaskar and Pradeep Sharma. They continued to work in the crime branch and nursed other plans – known only to the two of them.

ONE

The Emperor of Aurangabad Jail

Mumbai's most ferocious ganglord-turned-MLA, Arun Gawli, was convicted by a special MCOCA (Maharashtra Control of Organised Crime Act) court on 12 August 2013 and sentenced to life imprisonment for the murder of former Shiv Sena corporator Kamlakar Jamsandekar. Jamsandekar had been shot dead in March 2008, at his residence in suburban Ghatkopar.

Gawli was accused of having paid Rs 30 lakh to his men to kill Jamsandekar over a dispute regarding a piece of land. He and eleven others were found guilty by the court.

The court sent Gawli to jail for twenty years: ten for being a member of a murderous, organized crime syndicate and ten for extortion. While delivering the judgment, judge Prithviraj Chavan said, 'Instead of death, I am giving you life imprisonment.'

Arun Gawli's conviction set me thinking about his power and considerable clout back in the nineties, something I had personally witnessed during my first meeting with the gangster. This was in the confines of Harsul Jail in Aurangabad, in 1996.

Harsul is one of the largest jails in Maharashtra, and Gawli and his gang had found themselves cooling their heels there and eating spicy Aurangabad curry; it was the only place they could rest without crossing swords with other mobsters owing allegiance to other bosses.

At the time, I was barely two years into the profession and was accompanied by my wife Velly Thevar, by then an established crime

8

reporter. We took the overnight train from Mumbai to Aurangabad for the meeting, which had been set up by Gawli's aide-de-camp, Santosh.

The trigger for the interview was my amazing boss, Sai Suresh Sivaswamy, at the time the editor of the newly launched Express Newsline. The idea of a city pull-out edition along with the mother brand was just catching up. Bombay Times, unlike its tame avatar now, was posing a challenge to readers of its main newspaper, the *Times of India*, and in response, both the *Asian Age* and the *Indian Express* had launched their own city editions: The Mumbai Age and Newsline respectively.

Sai and I hit it off instantly. Unlike other editors, he did not bark out instructions but threw out challenges instead. 'Dum hai toh jaa Gawli ka interview jail me karke dikha (If you have the courage, go and get an interview with Gawli in jail)', he said to me. And so I set off brazenly for Aurangabad, unsure whether I would bag the interview in the first place and wondering how the hell I was to circumvent jail regulations.

I first landed at Dagdi Chawl to get a contact from the gang, and finally got introduced to Santosh. I was so naïve that when he asked, 'Daddy ko milna hai,' I actually thought he was asking whether I wanted to meet his father instead of Gawli. Santosh laughed and clarified: 'Mere daddy ka interview lene upar jaana padega!'

The meeting was set up. At the Harsul compound, we did not flaunt our press cards. Velly was essentially a reporter and I must say I have not seen a journalist quite like her. While I was waiting for my contact to appear and take me inside the jail for the interview, she was already walking around and listening to the stories of the people sitting on their haunches inside the compound.

She later told me, with much regret, that she had witnessed an amazing sight and, for the first time in her life, felt she had failed as a journalist. She had met an old man waiting with impatient eyes and an obvious eagerness for somebody. When she checked with the cops, they told her that the man had just come out of jail after spending almost a lifetime there. Velly tried to talk to him, but he was too preoccupied. Finally, after what seemed like hours, a frail old lady in a nauvari (nine-yard) sari wrapped in the traditional Maharashtrian style stepped out from the women's section of the prison. The man ran to her and they hugged and cried like young lovers.

Velly was moved but did not feel like disturbing their reunion. Also, she was too worried about what I was up to inside the jail to chase the couple for a story.

Velly's concern was not misplaced. Unlike her, I was a rookie. I was only twenty-seven years old and had never seen the inside of a jail except in Hindi movies. Harsul was an awe-inspiring fortress, swarming with security personnel, and I was very anxious about the interview.

While everybody else was frisked, my contact and I seemed to have escaped the guards' attention. After passing unchecked through several big halls and labyrinthine corridors, we were finally led into a large room. It was sparsely furnished, with only two chairs and a bench. The police officer who had led me and my contact into the room said, 'Please wait here. Daddy will come in a while.' I was flabbergasted. Why was a khaki-clad officer referring to Arun Gawli as Daddy?

We waited for Gawli to appear. After a few minutes, we heard the clanging of a big iron gate and light footsteps like those of a woman or a child. We looked up and saw a thin, puny man, less than 5 feet tall, frail but neatly dressed in a starched white kurta and pyjamas, a Nehruvian cap completing his attire. The man could pass for one of Mumbai's iconic dabbawallahs, except for his slight frame. He was clean-shaven, with a neatly trimmed Kamal Haasan-style moustache and well-oiled hair, and flanked by two cops who seemed to be melting in awe of him. He did not look like a prisoner. Gawli appeared well-dressed, comfortable and perfectly at home.

The mediator announced in a reverential tone, 'Daddy aa gaye.' Daddy has arrived.

I had to conceal my shock. I had seen photographs of the man, but nothing had prepared me for this. After having been fed a diet of Hindi film villains with their larger-than-life personas – booming voice and broad shoulders – this was an anticlimax. But his eyes were interesting. There was guile and many secrets in them: eyes that had lived life and thirsted for more.

'Namaskar,' I said, folding my hands.

Arun Gawli folded his hands in the same gesture.

'Haan bol, kya chahiye.' (Tell me what you want.) The way he spat out the words, it was like he was an emperor doling out largesse and I, a humble servant begging for an audience. I had to pinch myself to believe that I was standing before a TADA accused in a high-security prison.

'I want an interview with you, maybe 15–20 minutes of your time,' I replied.

The don seated himself in a chair and offered me tea and snacks. I refused, adding for good measure, 'I don't want anything from your money.' I felt brave after saying this but many summers later, I realized I could not show my antipathy to gangsters so blatantly. Now, when I am offered something, I tell them I have just had lunch or do not consume tea/soft drinks, etc., or I tell them I am unwell. I remember, as recently as three years ago, when my wife and I had gone to interview the sister of one of the most wanted men in India at her residence – my wife had come along because the journalist in her could not resist an interview with a female don – I refused to get up to greet her, and was chastised by my wife.

Any other man would have walked out of the interview after my self-righteous outburst, but not Gawli. His eyebrows arched, but he did not say anything.

The interview began and I found myself in my element, refusing to play ball and asking him all kinds of uncomfortable questions. We spoke about his rivals: Dawood Ibrahim and those who were baying for his blood, including Bal Thackeray, the Mumbai police, etc.

Twice, during the course of the interview, we were interrupted by a cop asking him to return to his barracks as the IG of prisons was about to go on his rounds. Both times Gawli screamed at him, shooing him away.

That was the first time I experienced the impotence of khaki. First impressions rarely die; to date, few policemen – a handful, really –

have managed to make an impression and rise above my general prejudice about them.

After the interview, Gawli warned me, 'Sambhaal ke likhna, be careful you don't write about the jail meeting.' It was more than a warning – a veiled threat, actually. But I was a reporter and reckless.

I returned and wrote the whole story in detail. Newsline ran the interview as an eight-column flyer across the page. "'I will join politics to save myself from a fake police encounter," says Gawli from jail', was the headline of my story. It created a big hue and cry. (Incidentally, Gawli went on to keep his promise and became a politician. The first time, he got a few thousand votes, but my cop friend, the late Anti-Terrorism Squad (ATS) chief Hemant Karkare warned me that it would take only a couple of elections more for Gawli to become an MLA. Karkare, one of the best policemen the force has seen, was so right.)

Ranjit Singh Sharma, then joint commissioner of police, crime, summoned me to the crime branch office and asked me to disclose how I had managed to get inside the prison and do the story. I refused to spill the beans. Sharma politely mentioned that he could issue summons against me under Section 60 of the Indian Evidence Act, 1872. I said, 'Sir, you can arrest me if you want. I can sit behind bars for a few months, but I cannot disclose how I got the interview.'

Mr Sharma was one of the finest crime branch officers the city had. When he realized that I was adamant and that a clash between the media and the police could get out of hand, he became concerned about me and warned me to be careful of the Gawli gang as they could make my life hell.

Later, when Gawli got bail and I met him with some foreign journalists at his fortress at Dagdi Chawl, he looked at me accusingly. 'Tumne mera boochch laga diya (you fucked me royally)', he said. Soon after my story was published, several jail officials got transferred and that had made his life miserable, he said.

I was lucky to be spared. Two journalists, one from the *Times of India* – my friend, Mateen Hafeez – and Anandita Ramaswamy of the *Asian Age*, had got roughed up by Arun Gawli and gang. Anandita had written a story about how Gawli's political party was going broke and not paying salaries to party workers. And then she did something reporters should avoid doing – after the story was published, she landed up at the infamous Dagdi Chawl for first-hand verification. The party workers roughed her up. They assaulted her physically, causing injuries and bruises.

Once upon a time, Dagdi Chawl was impregnable. It still is, to some extent. Gawli's top-floor terrace house in a six-storey building is so big that you could play badminton there. His drawing room is lined with various pictures and idols of a pantheon of Hindu deities and looks like the sanctum sanctorum of a temple.

Gawli's gang has a larger base than other gangs, with a lot of members in and around Mumbai and Pune. In Wadgaon Pir, where his in-laws live, he is revered like a saint. His other Maharashtrian peers have not been so lucky. Amar Naik is dead, Suresh Manchekar is dead, Sunil Sawant is dead, Chhota Rajan is absconding, Ashwin Naik is in a wheelchair, Anil Parab is in prison.

This is the story of the Maharashtrian mobsters who, in the words of Sena supremo Bal Thackeray were 'amchi muley' (our boys): sons of the soil, who greatly influenced Maharashtra's politics and drove the economy of the city of Mumbai.

TWO

Ghatis versus Bhaiyyas

A few decades before the Shiv Sena raised the bogey of 'Bhaiyya bhagao Mumbai bachao' (drive out the north Indians and save Mumbai), Arun Gawli had embarked on a similar mission, its forerunner.

Except for the Pathans, who never allowed a non-Muslim into their crime syndicates, the Mumbai mafia was a melting pot of cultures: a miniature Mumbai. When Gawli began establishing his supremacy in the Byculla region, he was first challenged by a local gang made up of a majority of north Indians – referred to by some as bhaiyyas – and so he became the first gangster to target the north Indian 'bhaiyya' gangsters. Bhaiyya means elder brother, but in Mumbai the Maharashtrians throw the word around as a pejorative to denote anybody who hails from the north of the Godavari.

In fact, the Mumbai mafia has never been racist or communal like the exclusivist American syndicates: in the US, you have the black mafia, Chinese mafia, Russian mafia, Pakistani mafia, Korean mafia, Italian mafia and so on.

Bombay has always been an amalgamation, a confluence of cultures, a cosmopolitan city that was under the control of some foreign ruler or the other since the fourteenth century, all of whom left their imprint on the seven islands. First, it was the Muslim rulers who annexed the islands way back in 1348 and refused to give them to the Mughal emperor Humayun. Sultan Bahadur Shah of the Gujarat Sultanate thought they were better off with the Portuguese, who ruled from 1534 to 1661. They married local women and established churches led by Portuguese Fransiscans and Jesuits. They called the place 'Bombaim'.

The British, who had always had their eye on Bombaim, got it as part of the dowry in 1661 when King Charles II of England married Catherine of Braganza, the daughter of King John IV of Portugal. The king gave Bombaim to the East India Company, who brought in artisans and traders to settle the new town. As early as 1661, the Parsis also migrated to Mumbai; in 1673, the British handed over a piece of land at Malabar Hill to them for the Tower of Silence.

After the swamps were filled by the 1800s and all the seven islands were linked to become one large island in 1845, more people came to the city and made it their own, thus contributing to its growth.

The local trains, the first of their kind, brought even more migrants into the city. Initially, it was the mills that attracted the hordes, but post independence, pharmaceutical and engineering companies brought more workers into its fold. Technically the Kolis, who were fisherfolk, were the original inhabitants, but most Marathi-speaking people, even if they come from different parts of Maharashtra, consider non-Maharashtrian Mumbaikars to be the outsiders. This view also stems from the consistently right-wing policies of the Shiv Sena, which believes that the sons of the soil (Maharashtrians from all over Maharashtra who speak Marathi) deserve more.

Incidentally, all Muslim gangs in the early years had north Indian bhaiyyas in their ranks. Different communities jostled for space in all spheres of life in cosmopolitan Bombay and this applied to the mafia too. North Indian bhaiyyas, predominantly from Uttar Pradesh and Bihar, were part of the Kanpuri, Jaunpuri, Rampuri and Illahabadi gangs. These gangs called the shots at Sankli Street and Madanpura in Byculla, which were essentially Muslim pockets. But they also had their fair share of Hindus, and conflicts were few and far between, except when women or wealth were involved.

The conflict between Arun Gawli, the Marathi-speaking gangster of the BRA gang (its name was taken from the initials of its three leading members, Babu Reshim, Rama Naik and Arun Gawli) and the north Indian bhaiyyas was not based on regional prejudices. It all began with territorial one-upmanship. The BRA gang was first challenged by Mohan Sarmalkar's gang in Byculla, known as the S-bridge gang – after the serpentine S-shaped bridge that connects Byculla East to Byculla West – and later rechristened as the Bhaiyya gang. Sarmalkar had considerable clout in Byculla West. He dismissed the BRA gang as inconsequential and refused to accept their supremacy. If the BRA gang had its headquarters at Dagdi Chawl and supporters in Peon Chawl, Laxmi Chawl and Cement Chawl, Sarmalkar had his headquarters at S-bridge.

Sarmalkar did not like the title 'S-bridge gang' because it limited his clout and jurisdiction to one location. He wanted a larger canvas and sought to call his bunch of thugs the Byculla gang. But Gawli was opposed to this.

Though Sarmalkar was a Maharashtrian and the leader of the Byculla gang, many of his top commanders were north Indians. Parasnath Pandey (the matka don of Byculla), Kundan Dubey and Raj Dubey were all north Indians. Sarmalkar also owed allegiance to Virar's Jayendra Singh Thakur, known as Bhai Thakur, who was a north Indian.

Gawli's master stroke was to quietly plant the seeds of mistrust among the Maharashtrian populace. He dubbed the Byculla gang the Bhaiyya gang and quickly usurped their title, rechristening his own gang the 'Byculla company'. Once he had prejudiced the local boys against the S-bridge gang, new recruits decided to join the BRA gang and scrupulously avoided the S-bridge gang.

Sarmalkar was aghast. He started proclaiming that Gawli was an Ahir and that he was from Madhya Pradesh, a neighbouring state, and as such, was not a local. The Gawlis are cattle-grazers and milkmen (gwalas) and are spread across Maharashtra's border with Madhya Pradesh and throughout the state. Sarmalkar, who was a hard-core criminal and boasted gang members like the Pandeys and the Dubeys, tried to claim that Gawli was a mill worker and did not know the ABC of crime.

Arun Gawli was the son of Gulab Puran Gawli and Laxmibai.

Gulab came from Ahmednagar, Maharashtra, while Laxmibai hailed from Khandwa, Madhya Pradesh. They had six children, of whom four were boys. Gulab Gawli had worked at Simplex Mill and had high hopes for his children. He was eager that his children acquire a good education. Arun managed to complete matriculation, which was a big deal in the late sixties and early seventies, but his father left his mill job around this time. The reasons are not known. His mother, too, had worked for over ten years at the cotton mills. In fact, most of the Gawli clan was employed as mill workers or government servants. Arun's sister Ashalata Gawli was married to Mohan Gangaram Bania alias Ahir, who was employed as a loader with Air India. Another sister, Rekha, was married to Digambar Ahir, who worked in the accounts department of the Central Railway. Vijay Ahir, a relative, worked at Khatau Mills before he became a corporator. One of Arun Gawli's brothers, Pradeep, who lived with his family at Dagdi Chawl, also worked at Khatau Mills, as did Sachin Ahir, son of Gawli's sister Ashalata. Gawli's connection with Khatau Mills ran deep and this later became the cause of a long and violent gangland feud.

After his father left his job, Arun took up a series of jobs with various companies. He joined Shakti Mills in Mahalaxmi after matriculation and later Godrej Boyce in Vikhroli. In 1977, he joined Crompton Greaves in Kanjurmarg.

It was at Crompton Greaves that Gawli first shook hands with the burly, well-built Sadashiv Pawle, later known as Sada Pawle or Sada Mama. In the company of Sada, Arun took to anti-social activities.

It was also here that Rama Naik and Arun Gawli met; they had earlier studied at the same municipal school in Byculla. Though Arun was Rama's senior, he looked up to him. Rama Naik lived in Lalvitachi Chawl at Cross Gully in Byculla. His penchant for getting into trouble meant he had to leave school before completing matriculation. He dropped out after Class 6 and took with him other troubled and trouble-making youths like Ashok Chaudhary alias Chhota Babu, Bablya Sawant and Vilas Choughule. His exit did not affect his friendship with Arun Gawli. Along with the other boys, they played kabaddi at the local Om Club.

At the time, Byculla was just making its mark as the Palermo of independent India. The Jaunpuri, Kanpuri and Illahabadi gangs were all big names in the area. Later, gangs headed by Nanhe Khan and Waheb Pehelwan along with the Johnny Brothers, who became active in the Clare Road area (which was essentially a Christian locality and ruled by the Johnny brothers), became prominent in Byculla.

With its history of gangs for more than fifty years, Byculla was the hunting ground of the Mumbai mafiosi. It was in Byculla that Arun Gawli and Rama Naik entered the lanes of the underworld. Once in, no one ever got out.

The internecine warfare between the S-bridge gang and the BRA gang escalated. Kundan Dubey was a known acolyte of Parasnath Pandey, and they had both served in the ranks of Sarmalkar's gang. Ironically, Kundan's sister Pushpa had fallen in love with Arvind, the elder brother of gangster Rama Naik, who was with the rival BRA gang. As Bollywod has shown us, such romances cannot survive without bloodshed. In 1976, Kundan got into a quarrel with Arvind on the streets and slapped him. Rama Naik's younger brother, Umakant, could not stand by and watch his brother's humiliation. He stepped in and soon a fist fight broke out between Kundan and Umakant. Kundan stabbed Umakant, who later succumbed to his injuries. Kundan was arrested by the Agripada police and jailed for a while before eventually being released on bail.

This incident marked the beginning of a violent battle between the BRA gang and the Bhaiyya gang. Until then, they had restricted themselves to street skirmishes and fist fights.

Kundan was now on the BRA gang's hit list. Soon after his release from jail, he barged into a gambling den at Parsi Wadi in Tardeo and killed two people; his reign of terror was beginning in the Grant Road area, earlier managed by his friend Shashi Rasam, the leader of the Cobra gang, whom he had met in jail.

The selective crackdown by the police on their matka (gambling) dens only exacerbated hostilities; it frustrated the BRA gang as the dens of their rivals were never raided. It was obvious that the others paid more hafta to the police. Arun and Rama never intended to join a gang – they would have happily run their matkas and liquor joints – but the raids made them furious. It was their sense of frustration over the injustice that forced Rama Naik, Babu Reshim and Arun Gawli to join hands.

Babu Reshim was the seniormost among the three and the other two looked up to him, discussing all plans with him and asking for advice. It was at his suggestion that they named their gang BRA. They soon started terrorizing the traders of the Byculla region by extorting money from gambling dens, liquor shops and those selling smuggled goods. Later, with the induction of foot soldiers into the gang, muscle power was provided to landlords and contractors to evict tenants for the construction of new buildings. This became their entry into the real estate business – Arun Gawli was the first don to dabble in land deals.

Many other dons in Mumbai tried their hand at the real estate and construction businesses. Haji Mastan tried very hard to get his fingers into the construction pie, with the help of the Dawood and Pathan gangs, but was unable to sustain it as the business required constant engagement. Dawood came into the field much later, initially content with rigging horse races at the Mahalaxmi Derby and financing films. However, Arun Gawli had foreseen that real estate would be the next big thing and concentrated his energies in the Worli, Byculla, Chinchpokli, Parel, Lalbaug and Dadar areas of south-central Mumbai or Girangaon.

Gawli understood the requirement for – and power of – muscle in this business. He started settling financial disputes and providing protection to his contractor friends. He demanded a flat 50 per cent fee for settling financial disputes or a certain number of flats in the newly constructed buildings. He was also the first don to demand 50 per cent of the money recovered in financial disputes. As the police could not intervene in such civil matters and did not get involved in settling financial disputes because of legal constraints, Gawli and other gangsters made a killing. These practices created a link between building contractors and gangsters, and the BRA gang became a force to reckon with.

Meanwhile, when Kundan Dubey was in jail, his sister fell in love with Shashi Rasam, leader of the Cobra gang. Shashi Rasam at this point thought he should patch up the relationship between the BRA gang and the S-bridge gang.

As it happened, Rama ended up in jail after a fight with another gang and met Shashi Rasam. Both were released in 1977. While in jail, Shashi tried to convince Rama to let bygones be bygones and bring closure to the Kundan episode by not testifying against Kundan in the Umakant Naik murder case.

But Rama was in no mood for any such reconciliation. He told Shashi in no uncertain terms that blood was thicker than water and that Kundan would have to undergo punishment as dictated by the courts. As expected, after the court trials, Kundan was convicted and sentenced to life imprisonment. Shashi was enraged, and this became the cause of their enmity. In Rama's eyes, Shashi was no more his friend; rather, an acolyte of the bhaiyyas, as he was in love with Pushpa Dubey, and for that he deserved to be punished. After Rama's release from jail, he – along with Chhota Babu and Arun Gawli – brutally stabbed Shashi at Bombay Central Bridge while he was returning from a visit to Pushpa's house. The police arrested Rama Naik, Choughule and Chhota Babu, but Rama did not divulge Arun Gawli's name. This not only took Gawli by surprise, it left him indebted to Rama Naik for life.

The conflict between the bhaiyyas and ghatis (the bhaiyyas referred to the Maharashtrians pejoratively as ghatis) continued to rage. The BRA gang wanted to take over all the matka joints, but it was Parasnath Pandey whose writ operated in these dens. Pandey was seen as an obstacle to BRA's growth, so one day Gawli and his men barged into his den and killed him, in full public view, brutally stabbing him with choppers and assaulting him with swords. The gruesome killing not only shocked everyone but scared the other matka operators, who immediately shifted their loyalties to the BRA gang.

The Sarmalkar gang was gradually getting decimated by their

rivals. The wild propaganda and the police were doing what Gawli had always wanted. Not that the system sided with Gawli; he, Babu Reshim and Rama Naik were tadipar (externed) from Mumbai for two years in 1979. While in jail, Rama Naik shook hands with don Varadarajan Mudaliar and Rajan Nair (Bada Rajan), who was the reigning don in the Tilak Nagar area. After Naik's release, they decided to capitalize on their newly forged alliances.

With Parasnath dead and Kundan in jail serving his life sentence, Sarmalkar decided to retreat from the arena. The remaining members – Hari Shankar Mishra, Mohan Gupta and others – also preferred to fade out. This gave Gawli complete control of the area and he began to call the shots.

Gawli, meanwhile, was carrying on an affair with Zubeida Mujawar, whose family belonged to Vadgaon Maval, near Pune. The family did not approve of their relationship, so the two had to finally elope and tie the knot; Zubeida came to Dagdi Chawl as Asha Gawli. Rama Naik and Babu Reshim did not approve of Gawli's marriage either, but Asha became Gawli's strength and de facto don in later years.

The bhaiyya bogey was later appropriated by the Shiv Sena and then the Maharashtra Nav Nirman Sena, who converted it into the Marathi-manoos-versus-bhaiyyas struggle. A paucity of issues had forced the Sena to reinvent itself around this time. Finding no new avenues, the party went back to its 'anti-outsider' credo, targeting people from the north, especially Uttar Pradesh.

In 2003, the Sena claimed that only 10 per cent of the 500 Maharashtrian candidates who appeared for the railway exams were successful because Biharis walked away with most of the jobs. Before the exams that year, Shiv Sainiks ransacked a railway recruitment office in Bandra, protesting against the huge number of non-Maharashtrians (read north Indians); a total of 6.5 lakh candidates from all over the country were set to compete for the 2,200 railway jobs in Maharashtra. The central government was forced to delay the exams. The Shiv Sainiks thrashed every Bihari who had come to

Mumbai for the exams – at Kalyan railway station, they caught hold of all north Indians getting off trains arriving from the north.

In gangland, the issue was never raised again, but the Shiv Sena made it an important tool in their political agenda.

THREE

Girangaon: The Village of Mills

The changing skyline of south-central Mumbai seems at odds with the lower-middle-class pockets that sit cheek by jowl with it. You can spot a Maharashtrian woman in an oversized cotton maxi buying vegetables next to a young woman headed to college or work, dressed in a spaghetti top and jeans. The social diversity is evident from Worli to Parel, from Lalbaug to Chinchpokli, at Currey Road, Bombay Central and Byculla, at Mahalaxmi and Lower Parel, where the old crumbling textile mills are giving way to swanky new buildings. For the post-liberalization generation, which did not witness the tumultuous events that led to the closure of the textile mills, south-central Mumbai is characterized by High Street Phoenix, Kamala City, One India Bulls Centre and India Bulls Sky or Peninsula Towers, to name a few landmarks. These are the signposts that now define what was once Girangaon; girni in Marathi means mills, gaon is village.

The entire stretch from Byculla to Dadar and Mahalaxmi to Worli was once referred to as Girangaon. The British found it difficult to pronounce these names, so they just referred to the entire area as Byculla. Today's android-fixated generation may not even be aware that the malls and high-rises were once thriving cotton mills that fuelled the growth of Mumbai and defined its character, even shaping its political and cultural history. But there was a time when Byculla was Mumbai's Manchester.

For the uninitiated, India Bulls Sky was Jupiter Mills, One India Bulls Centre was Elphinstone Mills and Phoenix rose from the ashes of Phoenix Mills; Kamala City was Kamala Mills, Raghuvanshi Mills is today's K-Lifestyle, Matulya Mills became Sun Palazzo, New Islam Mills is One Avighna Park, Piramal Spinning & Weaving Mills has become Marathon Nextgen, Modern Mills is now Mahindra Belvedere Court, Dawn Mills is today's Peninsula Towers, and so on. A majority of the eighty mills of south-central Mumbai are being transformed, some into corporate parks, some into malls, super-luxury stores and luxurious apartments, some into the offices of the media and advertising fraternity, and some into five-star hotels.

The denizens of these areas, who lived in chawls and one-room tenement buildings in the neighbourhood of the mills, are moving out or opting for boxed-in slum redevelopment homes. And the 250,000 men and women who worked in the mills are history. Some died, some became disillusioned, others simply lost their minds. Many committed suicide, some just melted into the background, some retreated to their native villages – while others ended up hawking vegetables beneath the very structures that gave them their bread and butter. Ironically, their children, denied a proper education and livelihood, work twelve-hour shifts in the mills-turned-malls. They are barely able to survive and there is no job security at all.

In the next ten years, even the lone relics of the mill era, the long chimneys that seem to reach out to the skies, will be dismantled, taking with them a slice of our history, of a time when the mills ushered in the industrialization and development of Mumbai and brought hordes of people from all over India to this city of dreams. For more than 150 years, the cotton composite mills were integral to the city's landscape. The textile mill boom changed the face of Mumbai to such an extent that the British put up a plaque at the Gateway of India, calling the city 'Urbs Prima in Indis' (most important city in India).

The first mill, The Bombay Spinning and Weaving Company, was set up in 1854 in Tardeo by a Parsi gentleman, Cowasji Nanabhoy Davar. By this time, the first train had already been flagged off from Bori Bunder (which was then named Victoria Terminus and is now known as Chhatrapati Shivaji Terminus) to Thane, and a year later, to Kalyan. Transport speeded up the process of industrialization. By the year 1870, Mumbai's south-central region had twenty-five composite mills. Both the British imperialists and the mill owners, all Indians, had realized that there was a big potential market for cloth made in India.

Prior to the advent of the composite mills, Mumbai got its cloth from the charkha and handlooms. More than twenty per cent of the population was involved in the hand-spun and hand-woven cloth-making process. The bleaching and dyeing of cloth was another long process, and this made the finished product very expensive. The other option was to buy cloth from the British. They took cotton to Lancashire and Manchester and then sent cloth back to India to sell, a finished product that was unaffordable for the masses. So, when Davar set up his first mill, the mill owners of Lancashire, Manchester and south England were furious. They demanded to know from their countrymen ruling India why Indians were being allowed to set up their own mills. They were sure that allowing Indians to have their own cotton mills amounted to hara-kiri, as Indians would naturally prefer to buy clothes made locally, which would also be cheaper. This, they said, would take away the profits of the Manchester mills.

The ruling class, however, expressed helplessness and retorted that the Indians would anyway got their hands on the technology because the Europeans and even the British making the textile machinery were eager to sell shuttle looms to Indians.

Textile mills multiplied because the reformers of the time, such as Lokmanya Bal Gangadhar Tilak, a Marathi manoos, emphasized the importance of indigenous industries. He wrote an editorial on the first textile mill in Pune in his newspaper *Kesari*, as early as 1885, advocating swadeshi and talking about the need for industrial development.

The workers at the mills initially worked twelve-hour shifts in the area that was called Girangaon, which stretched across a 12-km radius. When the mills came up in south-central Mumbai, it was access to the port that was a draw. Besides, there was ample land available and some mill owners got leases for ninety-nine years. Most were Indians: Parsis and Marwaris who had made their millions from trade in cotton and other products during the boom. In the year 1925, of the fifty-three mills in the city, only fourteen were British-owned. The Indians who owned these mills were the Tatas, Petits, Wadias, Currimbhoys, Thakerseys, Sassoons, Khataus and Goculdas, to name a few.

The mill area stretched from Byculla to Dadar on the Central Railway side, from Tardeo to Bombay Central, Mahalaxmi and Elphinstone on the Western Railway side. It was not less than 1,000 acres, and later became worth its weight in gold. But in the late nineteenth century, it was cotton, brought in bales to the burgeoning textile mills, that was worth its weight in gold.

The textile industry is cyclical by nature; each cycle seems to last an average of five to seven years, and a boom time is always followed by a downturn. Two historical developments led to a major boost for the Indian cotton trade and mills: the American Civil War and the war in Afghanistan.

The first of these happened in 1860. Before the civil war, Britain used to buy cotton from India as well as America. At one point, in the early part of the nineteenth century, they were buying a lot of Indian cotton. But the Indian cotton was not able to keep up with the gargantuan quantity of production that the newly invented textile machinery installed in Britain demanded. So the British began looking at American cotton, which they realized was of a superior grade. Southern American states like Louisiana and Arkansas, which practised slavery, exported the best cotton to England. After the civil war broke out in 1861 on the issue of slavery, there was a Union blockage on southern ports. The pro-slavery, cotton-growing states united under a confederacy and hoped to secede from the Union of America. The confederacy itself stopped cotton exports, hoping that Britain would be affected by the ban and would therefore help them fight the Union, which was against slavery.

But Britain did not take the bait. They instead looked east to India and Egypt, as did the French. This was the first boom time for cotton traders. Cotton became extremely valuable during the four years of the civil war. A cotton-starved Britain was guzzling Indian cotton and the Bhatia community and other cloth merchants like Premchand Raichand became the biggest cotton exporters. Raichand was called the cotton king. He minted millions and eventually built the Rajabai Tower, named after his mother, and invested in the reclamation of the Churchgate area. Raichand's affluence can be gauged from the fact that he donated Rs 2 lakh to the British for the construction of the tower (now within the Mumbai University premises) in the 1860s.

Other construction companies cropped up overnight to reclaim land from the sea. By January 1865, Bombay had thirty-one banks, eight reclamation companies, sixteen cotton pressing companies, ten shipping companies, twenty insurance companies and sixty-two joint stock companies. It came to be called the great Bombay bonanza. In just four years, the city's profits from cotton exceeded eighty million pound sterling.

The cotton came mainly from the Vidarbha region, which is now in Maharashtra. At that time, it was ruled by the Nizam of Hyderabad, who had control over a large territory consisting of the present Telangana, Vidarbha, Marathwada and four districts of Karnataka. In his overzealousness to help the British, the Nizam had once sent an army with the East India Company which wanted to conquer Afghanistan in the late 1830s. When they came back, the Company presented the Nizam with the bill. The Nizam was horrified, as he had presumed he was helping the Company. He could not pay, so he gave them Berar (Vidarbha) as a protectorate. Later, when the British Crown took over from the East India Company, they quietly annexed Berar with its rich, fertile soil that was excellent for cotton cultivation.

The cotton bubble burst in 1865 when the American Civil War ended and the British resumed buying American cotton. Egypt and India suffered huge losses; businesses went into liquidation and the reclamation companies declared bankruptcy. Premchand Raichand went bankrupt too. Eventually, though, the mills recovered and the demand for cotton continued to rise.

The next boom happened between 1914 and 1918. During the First World War, the British focused their energies on war efforts and their ships were used to carry arms and ammunition. Foreign-made cloth had stopped coming to India, so there was no competition. When the war ended in 1918, the mills were once again struggling. The great depression of 1919 did not help matters. But by 1925, they were back on their feet, and this time more mills had sprung up – taking the total number to eighty-three. (Between 1925 and 1938, fifteen of these mills shut down, unable to cope with the ups and down of the business.)

World War II broke out in September 1939 and Britain, with its colonies, geared up for war efforts. A Defence of India Act was promulgated and cotton was placed under the Essential Commodities Act. Around 65 per cent of the cloth produced in the organized textile industry – i.e., the composite mills – was reserved for military orders and the rest for ordinary people. Imports were halted and the textile mills made huge fortunes during the next ten years. The war ended in 1945 and Europe got busy with reconstruction. The Indian textile business now had great opportunities to boost exports. By 1955, however, the market levelled and depression once again set in; textile mills started incurring losses. The composite mills were subjected to higher taxation, strict labour laws, export obligations, shortage of raw cotton and many other hurdles after 1947. Also, industrial policy was relaxed post Independence and new industries such as pharma, engineering and fertilisers were making higher profits and attracting capital. By 1948, a new fibre – viscose – became available and started competing with cotton textiles. By 1955, synthetic fabrics such as nylon and polyester had made their entry into India. As the textile industry was not making profits, it could not modernize to suit the new standards and started closing down.

Strikes were frequent, from 1924 onwards. The *Labour Monthly*'s May 1924 report on one Mumbai textile strike is revealing.

One hundred and fifty thousand mill operatives, including thirty thousand women and children, have been on strike and locked-out of the textile mills of Bombay for nearly three months. All the mills of the district, eighty-three in number, are closed down. The question at issue is the payment of the annual bonus to the operatives, in addition to their usual wage. In July of last year, the owners put up a notice that the usual bonus, received by the operatives during the last five years and regarded by them as a form of supplementary wages, would not be paid. The men did not heed the notice, most of them being illiterate, and it was not until the end of the year when the bonus became payable that they realized the issue at stake. A strike was declared in the middle of January, followed immediately by a lockout on the part of the owners, in an attempt to force the men back to work unconditionally.

The monthly wage of a Bombay mill operative is 35 rupees for men; 17 rupees for women – for a ten-hour day. This sum is insufficient to maintain their bodily health and strength, or to provide them with the most elementary necessities. For this reason, during the height of the post-war boom period when mill profits soared to several hundred per cent, the annual bonus was granted as a form of supplementary wages. The cost of living has risen (according to official figures) 58 per cent since 1914; profits have risen from 674 lakh rupees in 1917 to 1,559 lakh rupees in 1921, with a slight fall in 1922-23. The cotton mill workers are proverbially underpaid and overworked, with the result that they were always heavily in debt to the money-lender. Their right to organise into trade unions was not legally recognised, and they had no regular labour organisations and no union fund. Their leaders, up to the time of the present strike, were drawn from the ranks of the bourgeoisie – lawyers, politicians, philanthropists and professional labour leaders, who were closer, in interest and sympathies, to the employing class than to the workers. They sabotaged every attempt to strike on the part of the latter, they took the side of the employers in every decisive issue, they used their influence to keep the men at work and satisfied with the old conditions instead of attempting to better themselves. The government, which affects to maintain its neutrality in labour disputes, has never hesitated to call out armed police and military to aid the employers in guarding their property and crushing a strike.

Strikes took place all the time in the Bombay textile mills as the workers fought for fair wages. In the early years, there was no unionism. It was the communist leader S.A. Dange who brought the workers under the communist umbrella and fought for the workers' rights. Many years later, in 1982, when Dr Datta Samant announced a textile mill strike, the 250,000 workers presumed that eventually there would be a rationalization of wages on par with that of the other industries.

The mills had begun a downward spiral long before Dr Samant called the strike. The textile workers, who knew they were underpaid as compared to workers in the pharmaceutical or engineering industries, decided to approach him to take up their case. They were tired of the official industry union, the Rashtriya Mill Mazdoor Sangh (RMMS), which was affiliated to the Congress-I but had failed to take up their cause. Dr Samant had fought for workers in other industries, and had a great following because his agitations always resulted in unheard of wage hikes. He was reluctant to call for a textile workers' strike as it was not his field of work. But the workers surrounded his house in Ghatkopar and refused to leave until he agreed.

Javed Anand, in his tribute to Dr Samant, says of the trade union leader, 'Samant could not be bothered to look at company balance sheets offered by managements as proof of the organization's inability to pay. He was convinced, like the workers were, that all balance sheets are dressed to lie. The fact that many companies which initially pleaded inability later agreed to pay more, added to Samant's and the workers' resolve not to let the balance sheets come in the way of their "exorbitant" demands.'

At the time of the strike, a skilled textile worker was drawing Rs 1,500 while an unskilled worker was drawing Rs 700/800. The strike got national coverage. Dr Samant had been a Congress supporter for a while, but Indira Gandhi had not liked his defiance during the Emergency and he had been jailed. She felt that if the textile industry workers got their way, so would the port and dock workers, and so on. So, later, when the workers were willing to call off the strike even without a hike in wages, insisting only on one condition, that the government scrap the Bombay Industrial Act of 1947, nobody paid heed to their pleas. Their only other demand was for RMMS to be de-recognized as the only official union of mill workers under the Bombay Industrial Act.

The government of the day refused to budge and the strike was never formally called off. The eighteen-month strike, one of the longest in India's labour history, proved to be the death knell of the already struggling textile mills. Most of them shut down and three lakh textile mill workers lost their jobs.

By the advent of the twentieth century, hardly any textile mill was running to full capacity and international brands like Finlay's, Calico and Binny's lapsed into history. Though the strike was blamed, every mill had its own reason for closure. Some closed because of the competition that was the result of globalization, some because they were labour-intensive and others because of family feuds.

The workers in these mills were predominantly Maharashtrians from south Raigad and Ratnagiri. The Konkan coast was very poor in those days and farmers had to fall back on one rice crop and mangoes. The cotton mills were the warp and weft of the migrant's life. For trade unionism, they would align with the communists, but as the communists did not believe in religion, the workers were soon under the sway of the right-wing Shiv Sena. The Shiv Sena found its early cadres among the mill workers of Konkan.

There were also workers from other Indian states who eventually put down roots here. Slowly, the chawls that were walking distance from the mills evolved into a multicultural space driven by common middle-class values.

The chawls and two-storey tenements, like the BDD chawls at Worli, housed workers in small, cramped rooms. Alcoholism was rampant, as was moneylending. Bootleggers and matka dens thrived. To escape the squalid living conditions, adults and children spent much of their time outside the house. Children lived and survived on their wits and often, when strikes were called, families were sent back home to the villages. Historians talk of communalism breeding in these places and Dr Samant attested to this. But there was something else that was bred here. Organized crime.

Gawli worked in Shakti Mills (the now infamous mills where a young photojournalist was gang-raped on 28 August 2013), following in the footsteps of his parents. Naik's family sold vegetables in Dadar, but his parents worked in the mills. Gangster D.K. Rao's parents worked in a mill, as did the parents of Anil Parab. Most importantly, by the early nineties, the Maharashtrian and non-Maharashtrian boys who grew up in Girangaon, working their way up the mafia ladder by stabbing and killing for money, realized that they were sitting on a goldmine.

South Mumbai was cramped and bursting at its seams and there was no place for expansion. The Bandra-Kurla Complex was being promoted as an alternative, but it lacked proximity to south Mumbai. The real-estate mavens, the mafia and the politicians realized that the only way for Mumbai to go was south-central. Girangaon had to make way for the new face of Mumbai, probably the next financial nerve-centre of the city. One by one, the mills that had survived Dr Samant's strike closed and began pulling down their chimneys. The money at stake ran into crores. Some mills were sold for Rs 400 crore upwards and others were pegged at Rs 600 to Rs 900 crore.

By the nineties, Girangaon had become the next Kurukshetra. The big players like Dawood had aligned with the builders, while Gawli and his ilk aligned with the mill owners. Everybody benefited, except the workers. And the new players, both in the mafia and state politics – and possibly even the politics of New Delhi – would come from the money of Girangaon.

FOUR

The First Meeting

The room is quiet, but there is the overwhelming presence of three heavily built, muscular men with forbidding expressions. In the centre of the room is a man in a wheelchair, wearing a half-sleeve shirt. His fingers are splayed on a white, sterile napkin that has been placed on his lap. He has a beard and his eyes are cold windows to his soul, contemplative, yet projecting annoyance. It is evident that our presence isn't appreciated. He is staring at us and for a moment we are sure he has seen through us and our hidden motives and intentions. His face bears creases, testimony to far too many years of the hard life, his deep cynicism and extreme hate and distrust of the world. This is fifty-year-old Ashwin Naik, brother of ganglord Amar Naik. It was only after a great deal of persuasion and cajoling that we were permitted into his sanctum. Not everyone is allowed in.

There are six telephones on the table. Needless to say, this is how he keeps the law and enforcement agencies flummoxed. How many phones can they tap?

Ashwin has distinctive mannerisms. He speaks with peculiar pauses and with an unusual punctuation, as if carefully weighing and contemplating every word that comes out of his mouth.

There is a photograph of a Shivling behind his table, and small idols of Ganesha and Laxmi are placed on the right side of it. When he sees us scrutinizing the idols, he turns, looks at them and says, 'My parents used to say: "Dekho bhagwan hamare peeche hi toh hain'" (Look, God is always behind us).

Upon a second look, we spot the visiting card of Sachin Ahir, lying next to the idols. Ahir is an MLA, a cabinet minister in the coalition government of Maharashtra, and it's surprising to see his card in Ashwin Naik's house, for Ahir is also the nephew of rival ganglord Gawli. There are lots of questions waiting to be asked, but we reserve the topic for future meetings – if we can coax more out of him, that is – and instead talk about his family, his upbringing, and the days that shaped his career as a ganglord.

Ashwin Naik became the don of the fledgling Amar Naik gang after the death of his brother in 1996. Amar was gunned down by Vijay Salaskar in a famous police encounter on 10 August that year.

On 18 April 1994, Ashwin too was shot on the premises of the sessions court by Gawli's sharpshooter Ravindra Sawant – only, the attack did not kill him. It left him permanently dependent on a wheelchair for movement.

When our discussion veers towards his childhood and his parents, Naik's face lights up. He speaks about his parents at great length, animated, smiling. He talks about their religious beliefs and their lack of education. He speaks of how ambitious they both were for their children and how they were determined that they should have the best education.

Ashwin had three siblings: brothers Ajit and Amar, and sister Alka. Only Ashwin had the opportunity to study and earn higher academic qualifications. None of his siblings managed to study beyond matriculation, though their father Maruti Naik wanted all of them to study.

Ashwin studied at Dr Antonio Da Silva High School and Junior College of Commerce in Dadar, and had been inclined towards technical education since Class 8. His fascination for aeroplanes and his leaning towards engineering saw him study aeronautical engineering. However, when he joined the Hindustan Aeronautics Academy, he had to quit within a year, unable to handle the harsh ragging of senior students. He then went to London and graduated as a civil engineer.

Ashwin has a few people with him today, among them his lawyer Bharat Mane, who helps him articulate his thoughts. A stack of newspapers is bundled on a rack in one corner of the room. There is a TV in another corner and he keeps surfing news channels. We realize that we are also under the watchful eyes of CCTV cameras.

He loves Bollywood films, Ashwin tells us proudly. He recently saw a Paresh Rawal starrer *Oh My God* and liked it very much. He is planning to see an action thriller, *Race 2*, at PVR Juhu today. When he sees our eyebrows rise in surprise, he assures us he will be surrounded by twelve of his most trusted men, protected even in the very public space of a theatre.

Ashwin says he was obsessed with Bollywood since his childhood. He used to bunk school to watch movies after saving his pocket money of 25 paise for over a week. He meticulously noted every expense in his diary, in a self-invented code language. This habit has remained with him until today. He makes notes in his diary that no one except him can decipher. The crime branch cops have had a tough time cracking his encryptions; during interrogations, the maximum amount of time has been spent decoding the entries in his diary.

Ashwin says he used to repair his friends' and neighbours' bicycles when he fell short of money for movies. But he confesses that he mostly just had fun because both his elder brothers treated him as a kid and pampered him.

As the eldest, Ajit Naik shouldered the responsibility of his house and family. He was a hardworking man, and toiled from 4 a.m. to 10 p.m. every day. There wasn't a single day he was not at the shop. He was well-respected in the Dadar market, and everyone took his name with great regard for his integrity and honesty.

Amar, on the other hand, was naughty and ended up in fist fights. Ajit tried to reprimand and reform him, but to no avail. Despite the friction between the older brothers, Amar and Ashwin got along well. Amar, though not proficient in subjects like English, was fantastic at maths. Contrary to popular opinion, he had few vices – he didn't even smoke or drink – but he became infamous because of the company he kept.

Then Amar began working at the shop, which had only been looked after by Ajit so far. Ashwin recalls, with a glint in his eyes, that that was when the problems began.

FIVE

The Vegetable Vendor's Vendetta

> In keeping silent about evil, in burying it so deep within us that
> no sign of it appears on the surface, we are *implanting* it, and
> it will rise up a thousand fold in the future. When we neither
> punish nor reproach evildoers, we are not simply protecting their
> trivial old age, we are thereby ripping the foundations of justice
> from beneath new generations.
> — Aleksandr Solzhenitsyn, *The Gulag Archipelago 1918–1956*

'No one will step forward unless he wants to get chopped up like a
carrot,' he said coldly, matter-of-factly, as if he was used to chopping
up the human torso on a daily basis.

He wielded the chopper like a vegetable knife, as though
demonstrating the act of carrot-cutting, ready to pounce and attack
anyone who dared take up the gauntlet and move a step towards him.

Amar Maruti Naik meant business, and this seemed clear not just
from his words but his demeanour. Amar's eyes were bloodshot, he
was gritting his teeth, ready to take that one step that would catapult
him from an ordinary youth to a criminal. The onlookers were clearly
nervous. It was evident that this twenty-four-year-old was willing to
kill or get killed; there was extreme hatred and madness in his eyes.

Five burly men faced him: menacing street thugs, bullies really, full
of bravura but no spunk. They realized that a wrong move by any of
them would propel the young man before them into action, and that

he might slice their heads off with one swift motion. They had never worked for a penny in their lives, and this man seemed like somebody whose sinews had seen hard labour. This presented a challenge; they were used to dealing with pliable vegetable vendors who grumbled but eventually gave in to their demands.

When Amar realized that none of his adversaries wanted to take the risk and meet his challenge, he moved to his left and extended his left hand to the man who lay face down on the pavement beside him, his white kurta soiled, his broken glasses beside him.

'Dada, uth dada, majhahaathdhar, dada uth,' Amar called to the man, who was writhing in pain. He bent down to hold his brother's arm, to lift him, but his eyes remained fixed on the thugs watching their movements.

Ajit Naik began to rise, leaning on his brother, but he seemed too weak to stand up; he stumbled and Amar, who was taking almost all his weight on one arm, lost his balance. This gave his opponents an opportunity to make the first move. One of them pounced on Amar from the side, while another tried to attack him from behind.

But Amar was faster.

He moved quickly to attack the person who had come from behind, slashing him with his chopper and managing to inflict a deep cut on the man's arm. But the attacker who held on to his neck stymied him. He moved his chopper from his right hand to his left, but found it difficult to get rid of the man whose hands were pressing against his neck.

The next moment, the man was shrieking with pain. Amar had used that age-old trick: squeezing his assailant's testicles hard. The entire Dadar market resonated with the sound of the man's agony.

A deep gash on the arm of one man and the horrifying howls of the other were enough to unsettle the goons. They decided to retreat. But as they fell back, their ring leader said, 'Tu thaamb, aaj aamhi lok tujha kheema karun taakin, mard ki aulaad hai toh ithech thaamb.' (You stay put here if you are a real man, we will come back and make mince meat of you). They took hold of their injured friends and left the spot immediately.

By now Ajit had come to his senses, and had heard their threat. He looked at Amar, who was still staring in the direction of his opponents.

Ajit shook him out of his angry trance. 'Amar, tu jaa. Leave, for the sake of our old parents.'

But Amar refused to go alone. 'Let's leave together,' he countered.

Ajit was reluctant to leave his shop during business hours and without shutting it down, but he wanted to get Amar out of that place. He knew the men would return in bigger numbers and with more weapons, and he would rather lose a day's business than his brother.

The brothers reluctantly left the shop unattended, to save themselves from the goons. They were not even sure which gang the men were affiliated to: the Potya, Bablya or Gawli gang.

The men returned as expected and when they did not find the Naik brothers, they ransacked the shop, flinging the vegetables on the ground, damaging their assets and taking whatever they found of any value. 'If anybody tries to follow in the footsteps of the Naiks, even God will not help you,' they warned the other vegetable vendors and shopkeepers.

The Dadar vegetable market is just outside the Dadar railway station, on the western side. Even in the seventies and eighties, it did business worth crores. The wholesale market, the Vashi Agricultural Produce Market (APMC), was yet to be inaugurated and Navi Mumbai was still in its infancy. The city's vegetable quota came from two main wholesale and retail markets, the Dadar and Byculla markets. Business was brisk here until the nineties, because they supplied vegetables to the entire city. And the ever-hungry mafia gangs operating in the Parel-Dadar stretch realized that they could partake of a slice of these considerable earnings merely by terrorizing the traders and vendors.

The Potya and Bablya gang began making the rounds of the market, and started taking money from vendors as vargani (contribution) for various causes. It started off with the Sarvajanik Ganeshotsav (community Ganesh pandals) and continued with a string of other festivals like Holi, Diwali and Gokulashtami. The vegetable vendors and traders were at their wits' end because the number of rounds and number of gangsters kept increasing every day – and everybody took the name of some don or the other. But they continued to hand them their hard-earned money, believing that it was better to be safe than sorry. Then came a time when the extortions became routine, festival or no festival.

Those who protested too much were beaten up mercilessly, as a result of which they had to be hospitalized and were deprived of their earnings for days or weeks. A few such cases served as cautionary tales for those who were frustrated enough to think of raising their voices against the extortion.

Amar had been coming to the shop only for a few weeks now; he was jobless and could not find any other vocation, so his father had asked him to sit at the shop. This was how he began to assist his brother Ajit, whom he worshipped despite their differences. Amar's skill at maths meant he took charge of the accounts. That was when he discovered that some amount of money seemed to be going missing, without being accounted for, consistently. He did not think his brother had any vices, so he decided to ask him about it.

Initially, Ajit was evasive. But when he realized Amar was not about to give up, he explained that he paid vargani to the gangs.

One day, Amar showed his brother, with the use of simple arithmetic, that if the thugs took Rs 100 every week from every shopkeeper, they made more than Rs 20,000 from the 200-odd shops in the market. And, look at it this way, Rs 100 every week meant that a shopkeeper ended up paying between Rs 5000 and Rs 10,000 every year, depending on the festivals and the number of visits. The gangs were enriching themselves at the cost of the hapless bhajiwallas. 'Why should we allow ourselves to be exploited?' Amar argued. Ajit told him not to think about it.

But Amar was furious at this gross injustice. How could a few men rule the market? He decided to stop paying vargani.

Once or twice, when the goons came, Amar grumbled and was slapped hard or his kurta was torn. They pushed him, shoved him, abused him and humiliated him publicly. Often Ajit had to intervene and save his brother from their wrath.

Ajit was a peace-loving man and he did not approve of Amar's protests. He told Amar that he didn't mind paying up if peace was maintained. 'Why should we bell the cat,' he often said, using the language of his English textbooks.

But Amar was in no mood to listen. He began picking fights with the extortionists when Ajit was not around. He realized that the goons came from various gangs and no one else was protesting.

Also, he decided to seek the help of the police. The cops acted against the Potya gang but turned a blind eye towards complaints against the Gawli gang, as they were receiving a hefty packet from them. In keeping with the tradition of corruption and injustice in the Mumbai police, they turned on the victim. Amar was soon making the rounds of police stations as the police were constantly coming to his shop, issuing summons for 'questioning' in some matter or the other. Then the summons began taking the shape of false cases slapped against him. In his absence, they manhandled Ajit and even bullied his younger brother Ashwin, who was still a teenager.

Finally, Amar felt that he had to end this torture once and for all. He could not live a life of subjugation, it was not in his nature. He decided to raise his voice and his hand. He was going to stand up and if that meant confronting the enemy, he was willing to do it. His argument was that the thugs who harassed them were not God's gift to mankind, but just ordinary men – with more failings than the rest.

Amar first tried to garner support against the gangs. In true blue-collar labour-leader style, he spoke of 'Kaamgaar anche ghaamache daam!' (The worker's valuable wages of sweat.) He had appropriated the slogan of Dr Datta Samant, who had used this line when he called for the cotton mill strike in 1982.

The day that Amar used the chopper, Ajit had seen the Potya men on their rounds and quickly dispatched Amar on an errand. Amar had left obediently, unaware of his brother's benign motives, but returned soon – to find Ajit being bashed up by five burly men demanding to know Amar's whereabouts.

The other vegetable vendors were terrified; nobody wanted to intervene. But Amar's reaction was swift, with the result that from that day on, he became a marked man.

At home, Maruti picked up a lathi and beat Amar until Ajit came between them.

But back at the market, Amar's carrot analogy had earned him fans among the vegetable vendors. It also earned him a handful of boys at his beck and call. His only motive had been to fight the high-handedness of the Gawli and Potya gangs, but it had reaped a legion of soldiers.

Gawli and the Potya gang rightly presumed that there would soon be a mass mobilization of boys against them. If Amar was allowed to get away with it, it would set a bad precedent and dent their clout in the market. So they decided to act.

Ashwin, the youngest of the Naik brothers, was seen as a soft target, so the Potya gang decided to abduct him and demand that Amar surrender. They wanted to beat him publicly, tame him, and teach him a lesson that others would learn too.

Ashwin was kidnapped and taken into custody as a hostage. He was barely twenty years old then and understood that he was being used as bait in the bigger battle against his brother. If Amar was close to Ajit dada, Ashwin doted on Amar; he would never allow his brother's enemies to score over him. He knew he had to do something before Amar was forced to submit himself to them.

Ashwin was looked after well enough in the goons' custody. He wasn't blindfolded on his way to their hideout, nor was he tortured or beaten. The boy realized that the men would not harm him; they were just using him. At 4 a.m. the next day, he opened a small window and jumped down from the first floor. Fortunately, no one heard him slip out and he was not missed until later that morning.

Back home, everyone was in a tizzy. Ashwin, as the youngest, was the darling of the family. Preparations were on for a full-scale attack when he arrived on their doorstep, unharmed. There was great jubilation, and Amar heaved a sigh of relief. He thanked God and then took a momentous decision. They had dared to touch his family and if he allowed this to continue, there was only misery in store for them.

It was better to take them on, he decided. He spoke to his father and Ajit, who for once seemed to concur with him. They had faced injustice and oppression. It was time to rise.

Their tacit approval was given. It was limited, however, to self-defence. They did not know that revenge is a double-edged sword, and that the line between predator and prey can get blurred very easily. No exercise in self-defence is devoid of violence.

Amar Naik started off by getting the boys on his side, anticipating an eventual face-off with the Potya and Gawli gangs. Vendetta was foremost in his mind. He had to do unto them what they had done to him. He had to rob them of their livelihoods and wealth and break their backbones. Matka dens and illicit liquor dens were big money in those days and they were run or patronized by the mafia. They were his first targets.

SIX

Gawli's Gumption

Arun Gawli had made his mark as an upcoming don in the areas of Byculla, Parel and Lalbaug and of course Dagdi Chawl, which was fast becoming the hub for all his nefarious activities. It is not clear if Gawli personally chose the place as his headquarters – like Haji Mastan had Bait-ul-suroor and Karim Lala had Tahir Manzil, near Novelty Theatre, or as Dawood and Sabir had chosen Musafirkhana.

Regular meetings and durbars were held at the chawl, and Gawli presided over them all. The only other person in the vicinity who was both feared and respected by him was Rama Naik.

Gawli had begun his operations here by employing a team for the black marketing of cinema tickets at Palace Cinema in Byculla in the mid-seventies. The operation was handled by Razaq Shaikh, who was responsible for ensuring the steady flow of money.

Shaikh had been a close friend of Shridhar Shetty, the owner of a Udipi hotel in Byculla East, until a conflict of interest over a woman had caused an irreparable rift between the two. Shaikh was sure of Gawli's support in his conflict with Shridhar, but Gawli's clout was not yet at its peak. Shridhar, on the other hand, had a brother who was well known among the association of Udipi hotel owners, which meant he was better connected than Shaikh. All that remained was the decider which would demonstrate Shridhar's clout and get Shaikh to back off.

44

And so it happened that, on a sunny day in March 1983, Shridhar followed Shaikh to Dagdi Chawl. When he reached Gawli's durbar, Shridhar hurled a volley of abuse at Gawli, hoping to belittle him. The ploy worked and Gawli appeared overcome by humiliation at the barrage of cuss words coming his way. Until then, Gawli had never been known to use weapons or lose his temper in public, but this was an unprovoked attack, and he was being abused in his own durbar.

In the blink of an eye, a Gawli aide, Taraman Ghatkar, reacted to the situation by slicing Shridhar down with a chopper. It is said that Arun Gawli joined Ghatkar in his vicious attack and helped stab Shridhar until he died. This, according to police records, was the first murder on the Dagdi Chawl premises.

The incident became too much for Shaikh to handle and he surrendered to the police, while Gawli went on the run. Ghatkar ran away, but was eventually caught by the police. The case was handed over to the crime branch and police inspector Madhukar Zende took it over. Zende was known to be a tenacious cop, and Gawli was advised to surrender in order to save himself the agony of running; Zende would eventually track him down and the penalty would be worse. After chewing on the idea for a month, Gawli finally surrendered to Zende.

Prior to the killing of Shridhar at Dagdi Chawl, Gawli, along with Reshim and Rama Naik, had been involved in the murder of matka operator and local goon Parasnath Pandey. The police had arrested Gawli and his cronies, but they had all managed to get bail and leave jail in a month – adding to Gawli's stature. As is often the case in India, the trial dragged on for years.

In 1985, when the case came up for hearing in court, all the accused were acquitted, except Gawli. He was not released as he had also been booked in Shridhar Shetty's murder, and this ensured his stay in jail for two years at least.

Criminals on the run don't have the opportunity to develop contacts over cappuccinos or access the internet for networking. For them, jails are the best places to strike up alliances and foster bonds.

Rama Naik, who had found a mentor in Varadarajan Mudaliar

during their imprisonment in the Emergency era, had got into bootlegging and smuggling through him. It was also around this time, in 1985, that Babu Reshim and Rama Naik had developed their contacts with a man called Rajan Nair – alias Bada Rajan – in Chembur's Tilak Nagar area, in the northeastern suburbs of Mumbai. In time, Rajan became their ladder to the Dawood-Sabir gang in south Mumbai.

In 1986, the Shridhar Shetty murder case came up for hearing at the sessions court and all three accused – Arun Gawli, Ghatkar and Razaq Shaikh – were acquitted. Even after three years, the prosecution was unable to convince the court of Gawli's involvement in the murder.

Arun Gawli returned to Dagdi Chawl to a huge welcome. The scale was unimaginable, like a politician's victory celebration. Some say it was equivalent to a krantikari, a freedom fighter, returning after being unjustly jailed; or, as some sycophants put it, a royal welcome given to a king by his subjects.

Gawli's reception was a slap in the administration's face; this was the man who had also killed a hotelier on the same premises and everyone knew it.

In Gawli's absence, Rama Naik and Babu Reshim had managed the gang efficiently. They had by now spread their tentacles to the matka and illicit liquor businesses.

One intriguing aspect of the gang's operations was its involvement in cultural activities in the city. Their exuberant celebration of festivals like Ganesh Chaturthi and Navratri extended to several days and included musical performances, visits to the cinema and other group activities. People gathered in large numbers and young men took days off from work or school to stay at home in their colonies and spend time together. The gang then started sponsoring the orchestra or other events and emptied their wallets, of course proclaiming the fact on huge banners, with their names flashing amidst words of appreciation and gratitude. This helped pump up the popularity of the Dagdi Chawl gang, as it was known in those days. It also helped propel Arun Gawli into the political arena.

By now, more than 200 jobless youth had joined the Dagdi Chawl gang. Rama Naik and Gawli then thought of an idea. They asked these young men to form teams and visit hotels, shops and offices around Byculla and ask for hafta. The demands ranged from Rs 100 to Rs 1,000, depending on the business and the turnover. Those who refused to pay or opposed the boys were taught a lesson. Their shops were ransacked and the owners so badly roughed up that others were thoroughly intimidated. This was how Gawli's reign of terror spread in Byculla, Madanpura, Chinchpokli and Lalbaug. Soon, the young men started getting more ambitious and extended their rounds to the Parel and Dadar markets. The money thus earned was used to pay gang members who ran errands.

The gang became richer and began drawing more people into its fold. Gawli's power was truly on the rise.

SEVEN

Mithun Mania

Chhota Rajan worshipped Mithun Chakraborty. Mithun had a certain panache, style and versatility that other actors lacked, and the don had become a huge fan of the Bengali dancing and action star ever since he watched his film *Suraksha*. Mithun continued his successful run at the box office with *Wardaat* and *Saahas*. All three movies were spy flicks, in which Mithun played a James Bond like character. Herein lay his appeal.

Chhota Rajan was born Rajendra Nikhalje. In Maharashtrian households, children quickly acquire a nickname and everybody, young and old, addresses the child by that name. In Rajendra's case, it was Nana.

Nana was so crazy about Mithun that he soon started to get his clothes fashioned after the star's; he even fashioned his hair like Mithun's, with a parting in the middle. He felt he could identify with the star, who was swarthy (like him), yet stylish.

He even cashed in on the hero's popularity; whenever a Mithun-starrer released at Sahakar Cinema, Nana personally ensured that his boys reaped a windfall in the form of tickets sold in the black market.

Then, one day, all hell broke loose. *Saahas*, which was released after *Wardaat*, was regarded as the final film in the Mithun trilogy by director Ravikant Nagaich. It had a 'houseful' opening, which meant that the tickets had been sold out. There was mayhem at the theatre compound on Friday. Subsequently, policemen were posted at the theatre on Saturday, in case of any further trouble. But Nana was ready and on the prowl; he was not going to let the police deprive him of business.

As the matinee progressed to the next show, and then to the third and last show, the ticket prices kept shooting up. A small argument with other Mithun fans flared into a scuffle; Nana was not willing to reduce the price of tickets for a Mithun-starrer. He believed he deserved every rupee that could be made.

The scuffle turned into a full-scale commotion outside the theatre. The constables posted on duty could not remain mute spectators; angry moviegoers who had been denied tickets were complaining to them about the black marketers.

The black marketers, however, were mere paper tigers. A few whacks from the police lathis and they crumbled and began running. But Nana could not bear to watch his boys being brutally beaten up. He grabbed a lathi from the hands of one of the cops and turned on them to defend his pride.

Assaulting a uniformed cop on duty was unheard of until the eighties – only lawless Pathans could get away with it. But Nana's bravura emboldened his men and five constables were beaten black and blue that day.

Nana's temerity was noticed by everyone in the Mumbai underworld. Until then, the bunch of thugs who sold movie tickets at Sahakar Plaza Cinema at Tilak Nagar had been known as Jagdish Sharma's or Goonga's boys. (Sharma was hard of hearing even then, though not mute, hence the nickname was not entirely accurate.) After that day, Nana's boys got their own identity.

Nana and his band of black marketers were arrested later by the police and beaten up in the lockup. But Goonga was specifically instructed by Rajan Nair, the reigning don of the area, to take care of the 'chokra log aur unka bail'. Within days, Nana and his minions were released on bail.

Now that they had carved a reputation for themselves in the area, everyone was scared of Nana's gang. The entire Tilak Nagar and Chembur area began talking about Nana in hushed whispers.

At this time, the mafia scene was dominated by Rajan Nair's gang – the Rajan-Rama company – in the northeastern suburbs. Rama Naik took care of Byculla, Lalbaug, Parel, Dadar and Worli. He also had connections in Bhandup and Kanjurmarg because of his affiliation with Ashok Joshi.

When Nana came out of jail, Rajan Nair called for the boy and praised his courage in front of everyone. 'Achcha hero giri kiya woh din (nice work that day),' he said, referring to the police beating and patting an elated Nana on his back.

Rajan Nair soon inducted Nana into his group, and Goonga, earlier affiliated with the Rajan Nair gang, became closer to Rajan 'Anna'. In the seventies and even the early eighties, the combined gang was regarded as far more powerful than even the Dawood Ibrahim gang or the Pathan mafia.

Nana had idolized Rajan Nair even before he had begun worshipping Mithun Chakraborty. He ruled the roost from Chembur to Ghatkopar, RCF to Kurla East, and parts of Sion.

Nana's father Sadashiv was a worker at Hoechst, in Thane. Nana had three brothers, Prakash, Deepak and Akash, and two sisters, Malini and Sunita. The family hailed from Lonar village in Satara.

Jobless and a Class 5 school dropout, Nana had not been able to find a respectable vocation for himself. He and his family lived in the lower-middle-class area of Tilak Nagar. The building was a two-storey structure, with ten rooms on each floor. Each house had two rooms, with a shared bathroom and a common verandah.

After dropping out of school, Rajan fell into bad company and joined a gang of boys led by Goonga.

From his teenage years, Nana had played cricket with people like Sadhu Shetty, Vilas Mane, Mohan Kotian, Avdhoot Bonde and others in the Tilak Nagar area, which was full of wide open spaces and large grounds. They called their cricket group the Diamond Cricket Club. Goonga was Nana's mentor and the ringleader of the gang of jobless youths in Tilak Nagar's Chembur area.

In the early eighties, jobs were hard to come by and young men in the lower-middle-class colonies were desperate. When they could not get a steady job, they began selling movie tickets in the black market. In the era of single-screen theatres and limited choices, black marketers thrived and made considerable amounts of money. Nana was barely twenty-five years old, but he was adept at avoiding the cops. He did brisk business.

After a while, he became so clever that Goonga elevated him as the head of the black-market ticket-sellers at Sahakar. Today's multiplex generation, so used to booking tickets on the internet, would have been worn out by the tedious task of getting a cinema ticket in those days. Each suburb had just one or two single-screen theatres and tickets were hard to come by. Though Ghatkopar East had the Odeon Theatre, Sahakar in Chembur catered to customers from Mankhurd to Sion East to Chembur, Shell Colony, Pant Nagar, Sixty-feet Road, Garodia Nagar in Ghatkopar East and, of course, Tilak Nagar.

Each theatre had two ticket counters, one for current booking and the other for advance booking. At the current booking counter, cinegoers could buy tickets just before the show started. If the window was closed, you could fall back on the boys hawking tickets outside the theatre. The price for these tickets was steep, sometimes double or even three times the original. The problem arose when the police swooped down on them suddenly, once in a while, especially when they miscalculated the popularity of a new release. In those days, only a big movie, a Rajesh Khanna or Amitabh Bachchan starrer perhaps, managed advance bookings and made the black marketers happy.

Slowly, the black marketers started working in collusion with theatre owners. They sold only a few tickets through advance booking and kept the current booking counter open for just a short while. A major chunk of the tickets was funnelled out to the black marketers. Profits were split between the theatre owners and the black marketers, who had formed a cabal. Each theatre had a group associated with it and outsiders were not allowed to do business there unless they were dealing with some standalone movie featuring B-grade stars.

Goonga and Rajan, along with their friends from the Diamond Cricket Club, were in control at Sahakar. Like other theatre owners, the management at Sahakar decided to bow to the wishes of the black marketers without any fuss. They opened the current booking counter only as a formality, and the income sustained the whole gang for months, until the time of the lathi charge.

Nana's infamy had grown in the last couple of years after his first brush with the law outside Sahakar. Then, one day, Rajan Nair was killed by a rickshaw driver at Esplanade court at the instance of Abdul Kunju, Nair's archrival. Nana was devastated, and decided not to rest until he had avenged his boss's killing. The murder of Rajan Nair alias Bada Rajan catapulted him into the big league. Nana was rechristened Chhota Rajan. The name stuck.

The first thing that Chhota Rajan's men did in Ghatkopar was enforce an impromptu bandh. All shopkeepers were asked to down their shutters. In those days, bandhs were the prerogative of the Shiv Sena or the communists – this bandh was a first for the mafia.

Meanwhile, Kunju was running for his life. Rajan chased him like an angel of death; wherever Kunju went, Rajan seemed to know he was hiding there. Chhota Rajan had taken charge of the gang, and finding Kunju and killing him had become a matter of prestige.

Finally, Kunju surrendered to the cops, thinking he would be safe in jail – but Rajan stalked him even in police custody. He fired at his target when he was being escorted from the court to jail. Kunju survived, with a bullet injury.

Rajan followed this up with an attack at J.J. Hospital, but Kunju, who seemed to have been blessed with a cat's proverbial nine lives, survived again.

Rajan's pursuit of Kunju impressed many a mafia boss across the city, including Dawood Ibrahim. Now, all the major gangs in northeast Mumbai wanted Rajan to join their gang. Kunju had managed to escape again, but his pursuer's stubbornness caught Dawood's attention.

Dawood had heard about Rajan while dealing with his mentor Rajan Nair in the matter of the Amirzada killing. When he saw his persistence, his planning and execution, he thought it would be worthwhile to work with the boy. In Dawood's mind, everything happened for a reason; there was a plan and an agenda that brought people from varied backgrounds together.

Dawood had something in mind for Chhota Rajan and he made his move before the Pathans or Haji Mastan could think of roping the boy in.

Acting swiftly, Dawood invited Rajan to his gang headquarters at Musafirkhana and subsequently into his gang. It is said that no mortal ever refused the invitation of Dawood, and for Rajan, it was a dream come true. Dawood was even bigger than Rajan Nair, of course, and for Rajan, who had lived on a diet of Bollywood films where mafia dons were larger than life, Dawood was the apex of mafiadom. He had an aura that was akin to the dons of Hindi movies.

That Dawood had invited him to his house so graciously floored him. But Rajan was alone in his delight. Not a single one of his gang members liked his association with Dawood.

They felt that even without an association with Dawood, they were in the big league, part of the syndicate. Joining hands with Dawood, they argued, would reduce their stature – though it would undoubtedly increase their clout. Rajan had a hard time convincing his team that the affiliation could lead to overflowing coffers. Plus, they would graduate from street ruffians to real mafia men.

That did the trick. Soon after, Rajan joined the Dawood gang and managed to get Kunju killed while the latter was playing cricket at Ghatkopar. Rajan had now become a name to reckon with.

Soon, Chhota Rajan rose to become Dawood's right-hand man – and the don then elevated him from the position of right-hand man to left brain. When Dawood escaped from Mumbai in 1986, Rajan stayed put and managed his finances and the gang's affairs with considerable skill and dexterity. He was a natural. His down-to-earth nature, lack of arrogance and humble background ensured that he managed people well.

Barely a year after Dawood's relocation to Dubai, he realized he needed his manager with him. Also, the Mumbai police had launched a massive crackdown on the gang and Dawood knew he could not afford to let Rajan go to prison.

In 1987, Rajan fled India and joined Dawood in Dubai. He continued to display his managerial prowess there and expanded Dawood's business in Mumbai.

But Rajan, a loyal fan, never felt a greater sense of accomplishment than when he met his favourite actor at a gathering in Dubai. He was awestruck and his first meeting with the star left him dumb; he hugged Mithun Chakraborty repeatedly and kept holding him by his arm.

Eyewitnesses recall that they had never seen Chhota Rajan behave in such a manner with anyone. He fawned over the actor so much that even Mithun, for whom being accosted by crazy fans was an everyday occurrence, seemed embarrassed.

Nana got himself photographed with Mithun that day – ensuring that his Tilak Nagar gang could see the august company he kept. From selling tickets for his idol's movies to breaking bread with him – that was the mark of true success.

EIGHT

Baptized by Bapat

Until the 1970s, the Maharashtrian mafia were yet to make their presence felt in the underworld. They had no real concept of territory, clout or influence, as they had no use for such things then.

The first gang to make its notorious entry into the Mumbai police's dossiers was the Golden Gang in the early 1970s. It started out as a small group of thieves operating around the Byculla railway station, where they stole goods from stationary trains. The gang had two outstanding qualities: they were extremely proficient in the practice of their vice, and even better at not getting caught. The group, which until then was without a leader, now wanted to be known as a gang, so they randomly chose the name 'Golden Gang'.

The name stuck. The members of the gang came from Byculla, Parel, Dadar and Chinchpokli. They were Maharashtrian youth who had not been able to pursue higher education and belonged to dysfunctional families. Their lives were anything but golden, and they believed that affluence might alleviate their sufferings.

Similarly, Amar Naik's nameless gang was originally formed by Ram Bhatt, whose stronghold spanned the Grant Road areas of Congress House and Kennedy Bridge, till Dadar. The one thing Amar Naik was uncomfortably aware of was his lack of resources in his war with the Gawli gang. As he was also overtly anti-Potya and anti-Golden Gang, he decided that aligning with Ram Bhatt, a local thug, was a safe bet.

Naik's gang was known for using the guerilla technique of weakening a rival gang's hold by attacking its matka dens. The gang had started using a cab as a getaway vehicle after covering the number plate with a piece of cloth. They also pillaged the matka dens while brandishing swords – but never used them on anyone. The sight of the swords was enough to terrorize the owners and they immediately emptied their coffers for Naik's gang.

Their confidence growing exponentially with these easy wins, the gang then went after liquor dens. A sword and a few proclamations – 'Aamhi bapat gang aahot' (We are the Bapat gang) – sufficed. Their individual identities remained secret as they entered the targeted shops and dens with their faces covered. The only thing the police had on them, in fact, was a small but significant detail – one of the members was referred to as 'doctor' by his mates.

The doctor in question was a man called Bhogale.

Bhau Torsekar, who had once been a senior of Bhogale's in college, recounts the following story. He lived in the same area as Bhogale, and often bumped into him. Once, Torsekar recalls, he found Bhogale and Amar Naik sitting in a restaurant enjoying missal pav. Spotting Bhogale, and with no idea that the man next to him was Amar Naik, Torsekar headed straight for the former, intending to give him an earful about his activities.

He said, 'I heard you are unleashing terror in the vicinity.' There was silence. Bhogale could not say a word.

Torsekar continued, 'And I heard about this man called Amar Naik. Naik tar lukhhach aahe, pan tula akkal nahi?' (Naik is just another loafer, but don't you have a brain?)

Naik was furious to hear himself referred to as a '*lukhha*'. His big aspiration had always been to be a gang leader, and here was Torsekar, a skinny little weakling, calling him lukkha. Naik rose to charge at Torsekar – but Bhogale stopped him.

He explained to Naik how he and Torsekar were from the same college, and told Amar Naik that Torsekar was only chastising him as he usually did and meant no disrespect towards the ganglord.

Naik backed off, but Bhogale decided to ask Torsekar why he had called them lukkhas. They were at Anand Bhawan, at Delisle Road (near Chinchpokli station) and Torsekar, between mouthfuls of missal pav, started explaining why he considered them lukhhas.

Torsekar was a well-read man. He was himself interested in stories of the mafia and had read extensively about the Sicilian mafia. He knew about Lucky Luciano's biography and legendary singer Frank Sinatra's connections with the mafia. He told Amar Naik bluntly that all his gang did was commit petty theft, which even a street thief could do, yet they used swords. This was hardly going to get them to an elevated position in the underworld.

Torsekar then began to relate the story of New York's Lapke gang (part of a fictional drama called *Gangs of New York*), which extorted large sums of money from bread factories in the city. New York consumes an enormous amount of bread every day, and the Lapke gang ensured that the bread factories flourished, just as they flourished in return. Lapke demanded a cent for each load produced by each of the factory owners, in return for protection. In a few years, he had earned a sizeable fortune, without any bloodshed.

Torsekar said this was the hallmark of a big gangster. Quiet menace, not pillaging shops with the laughable waving about of swords.

Torsekar's reasoning made sense to Naik, and he began to see how he'd failed to get the bigger picture. The ganglord was quick to apply the newly learned principle in the Dadar bhaji market. He introduced a 'bapat' price, which was 40 per cent of the original price of goods. Thus, a bapat rate became big currency in the Dadar area – and Naik started reaping cash and respect from it.

Now, Naik was a goon and made a show of ogling any women who passed through the Dadar market or were visiting Plaza Cinema. He was particularly drawn to a brahmin girl who was a regular visitor to the market. She had a mesmerizing gait. Torsekar recalls, 'It was almost like that of a supermodel walking the ramp.'

Her walk, unfortunately, also brought out the worst in the men of the Naik gang. Naik was particularly vulgar in his derision of the poor girl. He said the girl walked the way she did because she had a 50-paise coin stuck between her butt cheeks. The girl began to be called

Bapat. Whenever she came to the market, there were shrill whistles and catcalls and comments like 'Ae Bapat, kuthe challi? Ae Bapat, bagh kashi chalte! Ae Bapat bolavte mala!' (O Bapat, what are you up to? Look how Bapat walks! O Bapat, are you calling me?)

We asked Ashwin Naik about this story when we met him, but he just smiled, neither confirming nor denying it.

In 1983, 'doctor' Bhogale managed to procure a country-made revolver and it soon got about that Amar Naik had a sharpshooter in his gang. No one knew that Bhogale could not even shoot straight.

Over a period of time, Naik's clout and connections increased. In 1985, he began to enter into strategic alliances with other gangs in the area. His first alliance was with the Walji Palji brothers in the Prabhadevi area. The duo was notorious, and known to be extremely ruthless. For some inexplicable reason, they swore allegiance to Amar Naik.

Naik became so well connected that during the 1985 corporation election, his gang threatened to stop a Parsi councillor from contesting from Dadar unless he paid protection money. And he did not allow the Shiv Sena to put up any banners or hold rallies in Dadar, although it was their stronghold.

When the independent Parsi candidate agreed to pay up, he was allowed to contest in the area. He turned out to be the only candidate who held rallies in Dadar. No one else was allowed to enter the area for campaigning, and the police remained mute spectators.

Despite all his machinations, the Shiv Sena won the elections and it was then that Amar realized that the Shiv Sena had real clout. He decided that if he had to remain in power, he would have to ally with them. This, he figured, would be politically beneficial to him – and would also allow him to strengthen his gang.

Amar did not know that the sword that empowers can also kill.

NINE

The Byculla Company

This was his first assignment as a hitman. He had never held a gun in his hand before.

It had been a couple of years since he joined the Chhota Rajan gang, but he had never got an assignment. He liked to call himself Robin, which was not his real name. It was a mask that took attention away from his real persona. His short and unimpressive physique made him the butt of cruel jokes, and they called him Wangya – brinjal – instead.

Today, he planned to reinvent his past and earn his stripes. Henceforth, he decided, his name would inspire awe in the minds of everyone in the city and he would be elevated by several ranks in the gang hierarchy.

He had borrowed a cab driver's khaki uniform and tucked the gun into his trousers in the small of his back, as he had seen actors do in Hollywood.

He managed to enter the Andheri Metropolitan Court at 2 p.m. No security person, no cop, no lawyer tried to stop him, or even thought his movements suspicious. His diminutive build did have some advantages.

At exactly 2.10 p.m., when the court was in session, this tiny man walked in with aplomb, fished out his gun and opened fire on a man standing near the witness box: Hansraj Shah.

With this act, Anil Parab alias Wangya added his name to the illustrious list of failed gunmen in the history of the Mumbai mafia. Shah was injured, but not fatally. Though two alert cops, Sub-inspector Abdur Rauf Shaikh and Constable Yash Mahadev reacted swiftly and pounced on Parab, he managed to wriggle out of their grasp and sprinted past the onlookers. The policemen chased him. To deter them, he fired at them and they fired back. The bullets hit Parab, slowing him down. In no time, he was overpowered and the gun was snatched from his hands.

Parab was arrested and jailed, booked under charges of attempt to murder. After a few months of imprisonment, he was released on bail.

Hansraj Shah, the man he had targeted, was from Kanjurmarg, a northeastern suburb of Mumbai. He had shown exemplary courage by becoming a witness against the reigning don of the area, Ashok Joshi, who was like an elder brother to Gawli. Joshi had killed Shah's brother Nanji at the behest of Dawood Ibrahim and Shah had agreed to testify against Joshi. Dawood wanted to silence Shah, and he had asked Chhota Rajan to arrange for a shooter.

Shah was provided security cover by the police and was guarded at all times. The only time he was vulnerable was when he was inside the court premises. Courts in Mumbai in those days had hardly any security cover. The Mumbai mafia had attempted two hits on court premises earlier, and had succeeded both times.

On 6 September 1983, David Pardesi had shot dead Amirzada at the sessions court at the behest of Dawood. This was in retaliation for the killing of Dawood's elder brother, Sabir Ibrahim Kaskar. Rajan Nair had organized the hit job for Dawood by providing him with the shooter.

The manner in which Amirzada was killed had infuriated Alamzeb and the Pathan syndicate. They immediately got hold of Abdul Kunju to eliminate Rajan Nair inside the court itself. Within three weeks, on 24 September 1983, Kunju got a rickshaw driver, Chandrakant Safalika, to dress up as a customs officer and kill Nair in court. In both these cases, the victim was declared dead before reaching the hospital.

Chhota Rajan was confident that the closed courtroom was a good spot and never had any reason to doubt that the attempt to kill Joshi would fail. But the inexperienced Parab not only bungled the job, he also caused several setbacks to the gang by giving away information to the police.

Born in October 1964, Parab had not been interested in acquiring any formal education, dropping out after struggling till Class 7 at a municipal school. No one protested. Parab's father, Ramchandra, was employed at Morarjee Mills, and had a brood of seven to feed.

After the closure of Morarjee Mills, Parab shifted from the mill heartland of Lalbaug to Kanjurmarg in 1983. At this time, the Bhandup-Kanjurmarg-Vikhroli belt in the northeastern region was gangster Ashok Joshi's turf at one end and Krishna Pillai's on the other. Joshi was a local desperado who owed his allegiance to Rama Naik and Arun Gawli. It was still the early 1980s and Dawood Ibrahim's gang had so far picked fights only with the Pathans.

The other local gangs, several of them comprising Maharashtrian boys, were all linked to Dawood. Though Dawood was a Muslim, his sensibilities until that point were more Maharashtrian, or Konkani Muslim, as opposed to the Pathans, who followed north Indian Muslim traditions. His family was from scenic Mumka in Ratnagiri, Maharashtra, and they spoke Marathi at home.

Rama Naik, Babu Reshim, Ashok Joshi, Satish Raje, Rajan Nair and Chhota Rajan – who joined them later – were part of one gang, known as the Byculla Company. Within this company, Dawood was regarded as the top don in Dongri, Rama Naik was revered in Byculla, while Joshi dominated in Kanjurmarg. Joshi never trusted Dawood and remained wary of him till the end. Nevertheless, he did his bidding as they had some sort of an understanding.

In any case, in Kanjurmarg and Bhandup, if anyone was interested in joining the Byculla Company, they paid fealty to Joshi. Parab was one such youth, who was inducted into the Dawood gang by Ashok Joshi.

Barely 19, Parab had began enjoying the power that came from hobnobbing with gangsters and the fear that he managed to instil in common people. Even policemen kept their distance now, he realized, and ignored his petty crimes.

But now, Parab faced mixed reactions. Upon his return to Kanjurmarg, some laughed at his miserable failure in the courtroom. Others, however, hailed him as a braveheart for firing at the police and spending months in jail. Humiliated, yet just a little chuffed, Parab wanted to earn back his prestige and grow in the underworld. He was desperate for hit jobs.

At this time, Sunil Dattaram Sawant, alias Sautya, was a rising figure in the underworld. News of his daredevilry and recklessness had spread far and wide. He had been barely sixteen when he committed his first crime. It was not a crime committed for monetary gain; he had stabbed Bhau Marathe, the brother of a powerful Shiv Sena leader, in cold blood. The Sena had been spreading its wings at the time and had become an influential regional party. Bringing harm upon a member of such a party was reckless and foolhardy. But Sautya feared few things in life. He was built like an ox and stood tall at 5'8", with strong, broad shoulders. He had a deformity on the ring finger of his left hand, which the police duly noted as an identification mark.

Sautya was born on 26 January 1965. His father, Dattaram Sawant, was a native of Karaarewadi in Sindhudurg, and a railway ticket checker in Mumbai. Sautya had passed his matriculation from the Chikitsak High School at Girgaum, Charni Road, in south Mumbai.

From childhood, Sautya had been inclined towards crime. He formed a gang of Maharashtrian boys with criminal inclinations when he was in secondary school. Manoj Kulkarni, Vijay Thorat, Bachhi Apte and Santosh Lad were among the early members of his gang. They were well-built and strong and extorted money from liquor barons.

It was in Girgaum that Sautya first encountered Bhau Marathe. Marathe mostly had the upper hand in their spats, given that his brother was associated with the Shiv Sena. This so incensed Sautya that he decided to eliminate him. He eventually stabbed Marathe to death on 11 February 1982.

After the murder of Marathe, no one dared stand up against Sautya. Within two years of Marathe's killing, the gang had managed to garner great clout in the Girgaum area of south Mumbai. Rama Naik was then the don in the area beyond Girgaum and V.P. Road, and was considered a mentor by many Maharashtrian gangsters; like Arun Gawli, Sautya too revered Naik.

But someone else had his eye on him. Dawood always homed in on those who were exceptionally chaotic in their thoughts and actions. After inducting Chhota Rajan, whom he wanted to use more as a manager, he had begun looking for someone who didn't have any qualms about taking on hit jobs.

A daylight killing in Girgaum drew his attention to Sautya. A bootlegger named Satyavan Parab had refused to budge during Sautya's extortion attempts and, enraged by the disrespect and humiliation, Sautya murdered the man right there – proclaiming his dominion in the vicinity. Dawood was drawn to Sautya's aggression, and he wanted to bring him into his gang.

In the northeastern suburbs of Mumbai, Rajan Nair was also wreaking havoc and he was immediately roped in by Dawood. Through him, Dawood made subtle overtures which Sautya reciprocated with reverence. But he felt closer to Amar Naik than to Dawood and he did not want to jump ship. Within Naik's gang, Sautya's stature was guaranteed and he was gaining significant clout.

Sautya's gang had no non-Maharashtrian boys, and he held the Marathi ethos close to his heart. So when Dawood sent him a message, he neither refused the offer nor accepted it; he couldn't dismiss it outright, particularly as this was his chance to join a gang whose roots were similar to his.

Dawood understood. He knew how to get Sautya on his side – he simply had to wait for the right opportunity. Sautya owed allegiance to Sharad Shetty alias Anna, and felt close to him; Dawood decided to use this connection. When Sautya was arrested for some petty crime, Anna got him out on bail. Later, he revealed that it was Dawood's intervention that had facilitated Sautya's bail. The young gangster became indebted to Dawood. Naik, the don he looked upon as his mentor, had not helped him get bail, but Dawood had. He was willing to do anything for the don.

Parab, who was the same age as Sautya, decided to team up with him. The partnership worked for both men, perhaps because they were from the same Konkan Marathi background. (Maharashtrians from the coastal belt of Maharashtra, the Konkan region, have a distinct language and food habits – different from those who live in the landlocked, mountainous north-west.) They got along splendidly.

Dawood gave Sautya and Parab their first assignment. When two gangsters from the Pathan gang – Chhenu and Pappu, who owed fealty to Karim Lala – began acting smart, Dawood decided to eliminate them. The brief was clear: they had to be killed in their stronghold of Nagpada. Sautya and Parab accomplished the task, killing the duo with relative ease before disappearing on a bike.

Meanwhile, the Byculla Company, like all major gangs, had become too big and unwieldy and was hindered by issues of hierarchy. Discontent was simmering within the company. But it was yet to explode into rebellion. Dawood, who was making trips to Dubai by then, had begun promoting the gang as the D-Company. He wanted to be the big boss, and most of the time, his cavalier attitude irked the others.

Rama Naik, Ashok Joshi, Babu Reshim and Arun Gawli were not happy with Dawood's one-upmanship. They wanted to run the company like the cabals in the Italian mafia, and wanted consultation and discussion before any major decisions were made. But the ambitious don would not brook any interference and never consulted them. He believed he was the founder of the gang, and it was his prerogative to call the shots. Naik and Gawli did not approve of the company being tied to one man's identity, but they decided to remain quiet for a while. For the larger good and because the company was regarded as bigger than the individual, they continued being part of the syndicate, albeit reluctantly. One last straw, however, broke the camel's back.

In 1987, Rama Naik and Sharad Shetty became locked in a major dispute over some property in the western suburbs of Mumbai. The matter landed before Dawood for arbitration. Dawood ruled in favour of Sharad Shetty and Rama Naik could not accept the decision; he decided to part ways with the gang. The other Maharashtrian boys could not take the humiliation either and decided to secede.

The Byculla Company was now split into several factions. The cracks were clearly visible and the divide was vertical but still not along communal lines.

While Arun Gawli, Babu Reshim and Ashok Joshi aligned with Rama Naik and remained united as one gang, now called the BRA gang, Satish Raje, Sautya, Anil Parab and Chhota Rajan joined hands with Dawood. Thus a new grid of power was formed.

TEN

The Second Meeting

Today is our second meeting with Ashwin Naik at the Maruti Infrastructure office. Ashwin manages his business through this company, which he has named after his father. Our last meeting was in a guarded atmosphere, with less trust, more scepticism on display. He is now willing to trust us. He seems more cooperative, relaxed and willing to allow us a little window into his life. And we are all ears.

But he is in a hurry today. Not because he has any urgent business to attend to. He has plans to see another movie. We are still a little mystified at this wheelchair-bound ganglord wanting to watch every movie on the first day of its release and that too in a multiplex, where he is particularly vulnerable. We are sure he can afford to install a home theatre, but we decide to keep our counsel.

The last time we were here, he was getting ready to watch *Race 2*. Now, Abhishek Kapoor's film *Kai Po Che* is on the list. It is assumed that he will be guarded by ten to twelve men every time he visits a public place. Once again, he mentions *Oh My God*. He thinks it is one of the best movies to come out of the Bollywood stable.

He also keeps talking about his favourite actor, Aamir Khan. He absolutely loved *Three Idiots*, an Aamir starrer. 'Aamir Khan has fine sensibilities and this comes across in his acting,' he says. He dismisses Shahrukh and Salman Khan as mere entertainers, not actors.

Movies and cricket are high on Ashwin's list. He says he is a big fan of Sachin Tendulkar but Vivian Richards is his all-time favourite cricketer. 'There never will be another like Vivian Richards,' he says fervently. He remembers most cricket matches in detail – like the unforgettable Natwest 2002 final when Mohammad Kaif and Yuvraj Singh wrote themselves into the history of Indian cricket and became household names. That is one match he can talk about for hours.

We are dying to talk about his lady love, his wife of fourteen years and mother of his two grown-up children, Neeta Naik. But we are afraid of his reaction. After all, he was the key accused in her killing. We gingerly broach the subject of love, hoping for something. Ashwin's usually inscrutable eyes light up.

He talks of a time when there were many girls on the horizon. There was Lorraine, whom he once dated. He was with her when he felt drawn to another lady, who was painting at the beach. She wore a lot of jewellery and he had gone up to her and cautioned her: 'It's not safe to wear so much jewellery here, you might get robbed.'

The lady's name was Rita Panjabi. She was half-Indian and half-Lebanese. She found Ashwin fascinating, as he did her. She sent him a ticket to London, and they tried hard to make the relationship work. However, they soon realized that they were worlds apart on a lot of issues. There were cultural differences too, and eventually he felt that it was better to let go. After thirty years, Ashwin's eyes still gleam at the mention of Rita. The bereft heart is always willing to recall fond memories of love.

Would he talk about Neeta with such love? We try using a backdoor approach. What are his political leanings? He is happy to tell us that he worships Bal Thackeray. 'Bal Thackeray was the only messiah in a true sense for the Maharashtrians and the Shiv Sena is the only party concerned with the well-being of the Marathi-speaking people.'

'Is that why you exhorted Neeta Naik to join the Shiv Sena?' we ask. Ashwin does not reply. He refuses to elaborate and seems upset at the mention of Neeta. He isn't willing to continue the conversation any more.

He calls out to his buddies and asks them to prepare to leave for the movie. It's strange. A man can be such a romantic at heart and yet be disconnected from the topic of the woman he loved so much. We realize we have to rely on other sources for the Neeta-Ashwin prem kahaani.

ELEVEN

Civil Engineer Turns Criminal

The cars were moving smoothly on the Western Express Highway. Ashwin and Neeta were returning from a trip to Bangalore.

Ashwin was seated with his cousins and friends in one car, while Neeta was in another car with her father-in-law, Maruti. Earlier, at the airport, the couple were beaming from ear to ear, as if they had made some momentous decision.

It was Neeta Naik who first spotted the burly men at the Kherwadi junction. Kherwadi junction is one of the busiest intersections on the Western Express Highway, with Nirmal Nagar on one side and the Government Colony and Chetana College on the other. In the sixty seconds that it took for the light to turn from red to green, Neeta Naik spotted a few men getting off their bikes and out of their cars. They had pistols in their hands and they were moving quickly towards her husband's car. Alarmed, she immediately got out of her car and began screaming for help.

'Help! Helllllp! Arre koi bachao!' Neeta shouted at the top of her voice, as she raced towards Ashwin's car.

The gunmen were startled to see her and an elderly man (her father-in-law) running on the highway. This was a contingency they had not planned for. The signal by then had turned green, and the cars had already begun moving. The gunmen had no time to lose so they began firing indiscriminately at the windscreen of Ashwin's car. Ashwin reacted quickly and opened his door to duck behind the car.

It was a chaotic scene at the signal: a desperate woman trying to save her husband and pleading with the occupants of every passing car. The cars sped past her, the drivers simply looking the other way as they did not want to get into any trouble.

The Naiks' two cars had halted right in the middle of the road, disrupting the traffic. The shooters, certain from the damaged state of his car of Ashwin's death, swiftly got into their own cars and onto their bikes and disappeared through the lanes that led to Kalanagar and Chetana College in Bandra East.

The police, who were nearby in a wireless van, were alerted by the ruckus and rushed to the spot. Miraculously, Ashwin had not been hit at all. He had ducked at the right time – but the friend who had accompanied him from the airport had been injured.

After the initial shock, Ashwin walked towards a sobbing Neeta, calmed her down and got her into the car. They then resumed their journey. Neeta was still trembling with fear and sobbing continuously.

On their way back from Bangalore, they had been so happy. They had decided that they would leave Mumbai for good and settle down elsewhere. They were tired of being wedged between the police and the mafia. Every time Amar made a mistake, Ashwin was picked up by the police despite his being a qualified engineer with a clean track record. And when his brother scored over his rivals, Ashwin was a soft target for them to retaliate through.

This particular attempt had been made by Chhota Rajan, who was with Dawood at the time. It changed the equation for the Naiks and amongst the Maharashtrian mafia for ever. Neeta started to feel deeply insecure about Ashwin's safety and she began contemplating her options. Ashwin was fortunate to have come out unscathed this time, but would he always be so lucky?

Neeta finally made up her mind and told Ashwin to join the gang, regardless Amar's opinion. She realized Ashwin could never live a regular life and he needed the cocoon of the gang as a safeguard at all times.

'I breathe Ashwin, I don't need food and water. I only need oxygen and his fond memories to survive,' she told me many years later at her refurbished flat in Chinchpokli.

'That day, I realized my husband was not safe. I told Ashwin I wanted him alive and not dead. And I had no objections if he wanted to join hands with his brother and become part of the syndicate,' she said.

Neeta had tumbled into Ashwin's life after many failed attempts at finding that one true love. Ashwin Naik, unlike his notorious brother Amar Naik, was not conventionally handsome. He was a swarthy young man and had bulbous eyes. But he was charming and self-confident, with a sharp intelligence and a devil-may-care attitude that drew women to him.

Neeta happened to him by chance. With her high cheekbones and big, beautiful, doe-like eyes, she looked like Maggie Gyllenhaal. She was introduced to Ashwin one day when he was hanging out with his friends at Elphinstone College; she studied at Sophia's and they had common friends. The two were drawn to each other at the first meeting itself. Initially, it was romance on the rebound for Ashwin, smarting as he was from the Rita Panjabi affair. It did not take him too long though, to fall in love with Neeta's pretty face and cheerful personality. Neeta, on the other hand, was attracted to Ashwin's simplicity. Of all her friends, Ashwin seemed to be the most sincere and honest, and that acted like a magnet for her. Gradually, their budding friendship developed into companionship and the lovebirds began to seek each other out.

Ashwin's fondness for the movies meant that they saw numerous films together, and before they knew it, Cupid had struck. When they were about to graduate, they realized it was time to make a decision about their relationship.

They were both deeply in love, there was no doubt about that. And there was no trouble over compatibility. Neeta belonged to a conservative Gujarati family, while Ashwin was a mali (gardener) by caste, from Maharashtra. Neeta's father, Harilal Jethwa, was already involved in the hawala business while Ashwin's family, of course, was part of the Mumbai underworld. The decision to tie the knot was not hindered by considerations of caste, community or religion. Ashwin and Neeta were married without much ado.

Not long after they got married, they realized that crime was a cesspool that they were being dragged into. They wanted to start life afresh, go to a safer place. They travelled to southern cities like Chennai and Bangalore, before finally settling for the latter and making their home in the warm, welcoming city.

Years passed and Amar was constantly on the run, making trips in and out of Mumbai. The police continued to harass Ajit and Ashwin like they had in the old days.

The firing incident in 1992 on the Western Express Highway was the turning point. For the first time, the Mumbai mafia found a civil engineer in its ranks.

TWELVE

The Ambush

3 December 1988

The night always seems eerier in the wilderness than in the city. Especially if death is in the air. But this was not some dense forest, this was the Bombay–Pune Highway. There were no streetlights, so it was pitch dark. An uneasy calm dominated the whole scene.

The Maruti Omni van which had left Kanjurmarg a couple of hours earlier had begun slowing down near the Panvel petrol pump. The driver signalled with the dipper, which was strange because there was no one else there.

Ashok Joshi, who was like a brother to Gawli, was sitting next to the driver. He suddenly got suspicious. He took out his pistol and shot the driver in the temple, killing him instantly. He then grabbed his AK-56 and asked his men to get out their weapons. In such instances, a second can fuck your foes or finalize your funeral.

But Ashok Joshi and his three friends were a little late, even in their swift reactions. Chhota Rajan's hit squad, comprising Sautya, Parab, Sanjay Meher, Naresh Jukar, Diwakar Churi and Dinesh, descended on the car and showered it with bullets. Joshi tried to put up a fight, but he was outnumbered and outgunned by his adversaries. More than 200 rounds were fired continuously for five minutes, leaving five men dead in the car. Sautya's team suffered no casualties, not even any major injuries.

73

The killing was the result of meticulous planning by Rajan's men. They had followed the same strategy and used the same pawn employed by Gawli's goons a few weeks earlier, when they had killed Dawood's finance manager, Satish Raje. It had been decided unanimously that Raje should die as payback for Rama Naik's death, and this was the horrible fallout of that incident.

Raje was well aware that Dawood had left a plethora of enemies behind when he escaped to Dubai. It was not an easy task, being an aide-de-camp of someone like him, but he enjoyed being Dawood's Man Friday. As a mafia man himself, he was well-versed in the modus operandi employed by the sharpshooters. They usually halted their vehicle next to their target's car at a signal, peppered the target with bullets and drove off.

So Raje had got himself a heavily fortified car with tinted black bulletproof glasses as a precaution. Moreover, he sat between two bouncers while a third sat in the front seat. This made him feel secure. They were physically imposing and heavily armed; they could have easily taken on two dozen men on their own. Gradually Raje became complacent about his security and presumed that no one would dare touch him unless they wanted to get killed themselves.

Gawli's team managed to penetrate Raje's hitherto impregnable security cordon. On 21 November 1988, Sadanand Pawle alias Sada Pawle, Vijay Tandel, Paul Newman, Ganesh Vakil and other gangsters from Dagdi Chawl followed Raje from his den in Parel, having decided to strike near Nagpada Junction. When Raje's car reached the Mazgaon-Nagpada junction, two cars intercepted it. The gangsters executed their plan with precision and fled within a minute. Nine bullets were pumped into Raje, leaving him dead along with his bouncers. Not even the bulletproof windows helped. The windscreens were first shattered with hammers and then guns were pushed through the broken windows. The brawny bouncers and their guns could not save Raje.

With this move, Gawli had declared war against Dawood. Dawood then spoke to his best man, Chhota Rajan. His instructions were crisp: settle the score soon, and cause greater damage to Gawli.

The retaliation took place in less than two weeks, a rare phenomenon in the underworld.

Shyam Sunder Nair worked in a fabrication unit near Dagdi Chawl in Byculla and moonlighted as a driver for the mafia. It was he who drove Raje's car that night of the killing. Afterwards, he had been taken on by the Gawli gang and employed near Dagdi Chawl.

Chhota Rajan employed the same trick that Gawli had used. He approached Shyam Sunder Nair, who was now driving Gawli's men. Chhota Rajan and Parab bought him over to their side with gifts and cash.

One day, Ashok Joshi asked Nair to drive him to Pune. Nair, who had already defected to Dawood's gang, immediately informed Parab, who passed on the information to Rajan. Within hours, a death squad had been assembled to eliminate Joshi.

Nair was instructed to ensure that there was insufficient fuel in the car. As per the plan, when the needle on the fuel meter began going south, Nair, who was at the wheel of the Maruti van, told his boss that they needed to refuel. The Omni van, a favourite getaway vehicle of gangsters in those days, began approaching the petrol pump at Panvel.

Sautya was armed with an AK-47 and had more than ten men on his squad, ready for the assault. The guns were distributed even as the five cars speeded towards the Pune highway.

Dawood did not want to merely kill Joshi – he wanted his revenge to be as gruesome as the killing of Satish Raje had been. And it was. Parab later boasted that Joshi's killing was a feather in his cap. The brinjal-like hitman had begun improving his resume and was slowly transforming himself into a successful killer.

When Gawli had decided to zero in on Dawood's top confidantes who kept his coffers overflowing with cash, he had no idea what he was triggering. He had thought he would hurt Dawood financially by killing Satish Raje, his man on the ground in the city. He hadn't anticipated Ashok Joshi's elimination: emotional collateral damage, and a big setback to the BRA gang.

* * *

The whole cycle of vendetta had begun with the feud between Rama Naik and Sharad Shetty, and Dawood arbitrating against Naik. When Naik raised the pennant of rebellion, Dawood issued his execution orders.

Ironically, Rama Naik himself was killed in a police encounter by Sub-inspector Rajendra Katdhare. Katdhare had joined the police force in 1975 and had no major accomplishments to his credit until he killed Naik in an encounter.

On 24 July 1987, he was in his office at Nagpada police station in south Mumbai when he received a tip-off about Rama Naik's whereabouts. Apparently, Naik was getting a haircut at a salon in Chembur. Katdhare lost no time in rushing towards the location.

The ensuing events still remain a mystery. The media reported several different versions, and came up with various backgrounds to the incident. Katdhare himself claimed that he had warned Naik to surrender, but that the gangster had opened fire at him and tried to escape. Katdhare was forced to fire in self-defence, killing Naik.

It was speculated that Dawood had managed to arrange a tip-off for the Nagpada police about Naik's whereabouts. Normally, in such cases, the cops don't stop to try and identify the informer because they are pressed for time; they just follow up on the intelligence.

This proved to be a crucial mistake. Katdhare, ironically, had expected a reward for the mega hit. But the killing, one of the most sensational of its time, led to several inquiries, including a magisterial one. Katdhare's career ended even as it experienced its greatest high, and the Mumbai police force went under a dark cloud.

Katdhare may not have been able to enjoy his success, but others did: the White House in Dubai erupted in celebration. Sharad Shetty was overjoyed by the elimination of his rival and elated that he had managed to do it in such a manner that nobody could question or accuse him.

One person, however, wasn't in a festive mood; he was in mourning. He sat alone, reflecting on all that had happened and joining the dots. Arun Gawli had just seen the first strategic step

Dawood had taken to weaken his gang. The 'R' in the BRA gang was no more.

Raje's elimination in Dawood's stronghold of Nagpada, Chhota Rajan's quick avenging of the killing with Joshi's murder: the battle lines were drawn, and it was clear that only the strongest would rule.

What Gawli did not realize was that Dawood had begun to decimate his rivals from Dubai, even before Naik and Shetty had got locked in their dispute. He had not liked the idea of the BRA gang from the day it had been raised – and he had begun with B.

His first target was Babu Gopal Reshim, the 'B' in the gang. The man was a hardened criminal, but he set himself up for trouble when he molested a woman from the Kanjari community who was bathing in a makeshift bathroom in Kanjarwada in Byculla West. The woman raised an alarm and Babu had to flee the spot, but the entire community was angered by this affront.

When the community elders approached Dagdi Chawl for justice, Babu remained arrogant and got hold of a puny young man who was with the group and attacked him viciously because he felt he was behaving impertinently. As the 26-year-old, Vijay Utekar, lay writhing in pain, he swore revenge.

Utekar made several attempts to get even with Babu, but the goon managed to survive. Finally, fearful for his life, Babu decided to surrender to the cops; he felt he would be safer in jail. But he was mistaken.

No one could imagine that the fight between a tribal boy and Babu would assume such humongous proportions. Gawli too dismissed it as yet another skirmish between gang members. There was no reason for him to suspect that Vijay Utekar had links to the D-Company. Who could imagine that Dawood would seek out Vijay Utekar and collaborate in his efforts to take out their common enemy!

Utekar was agitated and, after several failures, and was willing to go to any lengths to kill Babu. When he heard his nemesis was locked up in a cell at Jacob Circle, he thought up an audacious plan. He first met with Chhota Rajan, who pledged to support him in any attempt on Reshim's life.

On 5 March 1987, Utekar arrived at Jacob Circle at 1.30 a.m., with Jagdish Khandwal, Kishore Maheshkar, Ravi Grover and Raju Shanker in tow. As he didn't own a vehicle of his own, he had hired two cabs to bring them there. One person was stationed outside to hold the cabbies at gunpoint, to ensure that escape vehicles were on hand. At first, Vijay tried to talk the guard, Uttam Garte, into believing that he wanted to deliver liquor to Reshim. The guard refused to fall for the bait, and an infuriated Vijay retreated and hurled grenades at the gates, blowing them to bits.

The five men stormed into the jail and rushed towards Cell No. 1 on the ground floor, where Reshim was. Vijay broke the lock on the door with a hammer, and one imagines Reshim was excited at first — someone was trying to rescue him, he must have thought.

Imagine his horror when he discovered the man at his door was none other than the vengeful Vijay! He pressed himself to the wall of the cell, but Vijay fired three quick shots and Reshim died a quick death.

Vijay was in no mood to let him off so easily. He took a hammer and smashed Reshim's head to a pulp. All that remained were mangled bits of bone and a mash of brain splattered across the cold stone floor of the cell and on Vijay's clothing.

Vindicated, Vijay fled with his accomplices into the night. The police, however, had a tarnished image to deal with the next morning. A brutal murder on their watch! The government set up a commission to investigate the happenings of that night and Utekar was hunted down relentlessly by the police. His fellow henchmen denied outright any connection with him, for fear of being implicated. He was now on his own, running for his life.

Finally, he was cornered at a hotel in Dadar, in October of the same year, and shot dead by Vasant Dhoble and Kishore Phadnis, policemen who had disguised themselves as milkmen. A bag full of explosives was apparently found in his possession.

Much later, when the dust had begun to settle, the khabri network went into overdrive over the person who had played a pivotal role in the incident but who remained camouflaged: Dawood Ibrahim

Kaskar. Apparently he had masterminded the entire plan, then took a backseat and enjoyed the proceedings.

A police dossier states: 'When the fact that Dawood had masterminded the killing of Babu Reshim came to light, the enmity between Dawood and Rama Naik and Arun Gawli groups increased.'

Dawood had used Vijay Utekar as a pawn to get rid of Reshim, and he had succeeded. Gawli, who learned this much later through his own inter-gang espionage network, was infuriated.

If Gawli had managed to kill Raje, Dawood had almost wiped out his peers and partners in crime – Joshi, Naik and Babu. It was three for one. He remained the only survivor of the severely weakened BRA syndicate.

Gawli was devastated and retreated into a shell. Advised to take a sabbatical from violence as he could not match the might of Dawood, he decided to take a step back but he did not want to show that he was scared either. He was uncertain whether he should raise the white flag of truce or hit back when he was ready again.

But Dawood, always several steps ahead, was far from finished. He knew he had to inflict the coup the grâce on Gawli, after which he could rest in peace.

There is a saying in the underworld: 'Jiski nazar game se hati, woh game se hata' (He who does not keep his eye on the game eventually loses it). Gawli had become oblivious to Dawood's diabolical plans to annihilate his gang, and this cost him dearly.

THIRTEEN

Manchekar and Mother

Today, Parel is Upper Worli and Phoenix has brought the world's luxury brands within easy reach. But long ago, when the sky-bound chimneys of the mills were the only markers of the area, and everybody was living the great textile mill myth, young men with little or no hope and nothing to look forward to except a life of drudgery and poverty, sought to emulate the local dada.

Dawood fans filled the bylanes of Dongri, and Rama Naik acolytes pounded the streets of Lalbaug, looking for the golden ticket that would help them rise above their lower-middle-class existence.

Some boys stumble into crime inadvertently and get caught in its web, but there are others who are sure about their trajectory from the beginning. Barely out of his teens, at eighteen, Suresh Manchekar was fired by his desire to become the top gangster in his area – the Dadar-Parel-Lalbaug-Byculla belt.

Born in 1964, he took to crime in 1982. As he was very young and a school dropout at that, he could not get a decent job and took to working at a garage in Sewri. But soon, he left that job and sought a partnership with Guru Satam, who had already established his criminal credentials in the area. Satam decided to indulge him.

Manchekar thought that the only way to make people fear him was to stick a knife into them at the slightest pretext, and he made this his method. Once he got noticed, he wanted to team up with the Bapat gang and later with Babya of the Golden Gang, but they both brushed him off. He seemed too young, and there was something objectionable about him. He had curly hair, he wore a look of perpetual astonishment in his eyes, his body language betrayed a severe lack of confidence – he was nondescript. In the mafia world, bravura was the basic qualification, and that is exactly what the 18-year-old did not have.

So, after flailing attempts at stardom in the organized mafia, Manchekar decided to strike out on his own. He had to overshadow Rama Naik's fame with little or no help from Guru Satam. Systematically, he began targeting people and spreading fear in the locality. Soon, money began trickling in, even as news of his terror tactics spread. Once, during a drinking session with Guru Satam, Manchekar began throwing his weight around and claimed that he was the boss. Satam, who was older than him, thought the idea preposterous. An eighteen-year-old upstart could not tell him to step down and proclaim himself head of the gang. The argument soon escalated into fisticuffs, and a younger and fitter Manchekar managed to thrash an inebriated Satam.

Satam was furious and decided to teach Manchekar a lesson. But he would savour the dessert of his revenge cold. He soon joined the Chhota Rajan gang, which was just beginning to come up in the late eighties. And he vowed that before he began serving his new boss full time, he would finish Manchekar.

He became a police informer and began squealing on Manchekar's hideouts, his people and his lieutenants. Unlike Rajan or Dawood, who were clever enough to keep the law enforcers in their pockets, Manchekar was a novice and still had to master the tricks of the trade.

He had not even realized that he had stirred a hornet's nest by antagonizing Satam. But now, the law enforcers were onto him and his gang.

Satam was constantly tailing Manchekar's gang and every little scrap of information he got, he passed on to the police. Between the local police and the crime branch, Manchekar and his gang were almost wiped out of Parel.

But Manchekar had realized that crime was his forte, and merely shifting out of his lair in Parel was not going to change him. He was going to go ahead full-steam with his ambition to become a don. He looked for a place away from the spotlight, from where he could operate safely. In the late eighties, the Kalyan–Dombivli area was yet to witness a large-scale construction boom. There were a lot of middle-class Maharashtrians and south Indians living in Dombivli and there was a huge industrial belt to one side; Suresh Manchekar decided he would shift base there, without loosening his vice-like grip on Parel.

The incessant police action and the frequent betrayal of people around him had taught him two things. Never trust an outsider, and conceal the real identities of your gang members. In a master stroke of sorts, and in what was a first of its kind, Manchekar turned the mafia business into a family enterprise. He appointed his sixty-year-old mother Laxmi Manchekar and his unmarried sister Sunita as finance and personnel managers respectively of his gang. His father Dhanaji was already dead, or he too would have been enlisted.

Ignoring protests from his brother Ramesh, Manchekar ensured that Lakshmi and Sunita began collecting the extortion money and allocating work to his people. He knew he could count on them to not betray him or reveal his hideouts to the police. To keep them loyal and ensure that there would be no problems, no rifts or jealousy amongst family members, he decided not to marry. Tiffs between daughter-in-law and mother-in-law or sister-in-law could prove to be his undoing, he decided. He did not want any obstacles in the smooth functioning of his gang.

Assured of full control over his finances, Lakshmi and Sunita rallied around him. Their trust and loyalty would not only serve Manchekar well, it would thwart any designs of the police and his enemies. Also, as they were women, the police would not be able to detain them at the police station beyond a few hours and could not subject them to third-degree torture. And thus Suresh Manchekar Incorporated launched the first family-run mafia enterprise in Mumbai, and the police were completely outsmarted by a wannabe ganglord.

The young man's experience with Guru Satam had taught him

another trick. He introduced yet another new angle to keep the police from sniffing out his gang by appointing decoy extortionists. He only got collection agents or negotiators who already had perfect covers and could never be suspected of being the henchmen of gangsters. This continued for years, until the cops managed to penetrate his shield and got their informants to dig deeper.

Ashok Pardeshi, for example, used to work as a ward boy at Wadia Hospital in Parel. The man was a paramedic by day and a Manchekar lieutenant by night. Builders and jewellers were threatened and asked to keep their bag of valuables or cash in the general ward of the hospital while Pardeshi was on duty.

The other decoy was Manohar Zingare alias Manya of Parel. Zingare ran his music and audio cassettes distribution business from the Kardar Studio compound in Parel. He used to collect money from people in the Kardar garages of Parel and pass it on to Manchekar.

Young Manchekar's move to Dombivli–Kalyan made him even more powerful. His wealth and clout began to increase, and the business and trading community, both in Parel and Dombivli–Kalyan, lived in constant fear. Manchekar knew from his early days that he had to shed blood to remain in control: fear is the lifeblood of this business. Earlier, he had stuck a knife into his enemies at the slightest pretext, but now he realized that he had to plan something special that would grab attention.

Manchekar looked around and settled on Shiv Sena corporator Vinayak Wable of the Sewri area in south-central Mumbai, who was a constant thorn in his side. Wable had initiated a drive against illegal hutments in Sewri; these had been constructed by Manchekar and he took large sums of money from slum dwellers for them. Wable's initiatives caused the municipal corporation to raze the whole slum pocket in the Sewri area. Despite Manchekar's threats, the corporator remained firm. Now Manchekar, along with a group of six men, shot Wable dead at Rafi Ahmed Kidwai Marg in Wadala, on 13 March 1991. Manchekar's personal participation in the killing enraged the Shiv Sena and the police. Except for Manchekar, all the others were arrested; by then, people were so scared that none of the eyewitnesses would testify against him. All six of his men were acquitted by the court.

In the meantime, Manchekar jacked up his extortion rates and people still paid up without any complaints. He began intervening in disputes between businessmen and builders, and making slums and extensions. In Parel, he was the undisputed don. People started coughing up money to his agents, no questions asked.

The cops had no way of tracing Manchekar or his lieutenants. Mobile phones were yet to come to India and the landlines used by Manchekar could not be tapped because the gang used public call offices. The calls were made to landlines and specific instructions were given for collections, leaving no trail. The crime branch was baffled and his rivals were totally mystified by the way Manchekar operated. They were making no headway in tracking him down.

Finally, it was his bête noire Guru Satam, who tipped the scales in favour of the police. Satam had thought he had flushed out Manchekar from Parel, but to his chagrin Manchekar had grown bigger and bigger. Parel was completely under him and this was bad news for Guru Satam. He could not forget the slight he had suffered at the hands of Manchekar. How dare that chit of a boy emerge as a frontrunner in what was once his backyard! Satam received intelligence about the Wadia Hospital general ward and Sangeetkaar (Zingare). He began working on his intelligence to crack Manchekar's other operations, and put his boss, Chhota Rajan, on to Pardeshi and Zingare. Rajan, too, sought to control Manchekar as the latter was eating away at his own gang's power base.

Rajan assigned the task of killing the decoy henchmen to two of his most ferocious killers. The squad, led by blood-slurping Kali devotee Baba Reddy, tracked down both the men and killed them in a span of four months.

FOURTEEN

Dawood's Killing Machine

'Shivaji is my hero and I live by the principles of that Maratha veer (braveheart),' thundered Sautya over the phone to Dawood. The don was listening to his top lieutenant give a sermon in Marathi on the traits of gallant men.

Sautya had studied in a Marathi-medium school and adored Shivaji, like most Maharashtrians, who had made a cult out of his philosophy of courage.

'Maaghar ghene Marathyancha raktaat naahin, me tyanchi maa bahin ek karin (Retreating is not in the blood of Marathas, I shall annihilate them),' Sautya said before ringing off.

There was a point to his long speech. By this time, Sautya had made too many enemies in the city. All the rivals of Dawood were after him, and Dawood had instructed Rajan to immediately take him out of Mumbai and get him to join them in Dubai. When Sautya heard this, he did not want to disobey his boss but neither did he want to leave the city. Rajan asked him to take up the matter with Dawood. Sautya rarely called Dawood directly, but because he believed that his running away from the city would be viewed as an act of cowardice, he decided to try and persuade Dawood.

With the vertical split in the gang, the Maharashtrian cadre in the D-Company had grown in stature and clout. Chhota Rajan had become the commander-in-chief and Sautya had become a virtual killing machine. Rajan had gone on a hiring spree, employing many young boys from Tilak Nagar and Chembur. It seemed as though he had decided to provide a livelihood to all the jobless youth of Tilak Nagar. He had the freedom to induct whoever he wished to, and delegate responsibilities as he liked. Also, he had Sadhu Shetty look after the beer bars of Mumbai, and Shetty soon got his entire cash-rich community under the aegis of the D-gang.

The hafta that began flowing in from the 3,000 bars in Mumbai itself ran into crores. Imagine if even Rs 10,000 came from each bar every month and multiply that by 3,000 bars – the sum amounts to a staggering Rs 30 crore a month. Going by this conservative estimate, the gang managed to rake in Rs 360 crore a year.

Rajan used to give Dawood the entire amount that was collected, then deduct a fraction to pay for the expenses of his people. Sadhu Shetty was also given a percentage of the money he was bringing in, and it made him so rich that he bought three bars for himself: Sridevi in Amar Mahal, Guruprasad on Sion-Trombay Road and Akash Bar in Sindhi Colony, Chembur.

As Shetty was close to his sister, he also acquired a couple of bars for his brother-in-law Prakash Shetty. Thus, Lady Luck began smiling on the whole of the Shetty clan and most of the homes in Tilak Nagar.

Shetty bought a bungalow for himself and a swathe of properties in his hometown, Mangalore. Another Mangalorean who looked after Rajan's growing businesses and wealth was Mohan Kotian. Kotian launched a fisheries company for Rajan and established an export firm, Ankita Traders. He also began taking care of Rajan's real-estate investments

In the mafia, top lieutenants are usually kept under close scrutiny for fear of a coup. Dawood, however, let Rajan be.

Meanwhile, Sautya was gaining a reputation as Dawood's Yamraj, the angel of death. He started to enjoy killing people; seeing their blood spill, hearing them shriek in pain and horror, gave him pleasure.

Soon, he was offered a partner to help in the bloodletting. He chose a man called Subhash Singh Thakur, from Khar. Educated till class 12, Thakur had worked as a machine operator in Sriniwas Cotton Mill. He belonged to a family of farmers.

Thakur had become a criminal purely because of the Mumbai police's obstinacy in booking him for a couple of murders that had taken place in Khar. Every time there was a murder, he and other young men were rounded up and thrown in jail. A crime branch cop even tried to kill him in an encounter, but he survived. The cops' desperate need to book someone for the murders finally turned Thakur into the criminal he hadn't been – and a bloodthirsty and ferocious one at that. As the adage goes, 'Man follows the path of his friends.' During his frequent visits to jail, Thakur rubbed shoulders with hardened criminals. This was bound to influence him. He went and met Karim Lala and expressed his desire to join the Pathan gang, but Lala directed him to Chhota Rajan, who introduced him to Sautya.

Sautya, who had watched him go in and out of jail, was fully aware that Thakur bore a deep grudge against the police. He asked Thakur to be his companion. Thakur knew that his frequent visits to jail meant that he had lost all credibility and claim to decency. Joining Sautya seemed to be the only sensible option left to him. It would ensure that the gang protected him from poverty and the clutches of the police. Thakur joined Sautya and became his most valuable protégé in crime. Much before the World Wrestling Federation (WWF) fighter gave himself the name of the Undertaker, Thakur called his team the Undertakers.

Dawood had, all this while, continued his assault on the Gawli gang and, in his zeal, he violated a cardinal principle of the mafia. Blood is cheaper than petrol, but family is sacred. While business may get dirty, the purity of blood has to be protected. But Dawood wanted to finish Gawli – his brains, brawn and blood.

Gawli loved his elder brother Kishore Dada alias Pappa Gawli. Stricken with grief at having lost so many close confidantes, he had sought solace in Kishore's company. As Kishore was not involved in any criminal activities, he felt no fear for his life and went about freely – until Dawood organized a hit on him.

On 22 January 1990, Kishore was shot dead outside Sitladevi temple in Mahim by a neophyte sharpshooter, Srirang Pawar, who could never have been traced back to Dawood. As it happened, the shooter was arrested but charges under TADA were dismissed after a review and subsequently he was acquitted of the murder.

A bereft Gawli was distraught beyond description at the bloodshed that had engulfed his kith and kin. He could not believe that Kishore's killing was the handiwork of the mafia. It was part of an unwritten code that family should not be killed. He began a process of reverse intelligence to establish the origins of the killing.

As Sautya was leading the death brigade of Dawood, Gawli felt he had to be involved in some way or the other. So, he first picked up an associate of Sautya, Ravi Kamathi, who was then tortured in the dungeons of Dagdi Chawl. Kamathi said he did not know if Sautya was involved, but that he had given instructions to give some weapons to Manoj Kulkarni.

When Gawli's men went to get Kulkarni, they realized that his sister's wedding was going on and the pandal was protected by several toughies. Gawli, in no mood to wait, was prepared for an all-out gun battle.

He spoke to Constable Prakash Joglekar, and bribed him to get two white Ambassador cars with beacons on them. His men drove up in these cars and met Manoj's father, Sadanand Kulkarni. They masqueraded as plainclothes crime branch cops and issued veiled threats to Sadanand. They told him that if his son did not promise to show up the following day, they would obstruct the wedding celebrations.

Sadanand did not want the wedding disrupted in any way. He immediately got his son, who was hiding in a neighbour's house. The fake crime branch men assured the father that they would take him in for questioning and return in a few hours.

The official-looking Ambassadors took Kulkarni to Dagdi Chawl, where he was brutally tortured. Finally, he broke down and confessed that he had been a side shooter – along with Sautya and Parab. Kulkarni was killed and thrown on the road, and Sadanand was informed, 'Your son has been released after a few hours.'

Meanwhile, equations and alliances were rapidly changing in the Mumbai underworld. All the splinter gangs that had clout in their local areas thought they had to join either Dawood or Gawli. This would give them stature and security.

In Satish Raje's lifetime, Dawood had never bothered to look at the Dadar, Parel and Lalbaug areas. Smaller groups were active here. Now, Babya Khopade of the Golden Gang at N.M. Joshi Marg and Guru Satam of Parel joined Dawood, while their direct rivals, the Amar Naik gang of N.M. Joshi Marg and the Pappa Nair gang of Parel joined Gawli.

Dawood immediately decided to strengthen his allies and issued orders to target the Amar Naik gang. Chhota Rajan put Sautya on the job. After receiving orders from Chhota Rajan, Sautya, along with Subhash Thakur, killed Sashi Singh Thakur in Andheri.

Within days, Sautya took Thakur for another job. Along with other members of the death brigade, they bumped off Lalu Mahadev at the Sun-n-Sand hotel in Juhu. Both men belonged to the Amar Naik gang and the killings were designed to curb their growing menace. Thakur had made his debut in the underworld.

As both of Amar Naik's aides had aligned with Gawli, their killing was a personal slight to the Daddy of Dagdi Chawl. Sautya's growing allegiance to Dawood also irked the Gawli gang and they make plans to teach Sautya a lesson.

They found his conduct treacherous. If Sautya held the ethos of the Marathi manoos close to his heart, why was he part of Dawood's gang? After all, he and Gawli had a common mentor in Rama Naik. At this point, Rajan and Sautya were two of the main pillars of the D-gang, and at least one of them had to be eliminated. Rajan was safely ensconced in Dubai and was beyond his reach, so he began making plans to kill Sautya.

Dawood, who had his spies within Dagdi Chawl, got a sense of Gawli's intentions and alerted Sautya at once. Sautya was furious upon hearing of Gawli's machinations and did not want to retreat. He first convinced his boss in Dubai, then began making preparations to take on his enemies.

In the underworld, they say offence is the best form of defence. The best strategy was to swiftly eradicate all the new men in the Gawli gang and leave it crippled, so Sautya began to target Gawli's men systematically. His first target was Paul Patrick Newman, who was killed at Ballard Pier on 28 July 1990. Newman was Gawli's right-hand man. This was another major setback for Gawli, just as the killings of Rama Naik, Reshim and Joshi had been.

The second massive assault was on Kanjur village, which still boasted an alliance with the Gawli gang and swore by Ashok Joshi. Sautya, along with Thakur and others, stormed the village, shooting indiscriminately with his AK-47 rifle. The attack left Ravindra Phadke, Joseph Perreira and four others dead. Sautya became closer to Dawood now, having nearly decimated the Gawli gang.

By 1990, the crime branch had understood the growing importance of Sautya in the Dawood hierarchy. They planned operations to track him down, but Sautya was always one step ahead. He knew that the police were feeling the heat with so many killings in the city and they would come after him full throttle. This time, he had to leave the country. As the airports would have a lookout notice with his photograph and all major railway stations would have increased security, roads were his safest bet. The Nepal border was porous enough to allow people with influence to infiltrate easily, he thought.

Raxaul in Bihar was Sautya's cross-over point near the Nepal border. From here, he, along with his associates, made the journey to Kathmandu. Sautya became the first man from Dawood's gang to set up base in the city. Later, he invited close associates like Prasad Khade and Bachhi Singh to join him. Subhash Thakur had numerous police cases against him because of the crimes he had committed with Sautya; by now, each had more than 20 murder cases registered against his name. So he too decided to cool his heels in Kathmandu until the police gave up the chase and normalcy returned to the city.

Gawli, on the other hand, had undergone a long spell of mourning following the killing of his brother. His seclusion had hit his gang hard. Gang members were getting killed and they had no protection from the ire of Dawood.

But they had to react to the killings or be decimated altogether. Finally, Gawli and his boys decided to retaliate. They would kill a family member who was close to Dawood, whose killing would leave the Dawood gang reeling forever. The gang had decided to make it personal the moment Pappa Gawli died, and therefore looked for a crucial member of the D-Company who was also close to Dawood's family. They found the perfect target in Ibrahim Parkar.

Parkar was married to Dawood's sister Hasina. He was a junior film artiste, and also owned the Qadri Hotel in Arab Gully, Nagpada. On 26 July 1992, he was at the cash register, going over the accounts. He stepped out late in the afternoon, accompanied by his driver Salim Patel. It was time.

Four men hurriedly approached him, drawing out guns from under their shirts, and fired at Parkar and Patel before running away. Parkar died en route to St George Hospital.

It had taken almost two years for Arun Gawli to retaliate, but he eventually managed a strike. It was now time for Dawood and his gang to mourn. A pall of gloom descended on that long trail from Dongri to Dubai.

Parkar's death brought a halt to the perpetual violence, but not for long.

FIFTEEN

Raavan

Ajit Naik, the eldest of the Naik siblings, who had remained a vegetable vendor and never had anything to do with crime, joined the Shiv Sena one day and began to closely work with Ramesh More, an MLA. Naik maintained a close rapport with More and Duttaji Salve of the Bharatiya Kamgar Sena. These contacts drew the Naik family closer to the Shiv Sena and also improved their prospects of getting a foothold in state politics.

The increasing proximity to the Sena was proving beneficial to Amar Naik in many ways, though he was uncertain about exactly how he could capitalize on the connection. Meanwhile, he himself had joined hands with Lalu Mahadev and Krishna Pillai. Both Mahadev and Pillai were men with substantial clout and manpower. Since they were not connected to Dawood or Arun Gawli, the alliance was beneficial for all of them. Additionally, Pillai had a stronghold in the Vikhroli area, which ensured that Amar would have a say even in the northeastern suburbs of Mumbai.

But when Dawood decided to wipe out his rivals, he targeted Mahadev and Pillai. Sautya killed Mahadev in a five-star hotel in the western suburbs, while Pillai was gunned down by Subhash Makadwala.

Pillai had a reclusive son, Kumar Pillai, who was not associated with gangland activities. But when he witnessed his father's death, he swore revenge. He vowed that he would not shave his head or don footwear until he had killed his father's killers. He subsequently joined Amar Naik, whose resources, he believed, would be helpful in tracking down his father's killers. A well-educated man, he managed to develop a good rapport with Ashwin Naik too. It is alleged that it was Kumar Pillai who first connected them to the Liberation Tigers of Tamil Elam (LTTE) and helped Amar procure the latest weapons from them.

After the loss of Mahadev and Krishna Pillai, Amar forged a friendship with Dashrath Rahane from Kranti Nagar in Girgaum. He needed replacements. Rahane reigned supreme in the steel market on V.P. Road in Girgaum and he often had skirmishes with Sautya, who was already displaying his clout in this area. Both Rahane and Sautya wanted the lion's share of the steel market and there was no arrangement that could be arrived at peacefully as they were on inimical terms with each other. Rahane's growing clout in Girgaum was irksome to Sautya and he decided to bump him off.

Avdhoot Bonde was Sautya's chosen man for the execution. Bonde, after careful planning, killed Rahane near Ganesh Talkies in Lalbaug on 19 October 1990. Rahane and his friend Surendra Nair had just emerged from a bar when the hit team that was lying in wait for him also came out. Rahane and Nair were too drunk to react or even think of defending themselves. A burst of fire from two guns ensured that both were killed on the spot.

This could have affected Amar Naik, as Rahane was a close aide, but his financial stability kept him strong.

Amar was twenty-nine years old at this time, and his parents were pressurizing him to settle down. Amar too was eager to get married. On 1 December 1992, he tied the knot with Anjali Aru, a graduate from Khalsa College and the daughter of Shriram Aru, a medical practitioner from Chunabhatti. Within a few years of his marriage, Amar gifted Anjali a white Maruti 1000.

Ashwin too gifted his wife Neeta a similar car. Both the cars were registered in Gujarat with similar serial numbers. (The registration number of Anjali's car was GJ-15-T-7732 while Neeta's car number was GJ-15-T-7766.)

Soon after, Amar's criminal record exploded. There were more than 26 cases registered against his name for various crimes. He was also detained under the National Security Act in 1986, though he was later released by the high court.

Amar's innovations in the world of crime were phenomenal. He appointed regional commanders for control of each area to ensure efficient functioning. Arun Jagtap was appointed for south Mumbai while Suresh reigned in Tardeo. Similarly, Appa Patil, Usman Matwankar and Kumar Pillai looked after Byculla, Mahim and Vikhroli respectively. After this change in set-up, Naik had more than 20 regional commanders all over Mumbai. Their job was to collect money and funnel the funds to him.

Amar had five passports registered under different names with which he travelled across the world: Singapore, Hong Kong, Bangkok, San Francisco, New Orleans, Detroit, Washington DC, Chicago, Atlanta, New York, Amsterdam, Brussels, Zurich, Stanford and many other places. (According to police dossiers, he had one passport in the name of Prabhu Krishna Shinde of Chowpatty. The second was in the name of P. Shinde from Osmanabad. The third was in the name of P. Shinde, but with a different number. The fourth was in the name of Jaywant Hanumant Rao Paygude, a resident of Pune. And the fifth was in the name of Ajay Bafna, a resident of Punjabi Bagh, New Delhi.) He travelled abroad from Mumbai and Delhi and used to book his tickets and transact business under three different identities.

Amar amalgamated the business of property development and illegal hawala racketeering efficiently. This earned him a lot of businessman friends as the money transferred from hawala racketeering was funnelled into property development, while the money earned from property development in India was easily stashed away in foreign lands with the help of hawala controllers. Both the businesses flourished in tandem and Amar churned out maximum profits by providing the necessary logistics for operations.

Amar quickly started buying property in the Dadar and Parel areas. He also had a significant property portfolio in his name in Kothrud, Pune. But the man was so clever that the police were never able to put together a complete list of his properties.

The police also came across several foreign remittances in the name of Neeta Naik, which they suspected had roots in Naik's drugs business. They found out that Anjali Naik had received $60,000 (Rs 15 lakh at the time) between January 1991 and January 1992. However, she had declared this to the income-tax authorities under the remittance in foreign exchange immunities scheme of 1991. Amar's many foreign trips, of course, gave the cops a hint about his friendship with influential drug cartels across the world.

The first time the police heard about his drug trafficking was on account of Shirbad Haji Khan, who was doing time in Arthur Road jail for violating the Narcotics Drugs and Psychotropic Substances Act (NDPS). It turned out that Khan's release had been organized by Naik, with the help of the high court staff and one of the public prosecutors.

Among other things, the cops discovered his fascination for sophisticated firearms. He owned an Austrian .9mm Glock, which is the standard personal weapon of Special Protection Group (SPG) personnel. The police had recovered a huge cache of arms including .9mm pistols, as well as several Israeli made .9mm UZI pistols, .9mm automatic carbines made in Germany, revolvers and nearly 500 rounds of cartridges from the house of Zarir Dorab Nalla Sheth, at Forjet Street in Fort.

Behroj Kaikashru Farshit, a close associate of Amar Naik, had given weapons to Zarir Dorab for safekeeping. Amar Naik had a lot of Parsi supporters, which was something none of the gangs had been able to garner earlier. Apart from Dorab and Kaikashru, he also had a gang member called Rusi Sevak Asli, who used to procure weapons for the gang. Investigations have revealed that the gang used to smuggle firearms from Pakistan through Chand Bhai of Shakipur Mina Bazar, which is 35 km away from Kanpur. The other supplier was Jehangir Patel, an arms dealer in Ahmedabad. Amar's alliance with Patel was seen as a move towards an alliance with the Pathan gang. He then struck up a friendship with Abdul Latif and Nari Khan, who later helped form an alliance with the Pathan mafia. Be it with the businessmen in the Parsi community, the Walji Palji brothers, Nari

Khan or the Pathan mafia, the police were never able to work out just how Amar went about setting up such efficient alliances.

It is, however, widely believed that his alliance with the Pathan mafia and Nari Khan proved to be his downfall.

Abdul Latif was a known Dawood Ibrahim loyalist and had quite a hold in Ahmedabad. That was how the crime branch and the Mumbai police realized that Amar Naik was now working in close connection with Dawood Ibrahim. The kind of sophisticated weaponry his gang possessed could have come from two sources, they suspected. One could be the Pathan mafia, which smuggled in weapons across the border from Afghanistan, and the other was rumoured to be the LTTE. Kumar Pillai, Ashwin's associate, owned a hotel named Peninsula in Chennai, and this was the basis for speculations that he had connections with the LTTE.

There was more to Amar's connections and influence though. Even as he was busy maintaining his clout and connections in the higher circles of the underworld, he remained rooted. The police were flummoxed to see that he had numerous sympathizers in the lower ranks of the Mumbai police. Shrikant Dattaram Lad of the local arms squad was caught for being a messenger for the Naik gang. Another cop, A. Kadam of the Khar police station, was found tipping off the gang about police campaigns against them. During raids on Naik, the police found a diary that belonged to him. It contained the names and numbers of many police officers, including IPS officers, as well as politicians and builders. The diary revealed Naik's close relationship with the Shiv Sena and showed his growing clout. The police felt they would have to clip Naik's wings immediately, before he got out of control.

What baffled them was Naik's elusiveness. While Arun Gawli could easily be arrested and Dawood's men could not dodge them for long – most of the gangsters landed in the police net sooner or later – Naik invariably managed to give cops the slip.

Unlike other gang leaders, Amar had no confidantes. He was a loner who trusted no one; he had no companions, no drinking partner, and always showed up without prior intimation. There was no way for the cops to spread a dragnet for him or plant a mole in his gang.

Amar used a bike, always wore a helmet, never drew attention to himself and melted into the crowd. From the way he dressed and the manner in which he conducted himself, it was difficult for anyone to suspect he was an outlaw. He appeared to be a businessman or a professional most of the time.

He was also good at disguises and could change his appearance like a chameleon. It was this trait, besides other facets of his personality, that earned him the sobriquet Raavan, after the arch-villain in the Ramayana, who was also a master of disguises.

Amar began to like his new title – he even began using the word Raavan as a code. Once, when he was dared by someone to face a cop and then escape, Amar bet heavily on his own ability to do so. He went to N.M. Joshi Marg and waited for an officer to emerge from the police station. When the cop came out and went to a nearby tea shop for a smoke, Amar went over and stood close to him.

'Saaheb, namaskar,' he said.

The cop looked at him, trying hard to place the man facing him.

'Namaskar, I don't recognize you, you are...'

'I am quite a famous person, saaheb... my name is Raavan,' Amar said, looking straight into the eyes of the officer.

'Raavan...' the officer repeated slowly, trying to remember where he had heard the name last.

Suddenly, the penny dropped and he looked up at the man in front of him.

Amar immediately pulled down his helmet, revved up his bike and zoomed off. He had won the bet and left the cops flustered.

The timid vegetable vendor of a few years ago had come a long way. Now, he could not only hold a cop's gaze, he could challenge him and vanish right in front of his eyes.

Amar Naik had become a menace and the police had to bring him to book. They could not allow him to mock them so blatantly.

The manhunt accelerated and more teams were pressed into service. The world began to get smaller and smaller for Amar.

SIXTEEN

Mumbai's Mickey and Mallory

What draws a man to a woman is the biggest mystery in the universe. Like Helen of Troy, many women have driven men insane with their beauty. But in the underworld, as elsewhere, women have been known to be a driving force for their men and their actions.

Gawli went on to become top don only after he married Zubeida Mujavar, who converted to Hinduism and became famous as Asha Gawli or Mummy. Asha's moral support made Gawli strong enough to face the Mumbai police, the ruling Shiv Sena government and his arch-enemy, Dawood Ibrahim.

It was Neeta Naik who exhorted her husband Ashwin to join his brother's gang, something both Amar and Ashwin had been dead against for years. And gangster Sautya's cruelty peaked after his association with Unita.

Sunil Sawant alias Sautya, already a dreaded hitman, scaled new heights of ferocity after he began philandering. His lust for women and thirst for bloodshed always spiralled out of control. People around him knew that most of Sautya's actions were driven by envy and greed. But his lust for women overpowered all other emotions, including ties of friendship, with shocking results.

Pappi Shirsekar, Sautya's best friend, had been arrested for murder and thrown in jail. Shirsekar's wife Unita Prajapati started coordinating with Sautya on legal matters and for financial help.

Sautya, who had never met her before, was now inexorably drawn to her. Subhash Singh Thakur did not like Sautya lusting after Unita – not only was she a married woman, she was Sautya's friend's wife. Thakur belonged to a family that attached a great deal of importance to maryada, which means dignity, decorum and by extension, loyalty. Soon, he and Sautya began to have arguments over Unita.

It was the nineties and Sunil Sawant and Subhash Singh Thakur had become Dawood's most ruthless killing machines. They complemented each other in every way and the opposition had no answer to this killer duo. By temperament, they were very different from each other. While Sautya could not live without his drink, Thakur was an ardent devotee of Shiva. Sautya's strength came from gallons of alcohol; Thakur relied on his faith.

Sautya realized that he could not have an illicit liaison with Unita as his friend would not allow it, and also that it could foment rebellion in the ranks of his gang. He devised a solution that only the most heartless of criminals could have come up with.

First, Sautya cleverly plotted Shirsekar's release from jail. He hired top-notch lawyers, bought over some eyewitnesses and worked hard on his release. When the case against him began to crumble, Shirsekar was given bail by the court in no time. He and his wife Unita were both extremely grateful and beholden to Sautya, and began singing paeans to his magnanimity.

Sauyta, however, had other designs, not known even to his closest friends. He sent his trusted aides to take Shirsekar out for a drinking session, rendering him vulnerable and totally off guard. While they were returning from their drinking session, one of Sautya's aides took advantage of the darkness to empty a gun into him before fleeing the place. Even Shirsekar's drinking partners were clueless about the assailant's identity and the killing was blamed on Gawli and other rivals of Sautya.

Once again, Sautya stepped in like a benevolent angel. He pretended to console Unita, ensured that Shirsekar had a decent funeral and remained helpful and compassionate throughout her ordeal. Then two things happened to Unita, transforming her into a different human being.

Even before the embers of her husband's funeral pyre had become ashes, she fell in love with her benefactor and agreed to marry him. Someone tried to warn Unita that Sautya was behind the killing of her husband, but she was beyond reasoning. And no one could tell if she had always secretly harboured a desire to become his wife.

Unita Prajapati was no ordinary woman. Subsequent events proved that her transformation was complete. She had turned from the hapless wife of a gangster to an all-powerful moll. She began to share Sautya's bloodlust. In fact, the Mumbai crime branch stumbled on to several statements by eyewitnesses which mentioned that Unita was present with Sautya at the scene of the crime. This was baffling. Why would a wanted gangster carry unnecessary baggage with him, which could slow him down and make him susceptible to arrest if the police chased him?

Unita also accompanied Sautya on his long road trips from Delhi to Kathmandu. Sautya never spoke of the nature of his relationship with Unita, but Subhash Singh later revealed, in his statements to the police, that Sautya considered himself incomplete without her. So, whenever Sautya, Prasad Khade and Thakur travelled in a car to far-off places like Gonda and New Delhi, Sautya insisted that Unita travel with them. A lawyer, on condition of anonymity, told me that Unita had acquired a taste for blood. So much so that she not only violated one of the cardinal principles of the underworld – no lingering after fingering – she even forced Sautya to break the rule.

A sharpshooter is supposed to scoot as soon as he has pumped bullets into his victim. But Unita loved to remain at the scene, watching life ooze out of the dying man, until he had breathed his last. The couple lingered at the spot, sometimes in the open, if they were not at immediate risk of discovery. At other times, they preferred to remain behind the dark tinted glasses of their getaway vehicle. No one before them had stayed long enough to see their victim finally succumb to his injuries. They were the Mickey and Mallory of *Natural*

Born Killers, Oliver Stone's crime-action film about two victims of traumatic childhoods who become lovers and mass murderers.

In the midst of all this, Sautya drifted away from his friend. Thakur's loyalty to Sautya also began to waver and he began distancing himself from him. Sautya, he felt, had found another partner in crime – and he had seen maryada being thrown out of the window.

SEVENTEEN

Mobster's Maryada

The mafia attracts all kinds. Men with temperaments that can shock even members of their own fraternity. Some who kill for pleasure, some who hone their skills but stick to their brief and just do their job. Some of them, like Subhash Singh Thakur, are religious, and take the high moral ground despite being killers, believing that if they give their word, they have to honour it, come what may.

Thakur was single-minded. Rarely has the underworld seen a man who could pick up a Kalashnikov with one hand, leave alone shoot with one hand. Thakur, who was fond of his daily physical regimen and took pride in his physique, was capable of doing both. He became a deadlier and more dangerous shooter than Sautya in no time.

The bright ones in the firmament always draw the attention of the big boss. Soon, Thakur began coordinating with Dawood and taking instructions from him directly. Dawood, who was in Dubai at the time, invited Thakur over for a visit. Thakur promptly got a passport made in the name of Raj Kumar, issued by the Mumbai passport office, and met Dawood in Dubai. He stayed in a hotel called Delhi Darbar for a week. At the White House, Thakur was introduced to the rest of his tribe in Dubai and he met everyone in the gang's hierarchy. He was greeted with a mixture of envy, awe and plain hatred because everyone knew that if Dawood had invited him, he must be very special.

The daggers-drawn looks came mostly from Chhota Rajan and his brood of Maharashtrian men, and Thakur immediately felt like an outsider. That he shared the same cotton mill background and faced the same problems that they faced did not matter to the Marathi-speaking boys. But Thakur decided he was not going to be upset. He simply shrugged off the cold vibes.

When the big boss calls you to Dubai, the trickledown effect is amazing. Back home in Mumbai and New Delhi, people unrelated to the mafia suddenly noticed him and realized that if he had the boss's ears, he was a man to be in touch with. They began approaching him whenever they needed help. Thakur had now become a power centre in his own right

Gradually, Thakur began to capitalize on all the contacts that Sautya had introduced him to and started making them his own. He struck up a friendship with B.B. Singh, who was the MP for Gonda district in Uttar Pradesh. He also became friends with an industrialist from New Delhi. Similarly, he cultivated good relations with politicians in northern India; the fact that he was from Varanasi helped cement these ties.

There was a palatial bungalow in the Randchor area of Kathmandu, which Sautya and Thakur had begun using as their base. As it was funded by Dawood, all his gang members, including Rajan, used it as a safe house whenever they were on the run from the Mumbai police after a killing. Kathmandu became a second home for most of the Mumbai underworld operatives, except for Gawli's men, who were content to remain in Maharashtra.

In the meantime, Dawood's men in Mumbai began approaching Sautya and Thakur instead of Rajan. Rajan did not approve of this violation of gang protocol, but he could not do anything. A Shiv Sena corporator from Bhandup, Kim Bahadur Thapa, idolized Thakur. Thapa was close to the Sena bigwigs and boasted that his friendship with Thakur made him feel invincible.

The safari-suited Thapa (he never seemed to wear anything else) held sway in the entire Bhandup area. At the time, Bhandup had a lot of hutments and it also housed international companies. There was a huge brothel area and a sizeable non-Maharashtrian, mainly Punjabi, population. Thapa was into extortion and every other conceivable racket that the mafia indulged in. But he was also very astute. He used his influence in Bhandup to get into politics. He contested elections for the civic corporation thrice and won each time. The Shiv Sena had no qualms about nurturing Thapa's political aspirations despite the fact that they knew he was connected to Dawood. Politicians and the mafia make natural bedfellows. The Shiv Sena knew that Thapa could collect his own funds for the elections and he always contributed generously to the Sena in return for a party ticket. People within the Sena could never understand why Bal Thackeray overlooked Thapa's Dawood connection. Some said it was his way of saying thank you to the Thapas of Nepal. (Champa Singh Thapa, his Man Friday, was from Nepal and served him till his death.)

Rajan was quietly monitoring the growing clout of Sautya and Thakur, but preferred to lie low. Then, one day, he called Kim Bahadur Thapa and asked him to shell out extortion money and allocate a share in the properties that he was developing, but Thapa rebuffed him. Rajan could not take this slight and finally had to take action. After all, it was his job to keep the gang's coffers full. He decided to eliminate Thapa and he didn't hide his intentions.

As for the Nepali strongman, he refused to be cowed down by the gangster's threats, and told Thakur of Rajan's threat.

Thakur called Thapa to his safe house in Kathmandu and tried to placate him. He also got him to talk to Dawood, who promised him amnesty. Word spread through the ranks that Thapa was now under the protection of Dawood Ibrahim. Rajan had to beat a retreat.

But Rajan's men in Bhandup refused to be reined in. Avdhoot Bonde was a local gangster who had built a house similar to Thapa's on a hillock, in an attempt at one-upmanship. Bonde's men began skirmishing with Thapa's men in the area.

After Dawood's assurance, Thapa had become so emboldened that he had stopped taking Rajan's calls altogether. He also kept tipping off the police about Avdhoot Bonde's activities. And if this was not enough, he began publicly ridiculing Rajan, which didn't go down very well with Rajan's men. It was bad for business. Rajan tried to tell

Thapa that they had a truce and he should stop bad-mouthing him, but Thapa remained reckless.

What followed changed the course of the Mumbai underworld. Friends turned foes, protégés rebelled against their mentors and cracks appeared in the most powerful mafia syndicate in the world.

Thapa's temerity gave the cue to others who felt they were closer to Dawood and need not kowtow to Rajan or his cronies. Rajan's men, who were now increasingly finding themselves ineffective and ignored by the moneybags in the city, decided to make an example of Thapa.

Petrol pumps or gas stations were a favourite with the Mumbai sharpshooters because they felt they had the advantage of space to manoeuvre their vehicles in and out, and the number of bystander casualties were usually low. Dawood's brother, Sabir Kaskar, was killed at the Prabhadevi petrol pump and Gawli's mentor, Ashok Joshi, met his end at the Panvel petrol pump. Kim Bahadur Thapa, the man who had been promised Dawood's protection, was killed in broad daylight near the Mangatram pump at Bhandup by Rajan's boys in May 1992. The killing sent shock waves through the city as Thapa was a known Dawood acolyte and he had been killed, not by his rivals but by Dawood's lieutenant. The traders and businessmen who generally kept their ears to the ground were puzzled by this development.

Dawood, though he had no fondness for Thapa, did not take the killing kindly. This was impertinence. No one was allowed to touch a person who had been given protection by the don. Dawood reprimanded Rajan, who tried to explain that his boys had got carried away and that he would punish them suitably by reducing their pay packets and incentives. But he could not bump off his entire team of hitmen – they were die-hard loyalists and useful to him, he said.

Dawood did not want to end his relationship with Rajan because of one killing, but he seethed with rage.

Things began to go from bad to worse after Thapa's sister called Thakur in Kathmandu and broke down on the phone. Thakur could not forget that he had promised andabhaydaan (bestowing amnesty) to Thapa. He promised Thapa's sister that she would have her revenge.

Thakur then called Dawood and sought his permission for his revenge mission against Rajan's men. Dawood gave the go-ahead. This is an established aspect of corporate management policy which is equally effective in the underworld. The head honcho feels secure and powerful in his position when his second-rung managers fight with each other and try to outmanoeuvre their rivals. This way, they focus all their energies and talent on decimating their opponent and the man at the top remains safe. No one would dream of toppling the boss in such a climate. So, when Dawood heard that Thakur wanted to kill Rajan's men, he could see several birds being killed with one stone.

Thakur had already made elaborate plans to get even with Thapa's killers. He may have distanced himself from Sautya, but he knew he would have to use his Maharashtrian friend to snare Thapa's killers, who were all Marathi speaking, like Sautya was. He asked Sautya for help and Sautya promised to give him his targets on a platter; he was happy that his friend had thought of him in his hour of need. Also, Sautya had an axe to grind with Rajan. Like in politics, in the underworld too, there are no permanent friends and no permanent enemies. Alliances are forged, broken, mended and salvaged all the time.

When Diwakar Churi, Sanjay Raggad and Amar Avtu, who were part of the team that had killed Thapa, reached Kathmandu to hide away until the Mumbai police's manhunt petered out, Sautya squealed to Thakur. Thakur was in Delhi at the time, living in the house of B.B. Singh. Thakur and Sautya made a plan to kill the trio; he said he would bring them to Gonda, and that Thakur should also reach the house of Pradhan Singh at Gonda.

Thakur immediately took the Vaishali Express from New Delhi station and reached Gonda in the morning. Guns and weapons had already been arranged by Singh. Thakur reached the place and even before the trio could say anything, he opened fire on them – and kept shooting until he ran out of ammunition.

Having fulfilled his promise, Sautya returned to Kathmandu with Unita, while Thakur returned to New Delhi, again by the Vaishali

Express. The dead bodies were left to rot in the compound of Pradhan Singh's house, which was actually owned by a parliamentarian.

After a couple of days, when Thakur called to ask Singh for an update on the incident, he was told that the bodies had been disposed of; all three had been stuffed into gunny bags and thrown into the nearby Sarayu river.

The Sarayu is regarded as sacred and finds several mentions in Hindu scriptures. They say a dip in its waters cleanses the soul of all sins. But all the rivers of the world would not be enough to cleanse the sins of the mafia.

EIGHTEEN

Dons' Divorce

When Subhash Singh Thakur killed the three Rajan lieutenants in Gonda district, Uttar Pradesh, he did not know that he was laying the ground for Mumbai's most violent gang war. Thakur had killed the gangsters for his personal satisfaction, not for the larger interest of the gang.

Rajan was distraught when he heard about the killing of his three men in cold blood – and the way their bodies had been disposed of. Thakur and Sautya belonged to his own tribe, yet they had not shown the basic courtesy of giving his men a proper funeral.

Rajan complained to Dawood, who remained as unmoved and unaffected as he had been by the earlier killings. This completely disillusioned Rajan.

He felt that ten years of his loyalty and subservience had been disregarded by Dawood, who was backing a new entrant like Thakur over him. Rajan became a recluse and turned to drink. He was frustrated and demoralized. He knew that ever since he had joined the company, it had grown by leaps and bounds. His efforts had paved the way for its enormous financial success.

Rajan had given the gang the structure of a business behemoth and he had watched it grow like a corporate, strengthened by the complex layers at each level of the syndicate. The exponential growth of the gang in terms of manpower and money was something that neither Dawood nor any of his other cronies had envisaged.

Rajan had brought his own trusted men into D-Company and made it invincible. The syndicate now boasted over 5,000 members. Sadhu Shetty, Mohan Kotian, Guru Satam, Rohit Verma, Bharat Nepali, O.P. Singh, Mama and scores of others had pledged allegiance to the Dawood gang, courtesy Rajan.

Rajan had also made new allies in the form of the Mohajir mafia of Karachi and the Turkish-Cyprus underworld. With Dawood at the helm, the Muslim mafia across the world had found it easy to strike up a rapport with D-Company. And, with Rajan calling the shots, the Maharashtrian boys had also began gravitating towards the gang.

But the jealousy of a few gang members was enough to change Dawood's attitude towards Rajan. Rajan, who sometimes drank too much, had failed to react appropriately to the killing of Dawood's brother-in-law, Ibrahim Parkar, by their rivals. Parkar was shot dead in July but by September, Rajan was still to formulate a plan for retaliation. The anti-Rajan lobby seized this opportunity to stoke the fire. They pointed out to Dawood that Rajan remained heedless of the pain he had suffered since the death of his brother–in–law.

This was when Sautya saw his chance and asked Dawood if he could avenge Parkar's killing. What ensued came to be called the J.J. Hospital shootout.

Parkar had been killed by Gawli's sharpshooters, Shailesh Haldankar and Bipin Shere, both of whom had landed in police custody. A few people had caught hold of them at V.P. Road and given them a beating, and they were both arrested by the police and taken to J.J. Hospital.

Dawood saw this as a litmus test for Sautya and Thakur. If they managed to kill those responsible for Ibrahim's death, they had a brilliant chance of rising up the ladder. If not they could kiss their ambition goodbye and he made this clear to them. The two men got down to work on their plan for revenge.

Sautya and Th akur led the attack on J.J. Hospital on 12 September 1992. The audacious attack saw a blatant use of AK-47 rifles. It left Haldankar and two policemen dead, and injured a police officer.

Rajan was not even remotely involved in this attack. It was becoming increasingly clear that Dawood did not consider him his aide-de-camp any more; Rajan might not want to leave Dawood, but his enemies in the gang had decided to write his epitaph.

Their divorce was speeded up by other factors, as if by divine design. Before Dawood or Rajan could take a final call about their association, the world around them exploded.

On 6 December 1992, the Babri Masjid was demolished by workers of the Hindu right-wing. This was followed by the worst communal pogrom the country had seen. Between December 1992 and January 1993, thousands of Hindus and Muslims lost their lives to the aspirations of a few men who were pursuing their own political agenda.

Pakistan was waiting for just such an opportunity to fuel communal strife in India. A month after the Babri demolition, 30 young men were flown from India into Pakistan and trained in warfare, and the use of sophisticated guns and RDX bombs. They were shown videos of Muslim women gang-raped in Surat during riots in Gujarat. The young men promised to retaliate by launching a massive strike on Mumbai. The entire attack was planned and executed by Tiger Memon. Dawood had a peripheral role to play in it.

During the planning of what would be the biggest attack on Mumbai during the nineties, Rajan was sidelined. He was surprised by the number of meetings Dawood was attending, and Shakeel seemed to be joining him in these meetings – which bothered Rajan even more. Tiger Memon and Mohammad Dossa were chosen to spearhead the whole operation.

On 12 March 1993, Pakistani's Inter-Services Intelligence (ISI), in collusion with the Mumbai underworld, unleashed the world's biggest terrorist attack so far on the city. The serial bombing, which included 10 time-bombs and two grenade attacks, ripped Mumbai apart, leaving 257 people dead and over 700 injured.

The entire blame for the blasts that shook Bombay and the country in 1993, was pinned on Tiger Memon and Dawood Ibrahim. Shiv Sena leader Bal Thackeray wrote scathing editorials calling Dawood a deshdrohi, a traitor, in his party mouthpiece *Saamna*.

Rajan was aware of the extent of Dawood's involvement in the blasts. But he decided to use this incident to prove his loyalty to his friend and boss. He began calling up and sending faxes to newspaper offices, defending Dawood. He labelled accusations of Dawood's involvement in the blasts as flimsy and motivated by a religious bias. In fact, he took on Thackeray himself and sent out the message that Thackeray should mind his own business and focus on politics, and that Dawood was no deshdrohi and needed no certificate from Thackeray. His daring defence pleased the don, but it was too little, too late. Dawood knew that Rajan was capable of handling the gang, but he would be faced with widespread mutiny within his own ranks if he tried to support him. Finally, he decided he would not pay any attention to supremacy disputes and called a meeting of his men to instruct them to behave maturely.

The meeting was called in the conference room at the White House in Dubai. Dawood explained to everyone present how business was more important than anything else to him, and how it would suffer because of these pointless scuffles within the gang. Someone in the room tried to object, saying it was Rajan who had tried to create a rift among the senior members of the gang. Dawood said he would ensure that everyone had equal power and flexibility, and that eventually everyone would report to him.

Rajan was pleased with Dawood's intervention. However, Shakeel and Sautya were unhappy. The period following the communal riots in Mumbai and before the serial blasts had seen a flurry of meetings. These had continued even after the blasts, and Shakeel had taken on the duty of organizing them, purposely leaving out Rajan in the scheme of things. When people asked about his absence, they were told that he was a kafir and a misfit among Muslim dons.

This hurt Rajan and he wanted to draw Dawood's attention to the gross injustice. But Dawood was focused on consolidating his position as a don and a global power player, and didn't want to be distracted by petty tiffs.

Shakeel and Sautya had by now begun consolidating their position in the gang. Sautya had inducted more than fifty men and ensured that every cog was well oiled. With this newly formed gang, he let loose a reign of terror in the western suburbs, from Bandra to Dahisar, extorting money from builders, real estate agents and liquor dens and filling Dawood's coffers with millions. According to a dossier prepared by former police commissioner Mahesh Narain Singh, '[M]ost of the killings in the western suburbs related to real estate and property dealing had been executed by no one else but Sautya.'

His growing power pushed up Sautya's testosterone levels. He was getting tired of Unita and her demands and now he began to look beyond her. During one of his trips to Uttar Pradesh, he met Razia, the sister of a gangster called Hanif Kutta, who hailed from Kanpur. Hanif was Dawood's childhood friend, so removing him from the path would not be as easy as it had been in the case of Shirsekar. Any wrong move could infuriate Dawood.

Sautya's overtures towards Razia were not appreciated by Hanif. Sautya then approached Hanif and expressed a wish to marry Razia, but Hanif declared that he could not marry his sister to a Hindu and demanded that Sautya convert to Islam first. Sautya, by that time, was head over heels in love with Razia and agreed to the conversion. He married Razia. It was said that the neo-Muslim Sautya often eulogized Islam in his talks, specifically mentioning the aspect of polygamy. This left his friends mystified. Was this the same Sautya who had once been a proud Maharashtrian and regarded Shivaji as his hero? Could the same man become such a turncoat only to marry a Muslim woman? His friends laughed at his changeable ideals.

The Mumbai police, meanwhile, had launched a nationwide hunt for the assailants involved in the J.J. Hospital shootout. Working on various tip-offs and processing cryptic paydirt, they managed to get some information on Sautya's hideouts. But most of their efforts proved futile, and they reached a dead end after visits to Greater Kailash in New Delhi and a farmhouse in Kanpur. Some say the cops did not make any breakthrough until they met Sautya's former wife, Unita. They claim a jealous and jilted Unita was instrumental in providing accurate intelligence to the crime branch sleuths. The information provided by her opened the floodgates for the Mumbai police. Their investigations led them to the house of B.B. Singh in Gonda, where they arrested Sautya's top confidantes, including Prasad Khade and Bachhi Singh.

Subsequently, they arrested Subhash Singh Thakur from another hideout and from him they learned some astonishing facts about Sautya's finances. Sautya had apparently made substantial investments through his sister Sunita Parab, who was eventually arrested under TADA. The arrests and the busting of his finances and hideouts crippled Sautya, who realized that he couldn't float around in Mumbai or India any more. He escaped to Dubai.

Sautya's relocation to Dubai proved to be the final nail in the coffin for Rajan.

Together, Sautya and Shakeel managed to isolate and sideline Rajan. In fact, they went a step further and began plotting Rajan's death. They wanted to kill Rajan and throw him off a ship.

Luckily, Rajan got wind of their plans and realized that there was no point in seeking Dawood's intervention any more. Perhaps they were even conspiring to kill him with Dawood's blessing! Rajan decided that if he had to fight later, he should survive today.

He immediately got his resources together and acquired an Indian passport in no time at all. It is said that an internationally famous Sindhi businessman who helped get documents and a safe address for the battle-scarred don. Rajan escaped from Dubai to Nepal and then to Kuala Lumpur in Malaysia. Now, he had only one motivation – to finish Dawood and destroy his empire.

In hindsight, ignoring Rajan and his growing frustration was one of Dawood's biggest mistakes. Dawood had many enemies, but as they say, a man's most dangerous enemy is the one who was once his closest friend.

NINETEEN

Ashwin's Assault

By 1993, Ashwin Naik had formally joined his brother's gang and was part of planning, strategy and management. Naik's exposure to foreign countries, his engineering degree and sharp mind soon made him a force to reckon with.

Among the mafiosi, a ganglord's skills are tested by the moves he makes and the alliances that he forges. Ashwin Naik's first move was to seek out Kumar Pillai of Vikhroli. Kumar Pillai was the son of Krishna Pillai, a powerful ganglord in the Vikhroli-Kanjurmarg area. Krishnan, like most Keralites, wanted his son to excel in academics. He sent Kumaran to the US, where he earned a master's degree in technology. Apart from being highly qualified, Pillai shared other similarities with Ashwin. They had both joined the underworld when they realized that they could not survive on their own, without protection.

Ashwin now wanted to focus on the finances of the gang. He wanted to augment the profits, not with the help of a chartered accountant but through people who knew about money and its operations in the real world; the enterprising Gujaratis came to mind. Help came in the form of none other than the Gujarati in his own family, his father-in-law, who was also a well-known hawala dealer. Harilal Jethwa ran his hawala operations in Dubai and other Gulf countries. With the help of Jethwa, Ashwin managed to maximize his profits. He trimmed non-essentials, and for once the gang seemed financially stable.

Gawli, who was sniffing out information on the debutant, was nervous. The alliance with Kumar Pillai and now Jethwa was making Naik's gang stronger. He had to cut off the monetary link to weaken it. He told his trusted aide Tanaji (Tanya Koli), 'Jethwa cha potlakar.' (Literally, make a gunny bag of Jethwa.) What he meant: kill Jethwa.

On 22 May 1993, Tanya Koli, along with other shooters, took out Jethwa. The murder came as a shock to the Naik family. Neeta Naik was bereft and the murder was seen as a major setback for the Naik gang.

To Neeta, it felt like the price she had to pay for exhorting her husband to join his brother's gang. She wept in Ashwin's arms. 'I thought you would be safe within the folds of the gang. And now my father is gone. What if they come for you too?'

Ashwin was enraged. He had always presumed that family members not related to the gang were spared, and this was a very personal attack. He wanted to hit back at the man who had deprived his wife of her father.

When he told Amar about his plan to eliminate Tanya Koli, his brother tried to discourage him. Amar had known a lot of hardship in his life and knew that the path he had chosen could lead to a violent death. But he didn't want his younger brother to tread the same path. Initially, when Ashwin had got involved in gang activities, Amar Naik had indulged him, hoping that he would keep away from the blood and gore. But now, Ashwin was demanding to get his hands dirty.

Amar finally gave in after he heard Ashwin's elaborate plans to bump off the offending hitman, and elicited a promise from him that he would not be physically present at the execution.

Like MCOCA these days, the draconian TADA was liberally used by the state government against all those who were involved in organized killings in the underworld. Soon after Jethwa's murder, Tanya Koli was arrested and charged under TADA. He was lodged in Amravati jail as the Arthur Road jail in Mumbai housed a large majority of Dawood's gang, while the Thane jail was filled with members of Gawli's other rivals.

At every court hearing, Tanya Koli was brought to Mumbai by a police escort on a train, on the given date, and taken back to Amravati the same day. Ashwin knew that killing Tanya Koli would be a formidable task as he wasn't a stationary target. He was constantly mobile, from the moment he was brought out of Amravati jail till he was dropped back to the jail. The only place where he was vulnerable was the court. After the Amirzada and Bada Rajan killings, security had been tightened for gangsters and the casualties could be high if they attempted the killing amidst so many police constables. Also, there was the possibility of getting killed, maimed or caught after the operation, with so many policemen around.

After prolonged deliberations, Ashwin decided that the only way they could execute the killing and escape was by targeting Koli while he was on the train. So they went over the route, the stations on the way, and zeroed in on Kalyan, where the train would stop for ten minutes on its twelve-hour journey from Mumbai to Amravati.

On 17 September 1993, Tanya Koli was brought to the Mumbai Sessions Court with an escort that comprised three policemen: Sub-inspector Dilip Nirapure, Constable Mankar and Head Constable Bhatkar. In keeping with the tradition of adjournments and further delays, Koli was remanded to judicial custody and the case was adjourned to 1 October. Ashwin did not have the patience to wait another fortnight to get Tanya Koli. It had already been four months since the murder of Jethwa. He decided that Koli had to be killed that day, as planned.

As the Vidarbha Express chugged into Kalyan station, it was already dark. Ashwin had chosen Kalyan because he knew that the terminus was huge, with many platforms; both suburban and outstation trains halted there, and a large number of people moved in and out constantly. The killers could disappear more easily here, especially under the cover of darkness.

Four assailants had been following Koli and the escort party on the train. The accused was handcuffed to the window of the luggage compartment just behind the engine. The assailants had noted the seating positions at the starting point at Victoria Terminus railway station. To ensure that no changes had taken place, they looked into the compartment when the train halted at Thane. They also wanted to be sure that nobody else had boarded the luggage compartment. They found Koli still handcuffed to the bars. Constable Bhatkar was in the opposite seat. Sub-inspector Nirapure and Constable Mankar were sitting next to Koli. The train reached Kalyan station at 9 p.m. and the assailants swooped on their prey. They fired at Koli indiscriminately. The man tried to dodge the volley of bullets, but he was rendered helpless by the handcuffs. He soon collapsed, his lifeless body limp, blood gushing from his organs. Bhatkar and Mankar also sustained injuries. Nirapure had the presence of mind to run towards the door of the compartment to catch the killers, but they had disappeared before he got off the train. Nirapure fired at the retreating men, and the ensuing commotion brought the railway police to the scene. They took the victims to Ulhasnagar Central Hospital at once, even as the chase continued on the ground.

Nirapure hadn't acted in vain. Both the city police and the railway police quickly teamed up to chase the fleeing shooters. Sub-inspector Mohite, attached to the Kolsewadi police station in Kalyan, was present at the station. He started chasing one of the men, later identified as Nilesh Ajgaonkar. Unlike the policemen in Hindi cinema, who arrive at the scene after the hero has wrapped up the fight, Mohite chased Ajgaonkar from platform to platform, and along the tracks, and eventually caught him. On platform 5, Sub-inspector Kamothe of the Kalyan Railway Police joined the chase. He pursued and arrested Deepak Naik. The assailants had made no contingency plan and even if they had one, they had forgotten what it was. They were nervous and unsure of where to run, and the tracks were dangerous. They could get run over by a train.

One of them dashed blindly towards the interiors of Kalyan and accidentally headed for Kolsewadi police station, which was more than a kilometre from the station. Constables Kadam, Oval and

Bijapure set off in hot pursuit and ended up catching another shooter, who was hiding in Kolsewadi tunnel number two.

The constables saw an injured assailant being carried by two of his accomplices. As soon as the marksmen realized they were being chased, they abandoned their injured comrade and ran for their lives, leaving him behind to be picked up.

In the meantime, the Kolsewadi police staff got the shock of their lives when they saw an injured man limp into the police station after dodging the police. Apparently, he had mistaken the police station for a government hospital, in an unprecedented goof-up!

The man was bleeding profusely and seemed completely disoriented. The constables took him under their wing and discovered he was Manish alias Gotya, one of the sharpshooters involved in the killing.

Back at the hospital, Koli was declared dead on arrival. The constables were admitted for treatment, and Head Constable Bhatkar later succumbed to his injuries.

Koli's killing shocked the mafiosi. Never before had a gangster under police protection been shot dead on a train. Ashwin had finally earned his stripes, despite the fallout for his men. Arun Gawli could not believe that a rank newcomer like Ashwin Naik had taken out one of his strongest hitmen. Ashwin now became Gawli's enemy number one taking precedence over his elder brother Amar.

Gawli was afraid of Ashwin's education and intelligence. Ashwin did not think with his heart, he applied his mind. The Mumbai police also took note of the newcomer, and Ashwin was promptly arrested by the crime branch.

Now that Ashwin Naik was contained for a while behind bars, Gawli decided to continue his attacks on Naik's financers. Sada Pawle was entrusted with the agenda of weakening and finishing off Naik's gang. Following his boss's diktats, Pawle summoned Babubhai Shah, the owner of Sheetal Stores on Grant Road, to Dagdi Chawl, but he refused to come. Pawle had called Shah to tell him to shift his allegiance and payments – from Naik to Gawli.

Sheetal Stores was a popular haunt for the créme-de-la-créme and the store was making a lot of money. Shah thought that because he knew Amar Naik, he need not be scared of the small-timer Sada Pawle. But Shah's refusal angered Pawle and Gawli, and in true mafiosi style, they planned to make Shah pay for his arrogance.

On 6 March 1994, Shah was brutally killed by Pawle and his men. Subsequently, his son Viren Shah quietly coughed up Rs 25 lakh for Gawli. The Mumbai police booked and arrested Gawli for the murder. But the deed was done and the message had been conveyed: Arun Gawli was no slouch and he could take on the might of all the Naiks put together.

Shah's killing rattled the Naik gang. Ashwin and Amar began drawing up plans to decimate the Gawli gang. Amar wanted to hit back at Gawli just the way he had hit at them, by striking at their financial nerve. But Ashwin was in police custody and it was left to Amar to take the battle into Gawli's camp.

Amar Naik knew that the biggest chunk of Gawli's funding came from the mill owners around the Dagdi Chawl area. Naik planned a major assault on Gawli's patrons. The mill owners who were colluding with Gawli and his nephew Sachin Ahir to fill the coffers of the gang would be his next targets, he decided.

TWENTY

Mills and Minions

The Khatau Makanji Spinning and Weaving Mill at Byculla was established in 1869, barely twelve years after the historic 1857 uprising in India, and fifteen years after the first cotton mill was established in the city. Built over a sprawling thirteen-acre complex, the mill has the dubious distinction of having changed Mumbai's skyline, shaped the destiny of two mafia gangs and somehow been responsible for the gruesome murder of more than a dozen men, among other things. It also boosted the careers of several ministers who were allies of the Congress in the state.

The story begins in the 1990s when the mill, with a workforce of more than 5,700, began registering an annual loss of more than Rs 54 crore, year after year. The chairman and managing director Sunit Khatau decided to contain his losses by selling the land on which the mill stood and moving his operations to the suburbs, to a less expensive plot in Borivli.

An astute businessman, Sunit Khatau, at fifty-five, was smarter than many of his peers and business rivals. Those were the days when mill owners were slowly coming around to the idea that they could construct multi-storey high-rises and chuck the workers in the bin after working out a compromise with the unions. Khatau had already bought a forty-acre plot in Borivli. The mill tycoon had a Plan B, which was even better from a business point of view. He could shift the mills to Mahad village, which was 170 km from Mumbai, where land was available at throwaway prices. With this move, he thought he could revive the business.

The liberalization policies introduced by the central government in 1992 had inspired Khatau to take such a bold step, along with the fact that he had Arun Gawli's support. According to the government procedure for such relocation, he needed to approach the Board for Industrial and Financial Reconstruction (BIFR) for approval. BIFR is an agency of the Government of India and part of the finance ministry. Its objective is to determine the health of industrial companies, to assist in reviving those that may be viable and shutting down those that are not.

Khatau started making the rounds of Mantralaya and the board offices and, in the documents he submitted, he undervalued the price of the 50,000 sq. mt. plot of land, putting it at just Rs 80 crore. When the government conducted its own survey to establish the true price of the land, based on the properties around the mill complex, they realized that it was worth at least Rs 300 crore.

After much consultation and wrangling, BIFR and the state government approved the plan, but with the rider that the recognized union should unanimously agree with it as well. The Khatau mill land sale was the first to get such a go-ahead from BIFR. Sharad Pawar was the chief minister of Maharashtra, and the government at the time was keen on allowing mills to sell or develop surplus land to raise capital for modernization. There were allegations that the government wanted to test the waters with Khatau mills, that eventually it wanted all mills to shift out of the area. Khatau got the green light for his project despite several hurdles that might have been daunting for any other businessman.

Encouraged by his success, Sunit Khatau approached the mill union, RMMS, whose leader was Haribhau Naik. An industry-level union representing the interests of the cotton textile mills in the city, RMMS was controlled by the Congress in those days. The Bombay Industrial Relations Act, 1946, had ensured that only one body could represent the mill workers' interests. At the time of the Khatau episode, RMMS had a membership of 150,000 workers, a board of

917 representatives and a managing committee of sixty-four people. Haribhau Naik was opposed to the Khatau plan in the absence of a proper rehabilitation package for the workers. It was a question of the livelihood of thousands of people. Haribhau refused to be party to such a decision, which threatened to jeopardize the lives of so many families.

Khatau realized that Naik could not be bribed or intimidated, so he decided to engineer his defeat in the next union elections. For this, he was even willing to use strong-arm tactics, including seeking an alliance with Arun Gawli. In the meantime, Khatau had already converted Shankarrao Jadhav, an aspiring union leader, into an ally. Jadhav, who was promised a great deal in return for toeing the Khatau line, seized the golden opportunity. But Khatau knew that Haribhau Naik could not be defeated easily as he was popular with the rank and file.

There are no records of when and how Sunit Khatau landed at Dagdi Chawl, Arun Gawli's den, which was just a stone's throw away from Khatau mills. It was well-known that Gawli called the shots in Byculla and the surrounding areas. Khatau is said to have paid him an advance of Rs 3 crore and promised him 5 per cent of the sale price. Gawli is reported to have negotiated for 10 per cent.

There is no record of officially computed numbers, but the approximate calculation by experts indicates that Khatau would have made Rs 500 crore. Gawli would have earned a cool Rs 50 crore, making him the richest ganglord in Mumbai. Land values in the mill area at that point were between 10 and 20 crore rupees an acre.

Gawli began to work on the workers' union. His first move was to plant his brother Vijay Ahir and nephew Sachin Ahir among the workers. Vijay and Sachin began to shadow Khatau as his personal bodyguard and aide-de-camp respectively. Groups of workers were threatened, bullied and intimidated and all ploys available were used to coerce the workers to sign a memorandum agreeing to shift the mill. The workers had been resisting in the hope that Haribhau would trounce Shankarrao Jadhav in the forthcoming elections. But, for the first time in the history of the Congress-controlled RMMS, Arun

Gawli took over the union. In April 1994, workers' representatives from fifty-four mills were forced to elect Jadhav as a puppet president and Gawli's nephew, Sachin Ahir, as one of the secretaries.

Once Shankarrao Jadhav replaced Haribhau Naik at RMMS, Vijay Ahir and Sachin Ahir managed to extract the much sought-after declaration, signed by the workers, allowing the sale of mill land and the shifting of the mill to another area. However, Khatau's victory was short-lived.

Union leader Dr Datta Samant and Haribhau Naik had sought the government's intervention in the matter, which they felt could be a precursor to more such sales. The government, however, preferred to turn a blind eye.

Darryl D'Monte, who documented the story of Mumbai's mill land in *Ripping the Fabric: The Decline of Mumbai and Its Mills*, says, 'According to reports, he (Khatau) had almost sewn up a contract with a construction company which was a front for the gang led by Dawood Ibrahim, who had set up base in Dubai. Dr Datta Samant made this allegation openly, saying the deal had been struck for Rs 400 crore. He said politicians and mill owners were responsible for the infiltration of criminal elements into unions.'

It was not just Datta Samant and the mill workers who were worried about this development at Khatau mills. Amar Naik, too, was angry, for Gawli was all set to monopolize profits in what he considered was his fiefdom.

In 1994, a gang earning a jackpot of Rs 50 crore could de facto run the city. Gawli's political ambitions were known to Amar, who was worried about the amount of ammunition and the political clout that Gawli could buy with that kind of money. His own gang could be decimated.

Amar Naik decided that Khatau could not get away without giving him a share of the pie. He made overtures to Gawli and began sending messages to Khatau.

The mill owner, who had just survived one major crisis, was highly perturbed by Amar's entry on the scene. He had not reckoned that he would have to concern himself with any other don after aligning with

Gawli. Also, he had seen that in the past couple of years, Gawli had shrewdly neutralized all his detractors. Khatau was impressed with Gawli's deployment of Vijay and Sachin to handle the sensitive issue of the workers, so he had no problem giving him a commission. But he did have problems giving money to Amar Naik. Just because the gangster happened to call the shots in the vicinity – the Chinchpokli and Currey Road areas – he didn't need to get a cut, or so he thought.

Khatau began discussing his options with Sachin and Vijay, his conduits to Arun Gawli. Gawli was in Yerawada jail at the time, managing to run the gang from behind bars as was the tradition. When the Ahirs conveyed Khatau's fears to him, Gawli told them to tell Khatau to ignore Naik's threats.

Amar's moles were closely watching these developments. They reported that Khatau had been seen visiting Dagdi Chawl at all hours. The Naik gang was getting desperate. Amar realized that Khatau had become evasive, refusing to respond to his messages.

The gang members held a meeting and Amar Naik expressed his fear about Arun Gawli becoming numero uno in the underworld after the Khatau money came in. All the other gang members felt that if Khatau was not going to share the booty with them, they might as well stop Gawli from getting the money. It was decided that Khatau would have to be killed, if they were to put a brake on the Khatau-Gawli deal.

Just as Naik had his moles in Dagdi Chawl, Gawli had his snitches in 144 Tenements in Chinchpokli, where Amar Naik held sway. When he heard that Naik had decided to kill Khatau and that they were staking him out already, Gawli decided to pre-empt the move by launching an assault on the Naik gang. He assigned the job to the dreaded Sadanand Pawle alias Sada Mama.

Sada Pawle was an ambitious gangster who did not recognize the power or authority of anyone except Gawli. His recklessness and temerity were legendary; he did not believe in the power of persuasion or dialogue. He always carried a gun tucked under his belt, unlike other gangsters, who preferred to keep it in the small of their backs.

Sada met his master Gawli at Yerawada jail and told him point blank that there was no point in killing the shooters of the Naik gang; he should be allowed to scalp the bosses. Gawli then gave the go-ahead to kill Amar. But Sada was more keen on killing Ashwin because Ashwin was responsible for the murder of Tanya Koli, who had been a close drinking buddy of his. In one stroke, he said, they would avenge Koli's murder and get Amar Naik off Khatau's back.

Sada Pawle left Yerawada promising Gawli that he would derive undiluted pleasure from the killing of Ashwin Naik.

TWENTY-ONE

The Third Meeting

By the time we meet Ashwin Naik for the third time, he has warmed up to us.

Earlier, he oscillated between a grim smile and a raging temper, corresponding to the questions asked. Slowly, he is beginning to smile at most of the questions.

He tells us that he enjoys travelling to Goa as the beaches and the weather there soothe him. He likes Scotch with plain water, a drink that he has every evening. He feels it helps him think. He also likes Urak, a local brew.

'I like to wheel around the Shivaji Park area, it has a calming effect on me. I top it up with a Subway sandwich and salad.'

We ask him if he has ever thought of writing a biography. He gives us a broad smile. 'Kaun apne pairon pe kulhadi maarega?' (Why would I want to chop off my own feet?) He suddenly gets worked up.

'These media people keep speculating about me and my family,' he says. In his opinion, the media has always portrayed him in a bad light, irrespective of the social work he does. He cites the example of a city tabloid that did a story about the possibility of his daughter getting married to the son of his one-time arch-rival, Arun Gawli.

'Journalists should respect the privacy of an individual. My daughter and I had to call a press conference to counter the false story.'

Ashwin tells us that the Mumbai police always thwarted his attempts at social work. They booked him in extortion and harassment

126

cases even when he was merely helping people. 'One fellow, Atul Potnis, duped me of Rs 6 crore in a supposed business investment. If I didn't do anything to this person who made a fool out of me, why would I torture those whom I am trying to help?'

It seems unbelievable that Ashwin would so easily forgive and forget a man who had cheated him of such a large amount. With his academic background, why would he want to still be associated with the mafia, we wonder. He does not tell us much about it, but talks about other, related things.

'I am very good with technology,' he says. Naik and Kumar Pillai are the only two members of the mafia who are fluent in English and have had a good education. Naik can draw up strategies that put the shrewdest mind to shame.

Though he is cagey, the ganglord makes one unexpected allowance: he shows us the bullet marks on his body. Ashwin is among the few gangsters in the city who has survived several attacks on him, and he cherishes the bullet marks like he would value trophies. He narrates to us the story behind each of them. But etched most clearly in his mind are memories of the day when Gawli's men crippled him for life in an attack at the sessions court premises in 1994.

TWENTY-TWO

The Crippling Bullet

Unlike the youth of previous generations, pounding the pavements and seeking out the government's Unemployment Exchange for a placement, young people in the nineties had more opportunities. The decade slowly ushered in progress, with liberalization. Anybody with adequate qualification, survival instincts and the ability to outsmart the next person could find a job in the up-and-coming sectors, which thrived on competition. However, for those who grew up in the cotton mill areas of south Mumbai, jobs were still few and far between – especially because they did not have the means or resources to study beyond school. The 1982 strike had ripped apart the social fabric, the livelihoods, childhoods, relationships and mindsets of an entire generation. Youngsters were pulled out of school, jobless fathers took to alcohol, women deserted their husbands, and everybody was snapping at everybody else. Values and morals took a beating and youngsters were willing to do just about anything for some hard cash that would put food on the table.

Ravindra Sawant was one such frustrated, jobless youth from Girangaon. He too had made several visits to the Employment Exchange offices in south Mumbai. An incomplete education meant he would forever remain on the waiting list, along with thousands of others, even for an unskilled job like that of a peon.

After drifting around for more than two years, Sawant heard from a friend about the prospect of making money through the mafia.

Upon further inquiry, he learned that one way he could earn a quick buck was by becoming a sharpshooter. If he swung the job, he could survive for at least a year.

The more he thought about it, the more he liked the idea. His friend Anil Gavkar promised to introduce him to 'Daddy' Arun Gawli, the reigning don of central Mumbai.

The pair travelled to Yerawada Central Jail, where Arun Gawli and Sada Pawle were serving time. They made a false entry in the jail register and met Gawli. As usual, Gawli had managed to get himself a special cell and was availing of several facilities which other prisoners could only dream of. He was known for holding grand meetings at his Dagdi Chawl residence, as though he were a king giving audience to his subjects, addressing their grievances. These were called 'durbars', a royal term used to refer to a ganglord's meetings in a comparison that rang true in terms of power at least.

After meeting Sawant, Gawli pointed him in Sada Pawle's direction and explained how he should get in touch with him for assignments as Pawle was soon scheduled for release from prison. Sawant was extremely pleased with the meeting. It was as if he had met God himself. He now imagined a happy end to his days of unemployment. After Pawle was released, he summoned Sawant to Dagdi Chawl. Their meetings became regular and Pawle provided him with money for his daily expenses. Within the premises of Dagdi Chawl, Sawant met many like-minded people, one of whom was Nagesh Mohite. The two soon became friends and started visiting Dagdi Chawl together.

One day, having received instructions from Gawli, Pawle called Sawant and Mohite and instructed them to eliminate Ashwin Naik. Ashwin had been arrested in the Tanya Koli murder case under TADA and was lodged at Adharwadi jail in Kalyan. He was regularly produced in the old building of sessions court No. 33 on the fifth floor. Pawle asked Mohite to conduct a thorough reconnaissance of Ashwin's court schedule and the long procedures and formalities that accompanied the hearings.

While Nagesh Mohite was busy trying to track the movements of the police personnel and Ashwin's escort party, Sawant was getting some target practice in a room at Dagdi Chawl. Pawle had provided him with a gun, and Sawant began honing his skills as a shooter.

Finally, the day arrived. It was 18 April 1994. Nagesh spotted Ashwin in the hall on the ground floor, waiting for his hearing. He was accompanied by constables Laxman Thorawat and Bhagyawan Nikam and commandoes Bhagwat Sondane and Sanjay Bhingardibe, who were armed with carbines. He raced back to Dagdi Chawl and informed Pawle that Ashwin was waiting and would be there for a long time before his hearing began. Pawle decided that this was the day to eliminate Ashwin. He gave Sawant a lawyer's black coat and white shirt. He also gave him a gun, a few bullets and clear instructions: Sawant was to shoot Ashwin at point-blank range, straight in the head, and ensure that he was dead before running from the spot. If he could not escape, he should immediately drop his gun and surrender to the police to avoid being shot at. After the briefing, Sawant left for the sessions court.

Mohite and Sawant entered court No. 33 and waited there for the hearing to begin. When Naik entered the court, Mohite pointed at him discreetly, giving Sawant visual confirmation of his identity.

Sawant now waited for an opportunity to strike. He was not prepared for the number of people surrounding his target, and hunkered down for a long wait. Around 3 p.m., Ashwin and five other accused were produced in court. Unfortunately for Sawant, the case was almost immediately adjourned to 22 April 1994.

Sawant had summoned all his courage for that day, but his target seemed to be dodging him. He watched as Naik, along with the other five, was taken to the ground floor. A van waited outside to take them back to Kalyan. Mohite started pressurizing Sawant, telling him to get Naik right then – or the opportunity would be lost forever. Sawant, who was already frustrated after waiting so long for a clear shot at Naik, ran downstairs and got to a spot in front of his target.

No one paid any heed to Sawant in his lawyer's attire as he stood behind a pillar. As Ashwin walked towards the pillar, Sawant aimed at his head but ended up shooting him in the neck. Ashwin, who was handcuffed, collapsed instantly and fell to the ground. Sawant, who wanted to make sure the job was completed, continued to fire at Ashwin. In the process, he got constables Thorawat and Nikam in their legs. While this was happening, Commando Bhagwat Sondane started firing in Sawant's direction and all hell broke loose. Sondane fired more than twenty-five rounds from his carbine. Sawant was shot on the right side of his neck and he too fell down. Still, the boy continued firing.

Meanwhile, Mohite took this opportunity to escape. By now, Sondane and Sawant were wrestling, rolling on the floor. Sondane snatched the gun from Sawant's hands. The commotion attracted the attention of other officials present at the court. Inspector Ratan Singh Rathod and Bhagwat, who were present in the TADA court for another hearing, ran to the spot. Sawant was outnumbered and Rathod arrested him. He was bundled into the van that had been meant for his target, and taken into custody.

Rathod ensured that Sondane, the main witness, was also in the van before taking Sawant to the Cuffe Parade police station. The Mumbai police have always had unresolved problems with the designated jurisdiction territory of various police stations. When Rathod's team reached the Cuffe Parade police station, they were welcomed by the Mumbai police's signature line on the issue of territory allocations: 'Aamchya haddhit nahi aahe!' (Not under our jurisdiction!) They were told to take Sawant to the Colaba police station. There, he was handed over to the duty officer, Ishaq Bagwan.

Meanwhile, Ashwin and the other injured were rushed to St George Hospital at Victoria Terminus (VT). Ashwin was later shifted to J.J. Hospital on Sandhurst Road as his injuries were serious. But he was still alive by some miracle.

Mohite rushed back to Sada Pawle and told him what had happened. The police, who had recorded the statements of the escorting party and Sawant, could not take a statement from Ashwin as he was in no state to talk. Soon, officers from the crime branch and ACP Vasant Gosavi of Colaba division rushed to the site of the firing and ensured that a thorough panchnama of the crime scene took place. They got an FIR registered under TADA, which was still effective in those days. A quick examination of Sawant's clothes produced five empty and one live cartridge still in the .38 revolver which he had used to fire at Ashwin Naik. His clothes were bloodstained and there were, of course, several eyewitnesses who could identify Sawant.

Strangely, in his defence during the trial, Sawant retracted the statement of guilt he had made while in police custody. He said that he had actually been returning from the Employment Exchange after getting himself registered and somebody had fired the gun at his neck and he had fallen unconscious. The prosecution had no trouble knocking down all his claims and proved, very easily, that he had not been returning from the exchange and that he was present at the spot and was the main accused. Sawant was convicted for firing at Ashwin Naik and was given life imprisonment. He was released after 15 years in jail.

Ashwin had to undergo treatment for a year-and-a-half. He was unable to provide any statement during this time. As soon as he was in a position to move around, he escaped from India. Gawli and Nagesh Mohite were acquitted; the prosecution was unable to prove that their actions amounted to conspiracy. Also, many witnesses turned hostile during the trial that lasted two years. The inexperienced gangster had managed to pull it off, albeit clumsily. It became his initiation into the world of crime.

TWENTY-THREE

Kill Khatau

'Kill Khatau!' Those two words signed the death warrant for India's top industrialist, Sunit Chandrakant Khatau.

Not one to tolerate a slight and keen on avenging the attack on his brother, Amar Naik had assigned the task of killing the tycoon to two of his most trusted aides, Dinesh Mithbaukar and Usman Fakira, and they began making preparations to write the most violent chapter in the city's history so far. They had roped in a few others and allocated work to them. Now they began to seriously make plans. They decided who the main shooters, the side shooters and the back-up team would be. They began arranging for weapons, accessories and other paraphernalia, and monitored Khatau's daily movements. Places where the murder could be orchestrated were shortlisted and debated, escape routes were discussed.

Khatau had managed to win everyone over to his side. RMMS, the industrial board, the government, ministers, Gawli and Sachin Ahir – he was feeling invincible. In his celebratory mood, Khatau failed to pay attention to his surroundings. He did not notice the two bikers discreetly following his Mercedes Benz as it left the massive gates of Khatau Mills at Byculla and, after negotiating its way through heavy traffic, moved towards Worli.

Khatau did not approve of Gawli's methods and had strongly remonstrated with Sachin when he heard of the deadly attack on Ashwin. But he was effectively silenced when he was told that this was a dirty business, and they did not need his advice on how to conduct it. Khatau was told in no uncertain terms that the manner in which Ashwin had been attacked showed Gawli's clout. Part of business, they insisted.

The daylight attack on big fish Ashwin inside the crowded court premises, while he was in the security cordon of the police, had shocked the cops, the underworld and especially Amar. In the annals of the Mumbai mafia, the attack on Ashwin is billed as a very big one, though he didn't succumb to it – as big as the killings of Dawood's brother Sabir Ibrahim, Gawli's brother Kishore, and Dawood's brother-in-law Ibrahim Parkar.

In the dead of night, when no one was watching, Amar used to visit his brother in hospital. Often, he left the place with tears in his eyes. Amar was aware that Ashwin had suffered a great deal since his teenage years, despite zero involvement in his elder brother's activities. The cops had often dragged him to the police station and detained him for hours, or his rivals had kidnapped him to exert pressure on Amar – yet Ashwin never fought with his brother. Amar loved his brother and was worried about what the disability would do to his psyche. However, knowing Ashwin as he did, he believed that his brother would survive and overcome this setback. What he desperately wanted to do was to finish off the people who had done this to his brother.

Amar made his first move within two days of the attack on his brother. His first target was Shankarrao Jadhav, who was a sitting duck. Jadhav, a nobody until a few months ago, had not only managed to upstage Haribhau Naik but had gone on to become the president of RMMS, thanks to Amar's rival, Gawli. As a Gawli acolyte, he deserved to be punished for his association, Amar decided.

On 20 April 1994, Naik's men accosted Jadhav's car near the Eastern Express Highway, just before the Kurla East intersection. Two men on a bike sprayed bullets and hurriedly escaped without checking the result of their actions. Jadhav was injured, but lived to tell the tale. When Amar heard that Jadhav had survived, he was livid. He was fast becoming a laughing stock in the underworld, he fumed.

A ganglord who could not even avenge his own brother! Amar had to salvage his pride. It was then that he decided to strike at the core of the problem.

Amar assembled his team of desperadoes and they began discussing the way forward. He wanted to kill Gawli, an idea that was unanimously approved. But there was a major hitch. Gawli had been booked under TADA and was safely ensconced in Pune's Yerawada jail. He was rarely brought to the city for court hearings.

Someone suggested Sachin's name, but Amar thought he was too insignificant to be scalped. His recent failure with Jadhav had made Amar abrasive; he wanted a big hit that would recompense the attack on Ashwin and, at the same time, cause major damage to Gawli's gang.

In a moment of resolve, he decided to eliminate Khatau. 'Kill Khatau!' he exclaimed.

Mithbaukar and Fakira scanned Amar's face, wondering whether he was blabbering because he was drunk. They had discussed this before, but in passing. Khatau was too big a fish.

'He has no right to live,' Amar said with finality, sealing the fate of Khatau and giving the final orders to his shooters.

For more than a week, the gunmen tailed Khatau and studied his movements. Khatau had no police security. Gawli, in his arrogance, had not provided protection to him either. This meant killing Khatau would be a cakewalk.

Once they were confident of pulling off the killing, three pairs of men on bikes prepared to tail Khatau's white Mercedes. On 7 May 1994, less than twenty days after the attack on Ashwin Naik, the killers zeroed in on Khatau. When the Mercedes halted at the Mahalaxmi railway station signal, opposite Race Course, the bikers closed in. One halted right across from the car, on the side, and one in front.

Eyewitnesses recall that the pillion riders on both bikes suddenly raised a sledgehammer, in one synchronized movement, and brought them crashing down on the windscreen and the windows of the car. Even before passers-by could react to what was happening, the two bikers whipped out guns, cleared space amidst the shattered glass to fit the muzzles, and fired several successive rounds. Despite all the commotion, everybody there heard the heart-rending screams of Khatau and his driver.

One of the bullets ricocheted and hit a biker in his thigh, causing him to fall off his bike. The other hitman and his friend immediately hauled him onto the pillion seat of the bike. The entire action took barely ninety seconds.

The signal turned green and vehicles began moving. Khatau's driver showed remarkable presence of mind and revved up the car, speeding towards Nair Hospital. But it was too late. Khatau was declared brought dead on arrival and his body was left at the morgue for the police to take custody of it.

The killing of a business leader can be extremely damaging for a state government. Other businessmen and traders put pressure on it as they feel the administration has failed them by not keeping the city free of crime. Ministers also dread the prospect of losing the next chunk of donations from industrialists during election campaigns.

Ordinarily, cases are registered by the local police station and parallel investigations are conducted by the detection wing of the crime branch or the DCB of CID. In this case, too, the Tardeo police station registered a case of murder against unknown assailants. However, the Khatau investigation was taken over by the crime branch on the very first day and scores of cops were pressed into service. All twelve units of the crime branch began working on the case round the clock. Hundreds of witnesses and other people were questioned, but the sleuths failed to make any headway.

The cops were clueless, except for one fact: one of the assailants had a bullet injury. He would have had to go to some hospital, nursing home or medical centre in the city for treatment. The cops began discreetly scouring hospitals in the vicinity. In four days, they checked more than 200 nursing homes and medical centres across the city, but could not find any sign of the injured gunman.

In 1994, there were no mobile phones, not even pagers. There was no electronic surveillance, no closed circuit televisions at traffic intersections, nothing that could get them close to their quarry. The only arsenal they had was an old-fashioned human intelligence network ('humint', as the American agencies term it), of khabris or informers. They began bribing their informers. All their hopes were pinned on some khabri bringing them information on a platter.

Finally, the elusive 'simsim' opened for the cops – with one little piece of information. One of the hitmen was said to be madly in love with a bargirl in Vashi. (The Nationalist Congress Party (NCP) had not been born yet and people were yet to hear of the maverick politician R.R. Patil, who later became the scourge of dance bars in Maharashtra.)

The cops posted their men in and around the bar at Vashi, waiting for the gangster to show up to see his favourite girl. Days passed but no one came to meet her. The police got tired of the stakeout and fed up of pretending to be rich men throwing money at the girls on the dance floor.

Then came the breakthrough. The policemen noticed that a waiter was bringing medicines on a daily basis and handing them over to a bargirl when the restaurant closed for the day. The cops immediately turned up at the nearby pharmacy and learned that the medicines included antibiotics, strong painkillers and antiseptics used for the healing of wounds. Jackpot!

On the seventh night of the stakeout, when the waiter delivered the medicines to the bargirl – a nondescript young woman who took the parcel from him with evident gratitude – the cops exchanged glances. The girl was quietly followed to a nearby one-room apartment and voila – they found their first accused. A heavily bandaged and recuperating Santosh Pagarkar lay sprawled on the bed.

Pagarkar's arrest opened the floodgates for arrests, and within a few days, the cops managed to apprehend ten men, including the four shooters from the Amar Naik gang. With almost the entire Naik gang in the net, they were hoping to arrest Amar too, soon. But Amar had fled the country to take refuge in London. His plan had proved costly, and he could take no further risks.

The ten accused were booked under TADA and the cops hoped for a conviction. But what followed shocked everyone.

A police dossier, which serves as a record of the entire incident, observes on page 171: 'However, the accused persons were acquitted by the TADA court as wife (Panna Khatau) of the deceased did not support the prosecution.'

The non-cooperation of Panna Khatau, the acquittal of all the ten accused in the killing, the failure of the judiciary in Mumbai and the unhindered escape of Amar Naik from the city mystified everyone. The police could not believe all the hard work that had gone into tracing the culprits, arresting them and prosecuting them under TADA had come to nought.

From his cell in Yerawada jail, Gawli was following the developments with unease. The killing of Khatau had changed equations within the mafia; it had impacted his coffers and the acquittal of the killers was unsettling. That Amar had fled to foreign shores also chafed; Gawli feared that he would turn out to be another Dawood, remote-controlling his kingdom while leading a lavish life in Dubai. It would be difficult to fight such an enemy.

Gawli had been so close, almost touching distance, to Mammon. But Khatau's killing had turned out to be Amar's master stroke.

One of the aides who first met the ganglord at the mulaqaat in jail and briefed him about the goings-on in the past few weeks said, 'Daddy just kept repeating one word as he stared into space: "Behanchod!"'

TWENTY-FOUR

Maharashtrian Mafia's
Anno Domini: 1994–95

Bal Thackeray, the founder of the right-wing Shiv Sena, had his fair share of idiosyncrasies. He never attended any public or private functions. From 1966 onwards, there was only one thing that he did consistently. He addressed the annual Dussehra rally at the huge Shivaji Park grounds in central Mumbai. Except on a few occasions, he never failed to turn up at the rally, where he raved and ranted at his opposition and exhorted the sons of the soil to rise and fight against 'south Indians usurping jobs meant for locals' or shouted his favourite slogan – 'Muslims go to Pakistan' – or vented against whoever his hatred was directed against at that point of time. The Shiv Sena's Dussehra rally gave direction to the Sainiks. (It was much later that Bal Thackeray decided that a daily newspaper espousing his views would reinforce the Shiv Sena's ideology.)

For many years, the Dussehra rally was something that not only Maharashtrians but other politicians waited for eagerly. The opposition parties in the state geared up for the next elections after they had listened to Bal Thackeray. Even national parties tuned in to his Dussehra rally. From Kashmir to Kanyakumari, everybody talked about it.

Thackeray's speeches were infused with rhetoric, vitriol and a dose of advice for the Marathi-speaking populace. He infused the spirit of Marathi pride in them, but in a roundabout manner. He derided them for their lackadaisical approach and exhorted them to be aggressive. His acerbic oratory and caustic speeches made headlines the following day, every time, in all the national dailies. In the era before 24x7 television news, thousands of Maharashtrians assembled at Shivaji Park to listen to Thackeray. Nothing could stop them from listening to their dearest leader. Not a single person budged even if they were pounded by torrential rain or if the sound system went haywire. Pakistanis joked that the rally was the only place in the world where a bomb hoax would not work. From the podium, Thackeray got away with making many a sensational, blasphemous pronouncement.

Even before the advent of the Shiv Sena mouthpiece, *Saamna*, on 23 January 1988, Thackeray had used the Dussehra rally to change his party's colours: from a chauvinistic regional organization to a Hindu nationalist party.

The year was 1994. The venue, as usual, was Shivaji Park in central Mumbai. The audience – card-carrying members of the Shiv Sena and the common Marathi-speaking populace – numbered more than a massive one hundred thousand. The Shiv Sena had spearheaded one of the worst incidents of communal violence in Mumbai in January 1993, after the demolition the Babri Masjid. The city was still reeling in the aftermath of the serial bomb blasts of March 1993 that followed the communal pogrom. So, when Thackeray declared, 'If they [Muslims] have Dawood, we [Hindus] have Gawli. These [Amar Naik and Arun Gawli] are aamchi muley [our boys],' there was thunderous applause even before he had completed his sentence. It was as if the audience approved of Gawli being a challenger to Dawood's might. Thackeray went on to talk about 'his' boys and the plight of the local gangsters, who were being hounded and taken out in selective police encounters or extra-judicial killings.

From that day onwards, Arun Gawli and Amar Naik were anointed as Mumbai's answer to Dawood. Political observers wondered why Thackeray did not extend his approval to another Marathi-speaking gangster, Chhota Rajan, who had openly rebelled against Dawood

Ibrahim and sought to bring him to his knees – unlike Gawli and Naik, who were busy fighting each other to corner the lion's share of the spoils.

Various explanations were proffered for Thackeray's exclusion of Rajan in his speech. Many said that Thackeray wanted to put an end to the tussle between the two Maharashtrian gangs and unite Naik and Gawli against Dawood's might.

Some said he did not mention Chhota Rajan because he was annoyed with him; soon after the serial bomb blasts, Rajan had behaved impertinently with the Sena supremo when the latter had dubbed Dawood a traitor. He had faxed letters to the print media in Mumbai signed with his original name, Rajendra Nikhalje. He had declared that Dawood did not need a certificate from anyone and that Thackeray should focus on politics. Thackeray never forgave Rajan for that jibe. Later, after his split from Dawood, Chhota Rajan tried to make amends. In several interviews, he expressed his profound reverence for Thackeray, but he continued to be cold-shouldered by Matoshree, the official residence of Bal Thackeray in Bandra.

The year 1994 became unforgettable not just for Thackeray's speech but for several other reasons. For the Mumbai mafia it came to be regarded as the Anno Domini (the year of our Lord, as it is known in the Julian or Gregorian calendar).

The Mumbai mafia is a world into itself; it has its own rules, calendars, principles and punishments. Until 1994, the mafia had used Dawood's escape to Dubai in 1986 as a reference point: 'While Dawood was still in Mumbai'; 'After Dawood's escape to Dubai'. This was also true of the police, lawyers, press reporters, politicians, academicians and whoever else talked about the world of crime. After 1994, the Muslim mafia and Dawood acolytes continued to use his departure as a reference point but other, equally significant signposts came to be recognized, especially amongst the Maharashtrian mafia.

The serial bomb blasts in March 1993 across thirteen locations in the city – aimed at landmarks like the Bombay Stock Exchange and Air India Building, several hotels, banks, shopping districts, and even the Shiv Sena's headquarters – were among the most sensational terrorist attacks in this part of the world. 257 people were killed. Chhota Rajan initially tried to defend his boss, but eventually rebelled against him and walked out. This split the gang straight down the middle and divided the mafia along communal lines for the first time.

Rajan had found some form of revenge at last. Dawood was no longer seen as a don or a smuggler. He was clearly perceived as a terrorist and an ally of the ISI and Pakistan. This perception was reinforced when he shifted base from Pearl Tower in Deira, Dubai to Clifton in Karachi.

Dawood was besieged now, it seemed, from all sides. India was demanding his head, Chhota Rajan was crying foul and Arun Gawli was sharpening his knives.

Back home, it seemed like the desi dons had acquired more muscle. Gawli, who had been cooling his heels in jail since 1992 under TADA, was now accused of masterminding the murder of former legislator Ziauddin Bukhari. Bukhari had once been close to Congress chief minister Sharad Pawar.

The mystery of Bukhari's murder was never unravelled, although it was widely rumoured that Gawli's men had been contracted for the killing. A day before his death, Bukhari had been heard threatening a minister at the Mantralaya. 'I shall expose you and your links with the mafia,' he is reported to have thundered, 'if you fail to fulfil my demands.' The minister's face was reportedly impassive. And the fallout came immediately after. Bukhari was found dead near the Byculla fire brigade. Gawli's men were later arrested under TADA.

Incidentally, Bukhari was the man who had given birth to the Young Party and made Dawood its ring leader in the early days. Later, Dawood and his brothers had drifted into goondaism and Bukhari dumped the Young Party and joined the Muslim League instead. Gawli's killing of Bukhari was interpreted as one more strike in his war against the Congress, Sharad Pawar and Dawood, not necessarily in that order. Thankfully, it was not interpreted as a communal attack, despite the fact that Bukhari was a Muslim cleric and the founder of Millat Nagar at Oshiwara in Andheri, a Muslim colony.

In 1994, Gawli's wife held a press conference at the Mumbai

Marathi Patrakar Sangh and alleged that Dawood had paid the city police to murder her husband, who might soon be liquidated in an encounter. She said that Gawli was being framed in the Bukhari case.

Meanwhile, Arun Gawli and Amar Naik's animus for each other increased, and there were more killings. While Gawli had tried to kill Ashwin Naik and ended up crippling him, Naik had virtually cut Gawli's financial jugular by killing Sunit Khatau. Naik was ahead, at least, for the moment.

Meanwhile, the Shiv Sena, which had begun inching closer to unfurling its saffron pennant at the Vidhan Sabha, eventually managed to win the state assembly elections in and ensconced itself in Mantralaya, the seat of the government, for the next five years. In its twenty-nine-year history, the party had never before gone beyond ruling the local civic body.

Soon after the Shiv Sena came to power, the Naik gang's fortunes changed. Amar had already escaped to England, and Ashwin, who was recuperating at J.J. Hospital (on bail, owing to medical reasons), managed to escape too, giving the gang a double lease of life. As if this was not enough, the Sena government, at its magnanimous best, gave a ticket to Ashwin's wife, Neeta Naik, for the corporation elections.

Neeta – her late father was a hawala dealer, her husband and brother-in-law ganglords – won the elections because she was smart, spoke English and was extremely intelligent. In interviews she gave before the elections, she had said that she was contesting because she wanted the police to stop harassing her family. 'I am tired of the midnight knocks by the Mumbai police. By being a corporator, I can shield my family from this constant harassment,' she said.

Gawli anticipated the same magnanimity towards his wife, Asha, but the Shiv Sena honchos gave him the royal ignore. Gawli interpreted this as step-motherly treatment. On the one hand, he was one of 'our boys', while on the other hand, his arch-enemies, the Naiks, were the only beneficiaries of the Sena's largesse. He felt that he was being used and manipulated by sugar-coated assurances; when it came to rewards, they would all go to his rivals.

Gawli was now fuelled by jealousy. The Naik family was gaining credibility and both Ashwin and Amar were absconding. This gave birth to a silent rebellion in the mind of the 'adopted boy' or 'favoured gangster' of Bal Thackeray.

In the underworld, like in politics, survival is everything. The family alone is sacrosanct, everyone else is expendable. And so began the next stage in the constant evolution of this parallel universe.

TWENTY-FIVE

The Demolition Squad

They looked like any other devout Pakistani Muslims waiting for the congregational prayers at the Saudi Masjid in Karachi to begin. In reality, the three men were Indian associates of Chhota Rajan – and they were there to launch an audacious attack on Dawood when he emerged from the mosque after prayers.

Farid Tanasha, Vicky Malhotra and Bunty Pandey were dressed in Pathani outfits and skull caps. It was the summer of 1998 and this was the first such plot to eliminate Dawood in his safe haven. Earlier, his rivals had attacked him only in Mumbai. He had subsequently left the city and relocated to Dubai, then to Karachi. No one had ever got this close to him before.

The hit squad had staked out the don's movements and discovered that he was a regular at Friday prayers whenever he was in Karachi.

Earlier, the three men had been given Indian passports by their handling officers, with assumed identities. They had travelled to Karachi via Dubai as though on a business assignment, all their papers in order. They did not want their mission to fail because of careless documentation.

They had been in Pakistan for more than a fortnight now, doing a recce of Dawood's plush bungalow, Moin Villa, near Clifton Beach. The villa was like a fortress, the lane leading to it guarded by Pakistani rangers. There were always hangers-on near the main gate and all

the other entrances were heavily guarded. Attacking Dawood at ⁀
bungalow was destined to end in failure.

The chances of getting him were higher at the mosque, despite t⁀
heavy cordon of security around him. A lone assassin could possib⁀
get close enough to kill him and then escape. It was decided that tl⁀
weapon to kill Dawood would be brought to them at the last minut⁀
once Dawood had arrived.

The moment Dawood reached the mosque for prayers, they mad⁀
a call to their contact to deliver the weapon. This is how it works i⁀
the Mumbai underworld, and they used the same modus operandi ir⁀
Pakistan. Unlike in the movies, where the shooter is shown carrying
a gun stuffed in the back of his trousers, the weapon generally shows
up after the shooter has been assigned the hit job, sometimes even
mid mission.

The team did not reckon for the fact that this was an unfamiliar
city. They kept waiting at the masjid, as Dawood got through his
wuzoo, namaz and other rituals; they could not react because their
errand boy was still on his way.

Finally, Dawood finished his prayers and left, without the
customary salutations to the Holy Prophet. The don was in and out
of the mosque in twenty-five minutes, and the weapon had still not
reached the potential assassins. They were left twiddling their thumbs.
Disappointed, they returned to India soon after.

The hit squad had been raised by Chhota Rajan especially to kill
Dawood and his cronies. This was the first such major operation
which, according to Mumbai crime branch officers, received the
complete support of the Intelligence Bureau (IB). There were several
attempts made on Dawood – one in 1995, without the IB's support –
but in 1998, the infiltration was done with the agency's help.

Ever since he had parted ways with Dawood, Rajan had been
consumed by the intense desire to take revenge. But Chhota Rajan
was a one-man army against Dawood Ibrahim and his gang. His
operations were modelled on a two-point agenda: surviving Dawood
and other gangsters, and retaliation. He was all set to decimate those
members of the gang who had been involved in the 1993 Bombay

blasts and had eluded the long arm of the law by finding loopholes in the judicial system.

He carefully planned the extra-judicial killings of those who had been acquitted. Rajan's handlers in the IB had been very clear about the terms on which his amnesty would remain alive and his safety ensured. Chief among these was that Rajan would have to eliminate members of the Dawood gang. The day he dithered on the terms, protection would be withdrawn.

Rajan had chalked out a plan and decided to raise an army of expendables, who would execute his orders without a second thought and also prove to be a useful vigilance arm. He had realized that he had to have a dedicated band of men who believed in his cause: toppling Dawood.

The squad he finally put together comprised a bunch of fearsome men. Balu Dokre, Sushil Hadkar, Sanjay Vatkar, Baba Reddy, Baba Mayekar and Vinod Matkar formed its core. Dokre was designated the leader of the group.

These were gangsters who evoked the deepest fear in people and they all belonged to Thane, a township much bigger than Mumbai, at the periphery of the metropolis. They had a reputation for being tough sharpshooters and they all owed allegiance to Chhota Rajan.

Baba Reddy, a devotee of Kali who ate raw meat and drank blood just as the goddess was believed to do, was among the most intimidating of the lot. They were so bloodthirsty that it was said they did not get a good night's sleep until they had killed an innocent man, woman or child. This gang, later nicknamed the Demolition Squad by the Thane police, unleashed unspeakable horrors in Thane. They held their weekly baithaks at a tandoori corner in Naupada, Thane, where they planned their next targets and inspired fresh terror.

Drunk on their new-found power and filled with total disregard for the law, the gang targeted a large boutique near Thane Nagar police station. They had earlier threatened the owners of the boutique and asked them to pay up, but the shop owners had steadfastly refused. Agitated, the gangsters barged into the store one day, demanding money. They even boasted of their supremacy in the area by daring the owners to call the police. They told them that the cops would not be able to touch them. 'Police hamara kya kar legi,' they said. (What will the police do to us?)

One of the owners, unwilling to believe the thug in front of him, called the police station to report the incident. Within minutes a police officer, Vipin Hasbane, along with two constables, reached the boutique. They were told that the gangsters had just left. They decided to follow and met the swaggering men at a little distance. They were on foot and did not seem worried that the police were following them; upon spotting the police team behind them, they simply opened fire.

Hasbane and his man ducked. Unfortunately, a seventeen-year-old Class 12 student was hit by a bullet. The Demolition Squad, of course, displayed no remorse as they escaped.

Another time, the gang barged into the house of a business tycoon at 11 p.m. One after another, they drew their guns and brandished them at him. What followed made the businessman nearly lose control of his senses. The barrel of one gun was shoved into his mouth, another into his nose and the third into an ear. Two more were shoved into the remaining orifices. They then demanded Rs 5 lakh from him at once. They warned him that if he was unable to accede to their demands, the guns crammed into his body would start going off, one after the other. The terrified businessman promised to give them what they wanted the next day and rushed to the crime branch office at Thane as soon as the gangsters had left.

In those days, the Thane crime branch had its office in a ramshackle chawl. One tenement was used as an arms depot and another for recreational purposes, while others were used as offices. When the businessman arrived in search of help, an operation was about to be conducted and the officers were busy preparing for it. The man was sent to the chief, Inspector Kailash Dawkhare, who wasn't really interested in listening to him as he assumed it would be one of those regular complaints involving an extramarital affair or something similar. When the businessman at last convinced him to at least listen to what he had to say and began to tell his story, the inspector was stunned. He assembled his team so that all of them could hear the tale of horror.

As soon as the officers had assembled, they smelt the strong, repugnant stench of excreta in the room. Looking around and assuming someone must have stepped on something objectionable on the way to the office, they were shocked when the businessman confessed that he had shat himself out of fear! Dawkhare's men then promised the businessman that they would protect him and, in fact, trap the gangsters and punish them. This opportunity could not be missed.

The Thane crime branch was not known to be as competent as the Mumbai police when it came to trapping gangsters or killing them in encounters. Nevertheless, a trap was laid the next day. Only, it was so obvious, even a rookie gangster would have been able to spot it. The Demolition Squad arrived at the businessman's house, but immediately figured out that there was something amiss. They retraced their steps and never came back to torture the businessman, who breathed easy at last. They were, however, never caught.

The Demolition Squad may have been heartless, but they exhibited a dubious patriotism with their first major killing outside India. Nepali MP Mirza Dilshad Baig, an MP of the Prajantra Party, was Dawood's friend and had given shelter to many of Dawood's men in his bungalow. Rajan had known this for a long time, and now he sent his squad to the bungalow to eliminate Baig.

The masterminds used an Indian girl to bait Baig into exiting his bungalow. Baig, a profligate womanizer, walked out of his bungalow straight into the arms of the squad standing at the front door. He was shot in cold blood. The Demolition Squad had managed to execute Baig after keeping watch over him for just a week. The killing not only rattled Dawood, it wiped out his support base in Kathmandu.

Subsequently, the squad also orchestrated the killing of Majid Khan and Mohammed Jindran, both accused in the serial blasts case of 1993. Then, encouraged by the lack of any attempts at detection by the Mumbai police and cheered on by Rajan, they killed film producer Hanif Kadawala, another accused in the blasts.

Rajan's hit squad killed at least six men who were accused in the blasts, and managed to strike terror and paranoia into the hearts of his enemies. Rajan began appearing on national television and giving interviews stating that he was a patriotic don, determined to finish off traitor Dawood and his men.

Following this, some of the blasts accused paid Rajan and brokered a truce with him, thus avoiding death for themselves.

By then Dawood had heard of Rajan's killing spree, and the aborted attempt at Karachi's Saudi Masjid. His security was enhanced and his movements restricted. The don had to secure his fortress before contemplating his next step.

Dawood's Man Friday, Shakeel, was infuriated by Rajan's increasing temerity. He knew that he had to soon launch a counterattack on Rajan, or else the D-Company's clout and power would start to diminish in the city. He began scouting around for a hitman who could patiently trace Rajan to whichever southeast Asian city he was in, and kill him. In this lay their best hope of survival.

TWENTY-SIX

Dance of Death in Dubai

Sunil Sawant alias Sautya's life had changed and taken a 180-degree turn. From the congested, narrow bylanes of Girgaum, he had moved to Kathmandu and then finally to Dubai. Dubai's expansive roads blew his mind. It was his first visit to a foreign country. He had seen Dubai only in movies and heard about it from friends. It soon became the city for him.

Dubai was growing steadily at the time. The first high-rise came up in 1991. Soon after, there was a big construction boom and a mad proliferation of high-rises. The city soon boasted more than 900 high-rises in an area smaller than Mumbai city. Anyone enamoured of money and prosperity loved it there.

Sautya had also begun enjoying life in Dubai. There was no dearth of wine, wealth and women, so his philandering ways could continue unabated. Dubai was, of course, a grander city, but most importantly, he was not a fugitive there. He could move around freely, like a citizen of the world. There were no police departments or agencies trailing him. Dawood was happy with him. In the hierarchy of the D-Company, he was rated as one of the boss's chief lieutenants.

Sautya felt on top of the world, totally invincible. In the mafia world, however, the higher the climb, the harder the fall.

Sautya, who had become Suleman after his conversion to Islam, was making plans to settle down in Dubai. He regretted having moved so late to Dubai, unlike his comrades-in-arms Sharad Shetty and Anil Parab, the two other Hindu gangsters who had remained with Dawood instead of aligning with Chhota Rajan. Both of them had managed to make a fortune in Dubai.

Shetty had established himself as a hotelier and owned a chain of hotels in the UAE. He owned two hotels in Dubai – Regent Palace Hotel and Regal Hotel – and was also head of the Rami Group of Hotels. He had business interests in many restaurants, nightclubs and hotels in Abu Dhabi too.

Parab had launched a business with an Arab national, Abdul Rehman al Raees, and opened a fancy department store. He also owned an electronics shop at Souk al Vassar in Deira. The small-time thug from Tilak Nagar had done well for himself; he now owned a fleet of Mercedes Benzes and BMWs.

Sautya envied the affluence and opulent lifestyles of his friends. He too wanted a settled life and steady business for himself, and he began working diligently towards this. He was thinking of partnering with Kafeel, a local sponsor in the Emirates, to set up a bouquet of showrooms in Dubai. An estate agent had taken him around Sharjah, which was a cheaper but very promising market. Personally, Sautya liked Deira, a plush upmarket locality in Dubai that could be compared to Bandra in Mumbai.

Sautya knew that Dawood could unlock any door for him in the Arab kingdom. Among other places, he had visited the Hyatt Regency shopping area with his Nepali broker friend, who had been showing him around. Malls were yet to make an appearance in Dubai. In the pre-mall era, Dubai had massive department stores or shopping corridors in five-star hotels.

While Indians and Pakistanis specialized in government jobs or in blue-chip companies, Bangladeshis in Dubai worked as waiters and held lower-level jobs in multinational companies. Nepalese and Filipinos mostly worked as labourers and menial workers at shopping centres and hotels. Sautya had managed to befriend several Nepalese people during his frequent visits to Kathmandu. These loyal Nepalese men now became his Man Fridays; they doubled as his bodyguards,

Maruti Infrastructure, the office of Ashwin Naik

Ashwin Naik flanked by researchers Akash Jain and Yesha Kotak

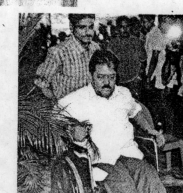

Ashwin Naik, 2011

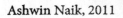

The main entrance to Dagdi Chawl

Bal Thackeray at the Shiv Sena's Dussehra rally at Shivaji Park. Also seen are Sena leaders Manohar Joshi and Madhukar Sarpotdar, 2008.

Rama Naik

Arun Gawli's rally at Flora
Fountain, attended by
1.5 lakh people, 18 July 1997

Bollywood sets with a Film Nagari theme at
Tilak Nagar Ganeshotsav, 2013

YESHA KOTAK

Arun Gawli, the
politician

PRADEEP DHIVAR/MIDDAY ARCHIVES

Arun Gawli after his
first arrest in 1977

Akhil Bharatiya Sena chief and
corporator Geeta Gawli, daughter
of Arun Gawli, at Dagdi Chawl, 2013

Chhota Rajan in a hat, dancing to a popular Bollywood
hit at a party in Dubai

YESHA KOTAK

Courtesy ACP ISHAQ BHAGWAN

Sunil Sawant alias Sautya

drivers, assistants, errand boys and also real-estate brokers. He had several around him, but his favourite was Shankar.

After the Hyatt visit, Shankar took him to Hotel Toofan. The Toyota car took a turn from the Corniche and entered Shaare' Naif to access Hotel Toofan's entrance. Sautya got out of the car and began walking towards the hotel. Shankar parked the car and followed him. Sautya was exhausted after an entire day of location hopping. Desperate for a drink and a meal at the hotel, he barely registered the sound of a car that came to a screeching halt nearby.

When the men got out of the car with their guns, Sautya was shocked. There was no reason for him to suspect that he was being stalked; this was Dubai, far from his home turf. He was completely unprepared for this confrontation with his own death. The man who had been touted as Dawood's killing machine actually quaked with the fear of death – as is often the case.

Three men fired at Sautya at once. He got a bullet in his arm and shoulder and tried to duck behind his Nepalese friend. But the volley of bullets continued, with the men closing in on him for better aim. Sautya, clearly desperate by now and aware that the bullets would get him sooner or later, pushed his loyal friend towards the armed trio and ran out onto the street.

The gunmen could not believe that Sautya would stoop to such cowardice. They pumped two bullets into Shankar and turned and ran after Sautya. One of them got back into their car and the other two chased him on foot.

For all the families of Sautya's victims, who had been killed in cold blood, Sautya's killing in a similar fashion on Naif Road would have been cathartic. A heavy-set, bleeding Sautya struggled to run on the pavement alongside a busy Dubai road, while a car and two short men chased him unhurriedly.

The debilitating Dubai heat, loss of blood and physical exhaustion slowed Sautya down. He tried to lean on a pole for support. When his pursuers caught up with him, Sautya saw them and cursed loudly, knowing there was no escape. He challenged them to a duel. But Sautya's killer, later identified as Guru Anchan alias Pandya, just stood there and pumped more bullets into him. Sautya held on to the pole, not letting go. Pandya then walked up behind him, whipped out a knife and slit Sautya's throat, getting the jugular. Sautya crashed onto the pavement, and lay in a pool of his own blood. The ambitious gangster was done for, his dreams ended in his dream land.

A few minutes had passed since the first shot was fired at Sautya, and the Shurta, or Dubai police, had been alerted. When the assailants saw the police van, they tried to run. Two of them managed to get into their car and escape, while Pandya was immediately disarmed and arrested. The duo in the car, identified as Shyam Sunder and Babu, were arrested after a chase.

Lieutenant General Dhahi Khalfan al Tameem, the police chief of Shurta for more than a decade, was furious at the way the Indians had perpetrated the killing – in the middle of the day, on a busy road full of people, and in such a gruesome manner. Tameem put his best man, Shaikh Abdul Jaleel, who was in charge of the Criminal Investigation Department (CID), on the job.

Subsequent developments baffled the entire Dawood gang and kept everyone confused for a long time.

Pandya told Jaleel during the investigations that they had killed Sautya at the behest of two Indian businessmen, Sharad Shetty and Anil Parab. He also told the police that Parab was the one who had supplied them with two revolvers, and that he had two more guns in his possession. The CID sprang into action and immediately arrested Shetty from the lobby of his hotel and Parab from his showroom.

Dawood was taken by surprise. He could not believe that two of his trusted aides were capable of plotting the killing of Sautya, who had been close friends with both of them.

Dawood was in Karachi, but he managed to place a call to Sharad in the CID lock-up, demanding an explanation from him. Sharad, who had by now figured out the conspiracy, explained it to Dawood. He convinced Dawood that Sautya's killing was the handiwork of Chhota Rajan, who had managed to execute the killing through a mole in the D-Company. Without a mole, it would have been difficult for first-time visitors to Dubai to smuggle in weapons and track down Sautya's whereabouts.

Dawood believed what Sharad told him and ensured that he was released the same day, but he did not show the same generosity to Parab. He remained suspicious of Parab, who had his roots in the Tilak Nagar gang and had been hired by Rajan. Also, Rajan had loaned Parab 50,000 Arab Emirates Dirham (AED) to start his business in Dubai. Parab fit the role of a mole, and to pay for this, he ended up spending three months in the Dubai jail.

Parab kept pleading his case with Dawood; he knew Dawood's clout with the Dubai government. Dawood ignored all his messages. Finally, the CID released Parab for lack of any evidence against him.

It emerged during the interrogation of Pandya that Rajan had not told the killers about Sautya's background. They had been told that he was to be killed because he was a Pakistani agent working against India. They had also been told that after the killing, they had to proceed towards Dubai Creek in Bur Dubai, barely ten minutes from Deira, where an abra, a wooden boat used as a water taxi on the creek, would be waiting for them. Dubai relies on old-fashioned water boats which regularly cart goods to neighbouring countries, including Iran and Israel. Even today, these abras are used by the smuggling cartel to ferry goods to Iran. They make a huge profit as business is brisk, especially with the US imposing stiff economic sanctions against Iran.

The killers were told that the abra would eventually drop them to the shores of Gujarat. The journey would take a few days. Rajan assured them that he would talk to his contacts in the smuggling ring to facilitate their escape. Plan B was that if they got arrested, they should name Parab and Shetty, who were Rajan's friends in Dubai. Both of them had agreed to help get bail for the shooters and get them released, the trio was told. These apparently sound arrangements emboldened the men and made them reckless, which is why they showed no hurry in finishing the job and running away from the scene. They had pursued Sautya patiently and even after shooting him, took their time slaughtering him in broad daylight.

Thus, by 5 August 1995, the Indian mafia wars had reached Dubai. Violence and bloodshed are bad for business, and Sheikh Mohammed was keen to attract business to the city. He did not want Dubai to be spoken of like Karachi or Mumbai. Tameem promised him that he would not allow anyone to commit any act that could disrupt the peace and security of the tightly controlled Arab kingdom.

In the course of investigations, the CID realized that the stories they had been told were pure fiction. Rajan had spun the yarn to persuade the shooters to take up the assignment. There was no abra waiting on the shores of Dubai, and Parab and Shetty had no hand in the conspiracy.

Tameem ensured that the case was fast-tracked and he issued a stern warning to Indian gangs in Dubai. The three shooters were awarded the death sentence. It came as a huge shock to them and their families that they received no help from Rajan while they languished in the Dubai prison. As a last-ditch effort, the trio converted to Islam and moved a mercy petition with the Dubai government. But Tameem ensured that no leniency was shown to them.

The police chief also ensured that an Interpol warrant was issued against Rajan, as the mastermind of the killing. Rajan, who had spent almost a decade in Dubai and had been instrumental in scores of killings in India, had never had a red alert Interpol warrant issued against him. It put paid to his plans of mobility.

Annoyed yet triumphant, Rajan sought solace in the fact that he had managed to inflict major damage upon Dawood's gang, killing one of his top men in his own lair. But this was only the beginning. The odyssey of death had just begun, across the seas.

TWENTY-SEVEN

Of Gangsters, Guns and Ganpati

Criminals are usually devout men, almost obsessively religious. The general feeling is that the whole world is gunning for them; only God understands them. The Mumbai underworld is replete with stories about gangsters' religiosity and their unwavering faith.

Varadarajan Mudaliar was the first don to unabashedly and publicly exhibit his devotion. He fed 1,000 devotees every year at an annual urs (celebration) at the Bismillah Shah Baba dargah at VT station. The lighting of his Ganesh Pandal at Matunga station was something the entire city came to gawk at, year after year. Initially, it started out as a small pandal outside Matunga station, but with the growth in his stature and influence, the pandal became bigger, swallowing a large chunk of public space outside the station. Crowds thronged to see the lighting at the pandal and like the Lalbagcha Raja, which is now one of the city's most visited pandals, it was Varadarajan's Ganesha that was the number one must-visit site for devotees every year.

Film stars often came to the pandal, and so did other celebrities. Jaya Bachchan used to frequent it when Amitabh Bachchan was battling for his life at the Breach Candy Hospital in 1982.

When the police decided to cut him down to size and diminish Varadarajan's powers, they asked him to reduce the size of the massive pandal. Eventually, it was reduced to 100 sq. ft. By then the Ganesh pandal had become a symbol of Varadarajan's diminishing clout. He felt humiliated and relocated to Chennai, where he died of a heart attack soon after.

Like Varadarajan, Gawli too is an ardent devotee of Durga and spends lavishly during Navratri every year. For as long as he was friends with the Shiv Sena, he displayed photographs of Bal Thackeray and his wife Meena Thackeray at his Durga pandal. The photographs were promptly removed after he declared war against the Sena.

Once again, the police reciprocated by restricting the size of the pandal and ensuring that music was not allowed to play beyond the 10 p.m. deadline.

When Chhota Rajan joined hands with Dawood and made his fortune, the first thing he did was conduct a puja at the Ganesha festival in Tilak Nagar in 1987. Soon after, he had to escape to Dubai. But he ensured that his boys erected a sprawling pandal on the Tilak Nagar grounds every year, and that the celebrations were on a grand scale.

Within a few years, the grandeur of the celebrations became the talk of the town. Rajan's people started modelling their Ganpati pandals on various famous edifices: the Red Fort, the Mysore Palace, the Ajanta-Ellora caves, Disneyland even. In 2013, they showcased Film Nagari. Over a period of time, they increased their budget, and now they spend millions of rupees as it has become a matter of prestige for Chhota Rajan.

The organizers pretend that they get the vargani (donation) from the residents of Tilak Nagar. But everyone knows that it is Rajan's Ganpati and that he has never compromised on the scale and grandeur of the celebrations at his pandal.

In the early nineties, the Tilak Nagar pandal, known as the Sahyadri Krida Mandal, audaciously displayed the initials of Chhota Rajan on its walls. This practice was, however, stopped when the Mumbai police launched a crackdown on the mafia.

In 2003, the police demolished a part of the pandal, claiming that it was larger than the specified size. A senior crime branch official went on to state: 'The shrinking in size of the pandal indicates the diminishing clout of Chhota Rajan.' According to a *Times of India* report titled 'Rajan's Ganpati show-of-strength diminishes', there was a police crackdown on the organizers when judge A.P. Bhangale of the MCOCA court, in 2001, ordered a suo motu probe into the funding of the Ganeshotsav – after reading an article that stated that the organizers had spent Rs 30 lakh on the decoration and celebrations. The probe failed to establish a link between Rajan and the Sahyadri Krida Mandal. Except once, when a pall of gloom descended on the pandal, the fervour of celebrations at the Tilak Nagar Ganeshotsav has never dimmed.

After the killing of Sautya in Dubai, Chhota Shakeel decided to get even with Rajan by attacking his financial muscle. Builder Omprakash Kukreja of Chembur was a known Rajan sympathizer. According to the police, he used to contribute Rs 50 lakh for the Sahyadri Krida Mandal's Ganeshotsav. A police dossier says that Kukreja also stored weapons for Rajan. Shakeel decided to cut off Kukreja's monetary support to Chhota Rajan. He wanted to avenge Sautya's killing and also spoil Rajan's Ganpati extravaganza.

On 18 September 1995, a month after Sautya's killing, three gunmen barged into Kukreja's office and started firing indiscriminately. The cops suspect an AK-47 was used in the firing, which resulted in the death of Kukreja and two of his employees – Deepak Bilkiya and Mohammad Ansari.

Rajan's gang was grief-stricken and this temporarily affected the celebrations. The Mumbai police never resolved the case nor did they arrest the shooters involved in the killing; the file was closed on 11 November 1996 and marked 'A': true but undetected.

Rajan, who knew that Kukreja had been killed to weaken him financially, decided to retaliate in a similar fashion.

On 13 November 1995, Rajan's men shot dead the managing director of East–West Airlines, Thakiyuddeen Wahid. The airline was India's first private domestic airline and it had expanded at a rapid pace. Rajan had always maintained that Dawood had invested heavily in the airlines, a claim refuted by Wahid and his family.

At stake was supremacy in a new era, in cash-rich Mumbai. Dawood wanted to prove that he was the top boss, while Rajan was determined to prove it was he who called the shots in Mumbai. Rajan went a step further and joined hands with Arun Gawli, at last. Together, they decided to uproot the Dawood gang from the city.

While the police maintained that Wahid's killing was Rajan's handiwork, they were not able to make any arrests to substantiate their claims. It was being speculated that perhaps Dawood himself had ordered the killing, because Wahid had refused to heed extortion demands. *The Week* even published an interview with 'an unidentified Dawood aide', claiming it could be that gang's handiwork. A threat to kill Shiv Sena chief Bal Thackeray was also made in the same interview.

The picture only became clear after Harinder Baweja, one of India's most intrepid investigative journalists, scored a scoop early in 1996. She managed to trace Chhota Rajan to Kuala Lumpur in Malaysia and spoke to him. In the profession for barely a decade or so, she was working as a special correspondent with *India Today* when she managed to get the interview with Rajan (excerpts below).

Q. Why did you leave Dawood?
A. He is not a man worth talking about. He betrayed both me and the nation. He got three of my men killed to try and reduce my power. He killed them in the worst possible fashion – by befriending them first, inviting them over and dining with them. He thinks he has reduced my power and strength, but three people are not going to make a difference when there are a thousand others with me. It was the manner in which he did things that smacks of betrayal.

Q. And why do you say he betrayed the nation?
A. He was the brain behind the Bombay bomb blasts in which hundreds of innocents lost their lives.

Q. You are making a very serious charge. How do you know that he was involved in the blasts?
A. Because at that time (March 1993) I was in Dubai and Dawood was in Karachi. He returned 2–3 days after the blasts and was inundated with calls congratulating him. I asked him about his involvement and,

of course, he denied it. You see, by March we were in any case falling out with each other. Differences had crept in after the killing of my three associates and I was not part of the many closed-door meetings in which Tiger Memon and Dawood were together. There was also talk of landings in my presence.

Q. Why were you not part of the conspiracy?
A. I was not in the inner circle any more and if I had had any idea, I would not have allowed it to happen. Perhaps Dawood suspected that.

Q. How could you have prevented the blasts, said to have been planned with the help and support of Pakistan? It wasn't a one-man operation.
A. I would have told the department or contacted someone in the Indian government. I would also have put my own men on the job.

Q. How did you finally leave the gang and escape from Dubai? They must have been keeping an eye on you.
A. Not just that. My passport had gone to the Indian embassy for renewal and I never got it back.

Q. But didn't you have a receipt?
A. I had a receipt – in fact, I still have it, but Dawood told me that the embassy had instructions not to renew my passport. The truth, however, is that he got it renewed but never gave it back to me. Along with mine, he had given his brother Noora's passport, which came back renewed. It was his way of pressurizing me. Anyway, it may be news to him, but I still have an Indian passport issued in Dubai.

Q. How could he get it renewed? You mean he had contacts even in the Indian embassy?
A. Yes, money means a lot in this business and can buy you anything.

Q. So how did you leave Dubai?
A. I got myself another passport. But don't ask me how because I will not spell it out.

Q. You finally parted company after the blasts and have now become his opponent. The Bombay police believe that your gang is behind the killing of Thakiyudeen Wahid, the managing director of East–West Airlines.

A. I gave the instructions for Wahid's killing. He was Dawood's financier in India. I got him killed because I want to take revenge on Dawood for the bomb blasts. Before that, Sunil Sawant, another very close associate of Dawood, was bumped off on the streets of Dubai. I want to eliminate all the people who have let down the country by conspiring to blow up Bombay.

Q. But Dubai is supposed to be Dawood's headquarters. He has been controlling the Bombay underworld from there for so many years.

A. Dawood is only a media don and he has been in Pakistan for over two years now, not having the guts to go back to Dubai. I have my contacts and resources and have proved that I can get at him, even if it means planning an operation in Dubai. Sawant was Dawood's main hitman and we got him despite all his security guards. Now I am looking for Dawood.

Q. But you say he is in Pakistan...

A. So what? I know where he is and we have already made one attempt on his life in Karachi. There are smugglers in Pakistan who are opposed to him because he is stepping on their turf. He might think that Pakistan is safe because it is an Islamic country, but there are people there who want him as badly as I do. I will not rest till I finish him off. He is my nation's enemy and has to be taught a lesson.

Q. How are you any different? After all, you are also working against the nation.

A. I have never harmed the nation. My fight is against Dawood.

Q. But you are also a killer, a criminal...

A. I am killing Dawood's men. In fact, I am making the police's job easier and am doing the country a good turn by getting rid of those who conspired to destabilize it.

Q. It seems odd that you should go on about the country when you admit that you will continue to indulge in killings. What about Wahid's killing?

A. I gave the instructions for Wahid's murder. He was Dawood's financier in India. East-West Airlines is, in fact, owned by Dawood. Wahid used to come to Dubai – where I also met him – often and Dawood told me that he was starting an airline. It was important to kill Wahid for that was another way of reducing Dawood's power.

Q. So you killed Wahid to avenge the killing of Kukreja, who was supposed to be your financier.

A. He was not my financier. These are only filmi stories. I have never met Om Prakash Kukreja in my life. His brother Mohan was a friend of mine and I used to speak to him occasionally on the phone.

Q. The Bombay police has announced an award of Rs 2 lakh for anyone who provides information on Wahid's killers. Why don't you claim the award?

A. I don't want that money. It is compensation enough that the operation was successful. There can be no greater satisfaction than that.

Q. Apart from killings, what are your other activities? The police believe that you smuggle narcotics.

A. I have never touched drugs in my life. I don't believe in earning money through spoiling people's lives and hurting them.

Q. You have hurt Wahid's family.

A. What about the hundreds who were killed in the blasts and what about their families? They were truly innocent. Wahid should never have involved himself with Dawood.

Q. You were also very close to him till only two years ago...

A. Yes, and that is the only regret I have. Not that I am part of the underworld but that I associated with a man like Dawood.

Q. Are you sure he is in Karachi?

A. Yes. Initially, just before I left Dubai, I had his telephone number there and even called him to see if I had been given the correct number. That number has obviously changed but I know from my sources that he is still there. The number, in fact, was given to me by Sunil Sawant. I called him once to wish him on his birthday (26 December). He does travel out of Pakistan once in a while but Karachi is his base. Gone are the days when celebrities used to seek his company. When even saints like Chandraswami wanted to meet him.

Q. Chandraswami has gone on oath before the Jain Commission saying that he has never met Dawood.
A. That is the biggest lie I have ever heard. I was very much part of the Dawood circle in late 1989–early 1990 when Chandraswami came to Dubai. I was the one who went to pick him up at the airport. He stayed in Dubai for three to four days at Chhota Shakeel's (a close aide of Dawood) house, where Dawood used to come and meet him.

Q. What happened in those meetings?
A. I don't know because they used to sit alone in a separate room. Chandraswami used to play astrologer and he always maintained that he would predict the future but in private.

Q. Did he predict yours as well?
A. Yes, he told me that I would have no problem with Dawood but that I would fall out with his brothers. Obviously that was all wrong.

Q. Your fight is not with Dawood's brothers?
A. I have nothing against them so far and I know that Dawood didn't involve his brothers in the conspiracy. In any case, neither he nor I want to involve our families in the war. My brothers are happily staying in the village along with our mother.

Q. Why did Dawood and Chandraswami meet?
A. I don't know the details but what I do know is that Dawood was keen on meeting Adnan Khashoggi. Dawood and Chandraswami flew to America from Dubai. I was also supposed to accompany them but I didn't get a visa.

Q. Did they return together as well?
A. No, Dawood came back with a lot of photographs of the three of them together and I remember him criticizing Chandraswami saying he is no godman, he only talks of projects and money.

Q. Did Babloo Srivastava arrange the meeting between Dawood and Chandraswami?
A. No. The meeting was arranged by Bombay-based friends of Dawood. Chandraswami flew to Dubai and I received him at the airport. All that, however, is in the past now, for even in Pakistan Dawood is not living freely. He is pretty much in hiding, but how long can these rats stay underground? I will teach them a lesson even if I have to pay with my life.

Q. You are involved in the property business in Bombay in a big way. According to estimates, you make several crores through contract killings, property business and protection money.
A. Several crores a year, not in a day.

Q. What will you do with so much money?
A. I need the money to weaken Dawood's gang.

Q. You can weaken him by surrendering and cooperating with the police ...
A. I don't trust the government because a lot of them are mixed up. Dawood is capable of buying officials and turning them against me.

Q. You must be using the same tactics – building contacts in the police and political circles.
A. I don't believe in using money because the person who takes money from me can sell himself to anyone, Dawood included. Nor do I have any political godfathers. Yes, I am a supporter of the BJP and the Shiv Sena. One of Dawood's aides said recently that Bal Thackeray was number one on their hit list. All I want to say is that if necessary we will provide protection. No one can touch Thackeray saab. Dawood won't be doing his own Muslim brothers a favour by trying to touch Thackeray, for then all hell will break loose.

Q. So, you have approached the Shiv Sena.
A. No, I have not. But they only have to give us a hint and we will be at their service.

Q. So it is true that there is some sort of a communal divide even in the underworld?
A. Not in my mind. I still have a lot of Muslims working with me and I consider all Muslims my brothers. Dawood too has Hindus even in his inner circle, like Sharad Shetty and Anil Parab.

Q. Why are you talking of religion and Hindu-Muslim amity? As far as the police is concerned, you are an underworld hitman who has jumped bail.
A. All of us in the underworld are hitmen. And why can't I speak on behalf of my country? I am not interested in destabilizing the country through blasts and provoking communal riots.

Q. So killings are okay if the aim is settling personal scores?
A. I have been let down by Dawood. That doesn't hurt me as much as the blasts do. I will stop only after I have finished Dawood and Tiger Memon and I have set a target of a year for myself to accomplish that.

Q. How do you manage to remote control?
A. It is the age of communication. The telephone is my weapon.

Q. Have you met Tiger Memon?
A. Several times. He used to come to Dubai often to meet Dawood. He also came to attend my wedding in 1988. Dawood and Tiger have a long association. He was in Dubai even during the riots and before the blasts; Tiger and Dawood went to Karachi together where they stayed at Taufiq Jalliawala's house.

Q. Dawood has established and earned for himself the title of don. You talk very confidently of catching up with someone who was once your boss.
A. I am very confident. It is you press people who have made a

petty smuggler and criminal out to be a don. Today it is not his writ but mine which runs in Bombay. Dawood, in fact, is under pressure. His men are hiding in Bombay and if we can penetrate Dubai too, which was once his unchallenged domain, then what kind of a don is he? He is now only a fugitive who won't be able to run for too long. It is not me alone but Arun Gawli too, for we have joined hands and together are more powerful even in Bombay. All our actions and activities are coordinated, for we are now working together.

Q. You are also on the run. Are you scared of Dawood?
A. I am not scared of him. In fact, I'm prepared to take him on face to face. If I am in hiding, it is only because I have an unfinished agenda. The day I get him, I will come back to India and surrender. You might think I am in hiding but as far as I am concerned, I am being practical. Why should I offer myself to them when I know that they must also be in search of me? After all, they have managed to kill my friends and associates too.

Q. Subhash Thakur, one of Dawood's associates who is now in custody, has said that Dawood wanted him to eliminate you.
A. That is true and I knew about it. They had, in fact, planned to throw me off a launch but I didn't go to that launch party. I kept a distance after three of my associates were killed and finally left Dubai in July 1993.

Q. How long will you continue to hide? Aren't you fed up with the kind of life you're leading? Running from the law is also an offence.
A. I cannot surface as long as there is a threat to my life. I will return once my task is over and then I am willing to face trial and go to jail if necessary. But only after I have taught Dawood a lesson.

Q. Is your family prepared for this?
A. After all they are also keen on returning to their country and living a normal life.

Q. You've never thought of taking up a job?
A. I was working with the German pharmaceutical firm Hoechst where my father also worked as a storekeeper. Later, because of the company I kept, I became involved with the underworld. It's been a long journey. From selling cinema tickets in black to travelling to Southeast Asia.

(Courtesy *India Today*, 31 January 1996.)

TWENTY-EIGHT

The Afghani Affliction

Death comes in all avatars: in the form of a business associate, a friend, or even in the guise of a bewitching beauty.

Ayesha Qandahari was a woman of indescribable beauty, an Afghani with flawless skin, big, dark eyes, long eyelashes, a mesmerizing smile and a perfect-ten figure. Men would kill to possess her. But it seemed that those who made love to her were destined for certain death.

India's biggest druglord, who dealt in heroin, Nareyi Khan alias Nari Khan, was totally smitten by her charms. (Incidentally, Nareyi means 'on the way to heaven' in the Pashto language.) Nari believed his name took on its real meaning when he met Ayesha. He threw money at her to woo her.

Nari's affluence and naiveté caught the eye of Ayesha, who was married to Jannat Gul Qandahari, a well-to-do Pathan who was not quite in the league of Nari Khan.

Before Nari Khan came into their lives, the couple had been happily married. All that changed when Nari set eyes on Ayesha's beauty for the first time at one of the Pathan gatherings. He became besotted with her and immediately wanted to marry her.

Ayesha was dazzled by Nari's wealth and agreed to ditch her husband. Gul, a simple Pathan, was too much in love with Ayesha to divorce her just because she fancied another man. He was just not willing to let her go. Seeing that Ayesha was impressed with Nari's wealth and opulent life style, Gul put his entire wealth, including his flat, car and other assets in her name to stop her from leaving him. But Ayesha was not impressed by the gesture. A heartbroken Gul hit the bottle and was reduced to a Devdas-like state.

Ayesha began a torrid affair with Nari and Gul finally left her and took refuge at the Aga Miyan dargah in Akola. It is not known whether he formally divorced her. In any case, Ayesha and Nari were too involved with each other to care. But the story continued, ominously. After Gul was destroyed, it was Nari Khan's turn.

Towards the end of 1994, Nari attempted to deal in one of the biggest heroin consignments ever, of 355 kg, and got busted. The Narcotics Control Bureau (NCB) sleuths raided his house in Mazgaon, near Dongri in south Mumbai, and seized the contraband. They booked him under the Narcotics Drug and Psychotropic Substances (NDPS) Act. Nari's downfall had begun.

Ayesha did not want to dump Nari yet. She began coordinating with her lawyers to take care of the legal paperwork. Nari was pleased with her dedication – little understanding her foresight – and remained enamoured of her.

Soon, Nari's obsession with Ayesha became known to the NDPS community. This was a close-knit group of people who frequented the three specially designated NDPS courts on the first floor of the old building in the City Civil and Sessions Court precincts, near Fort in south Mumbai: lawyers, police officers from NCB or the Anti Narcotics Cell of the Mumbai police, orderlies, paralegals and others who were involved in the cases.

Often, the NDPS cases were only heard in two courts, while the third court remained vacant. The cops began using it to eat their meals, as a place where the accused could wait, or where relatives could meet undertrials. Nari bribed the constables into allowing him and Ayesha sole access to this court; he told them to lock the door and stand guard outside. Nari and Ayesha's love nest thrived at the expense of other undertrials, who were denied access to the comforts of the empty courtroom. Every time Nari was called to the court for a hearing, Ayesha and he ended up making love in that empty courtroom. The hectic love-making left Nari Khan totally drained but satisfied with life, as he confided in his lawyer. He had no complaints about his protracted trial, as long as he could see his jaan. Several months later, one spunky lawyer discovered his use of the empty courtroom and complained to the judge, who promptly put an end to it.

Ayesha had managed to win Nari's trust to the extent that he gave her power of attorney to withdraw money from his bank account or even liquidate his assets. She had been waiting for just this moment.

Around this time, Ayesha was drawn towards a handsome young man, Khalid Usman, scion of a Bandra-based tycoon. Khalid often took her for a spin in his Mercedes and spent money lavishly on her. It took Ayesha no time at all to become cold and indifferent towards Nari, who was flummoxed by her sudden transformation.

Nari was lodged at the Arthur Road jail. His cellmate Askandar Shah recalls, 'He was so distraught at the woman's betrayal that he wept for hours, even his long beard got soaked with tears.' He spent weeks and months nursing his grief and hoping that someday Ayesha would return to him, knowing that no one could love her the way he did. But he cried in vain. Ayesha had dumped him for good, never to return.

Now, Nari was no Jannat Gul Khan to end up at the dargah of a Sufi saint. He was an internationally connected druglord with unlimited resources at his disposal and powerful connections. Naved Khan, the fugitive drug baron, had introduced Nari Khan and Amar Naik to each other. Naik and Nari had business associations and met frequently in Ahmedabad, where the Pathan syndicate had massive clout, a safe base and hideouts. It was with Nari's collusion that Naik had managed to make it big in the drug business despite being a Maharashtrian.

Nari shared his cell in jail with men from the Amar Naik gang, who were accused in the killing of industrialist Sunit Khatau, and they treated him quite deferentially. During one of his hearings, Nari met an errand boy of the Naik gang and ordered a hit: he gave them supari to kill Khalid Usman and Ayesha.

It was now Khalid's turn to feel the kiss of disgrace. A man who had never seen infamy in his life and who hailed from a respectable family, ended up tarnishing their image irreparably.

Nari's declaration of a bounty on the head of Khalid and Ayesha reached the ears of the crime branch. They realized that a gang that did not hesitate to kill an industrialist like Khatau would have no qualms about killing anyone. The intelligence was strong, so they resorted to the age-old method of protecting their informers — putting them in jail.

The cops told Ayesha that the only way to protect Khalid was to detain him in a false NDPS case. He could be acquitted later and walk free. Ayesha was too scared to not agree to the arrangement. The crime branch cops then framed Khalid in a false NDPS case and threw him behind bars.

Khalid was saved, but Ayesha was still vulnerable. A senior cop befriended her and began giving her company. It must be said that this time Ayesha was trying to save herself from a jilted lover and was not drawn to the cop because of his money.

Khalid's family was very upset at the turn of events. They hired top-notch NDPS lawyers to get their son released. It was advocate Ayaz Khan who managed to demolish the false case and get Khalid an acquittal, but not before he had spent months in police custody.

Nari, meanwhile, was burning with the fire of revenge. He could not tolerate the fact that Ayesha was alive and sleeping with men of her choice and having fun with his money. He wanted to retrieve his assets and kill her as gruesomely as possible. He hired the most expensive battery of lawyers to get himself bail or acquittal.

Ayesha, who heard of Nari's plans through her cop boyfriend, began working on ensuring that Nari was convicted. She wanted him to spend the rest of his life in jail. She came up with a diabolical plan, which impressed even her boyfriend. If the presiding judge was threatened in some way, on behalf of Nari, she said, he could be misled into thinking that Nari was actually guilty and he would convict him.

They began working on the plan, but Ayesha, who had fooled so many people around her, could not deceive the judiciary. Her game plan was exposed and the judge acquitted Nari Khan of the NDPS charges.

Nari was now a free man, and ready to execute the killing of Khalid, Ayesha and her current boyfriend. He decided to use his friend Naik's lethal operatives and began hatching a plot to kill Ayesha after raping and disfiguring her.

Nari had by now managed to make inroads into the Naik gang and knew most of the gang members. As Amar Naik dealt in drugs and was in touch with the drug cartels of the Pathan gang of Ahmedabad, he was only too happy to assist Nari and get closer to him in the process.

It was an association of mutual benefit. Nari needed Amar to kill Ayesha and her boyfriends and Amar needed Nari to bolster his drug trade. There was implicit trust between the two, born of their need.

But when the roulette of destiny starts spinning, no one knows who will win and who will lose.

TWENTY-NINE

Gawli's War on the Shiv Sena

For the first time in the history of the state of Maharashtra, the Congress–I was routed in the state assembly elections in March 1995. The Shiv Sena, which had only dreamt of such a day for 29 years, managed a jubilant victory with its alliance partner, the BJP. Political observers noted that the BJP–Shiv Sena combine rode to victory on the back of a communal wave post the Babri Masjid demolition, which had polarized the state and the country. Marathi-speaking people in the state were excited; they were expecting several benefits to come their way, and some clean governance. Particularly for those from the coastal Konkan belt, the victory seemed very personal as they had always felt sidelined by the Congress-I government, which leaned more towards western Maharashtra and the sugar belt. The bulk of Bal Thackeray's supporters came from those coastal parts – Ratnagiri, Sindhudurg, Sawantwadi, etc. – and most of them were mill workers.

Gawli, too, believed in the Sena's promise of more power to the sons of the soil, even if they were on the wrong side of the law. So, when he managed to get bail and leave Yerawada jail, he landed up at home looking much more confident and happy. Dagdi Chawl was bedecked like a bride in his honour.

Gawli wanted to capitalize on the Sena's promise of patronage. He had begun to idolize Thackeray and spared no opportunity to express his profound reverence for the Sena supremo. Thackeray's photograph

174

was prominently displayed at all public functions at Dagdi Chawl. For once, the gang felt invincible, with the blessings of a godfather upon their heads.

Gawli knew that even if the Sena government spared him by not slapping unfair cases against him, he was not safe from Dawood's machinations. He was advised by his think tank – his wife and top gang members – that he should seek police protection against Dawood. Gawli quite liked the idea. Having the police around him would stop the rest of the police force as well as other gangs from touching him. He sought the Sena boss's consent to seek security cover. As expected, he was given the go-ahead by Matoshree, but was told to make a formal application to the police and the home department.

All such applications for security go through a process of screening and clearing by various departments of the Mumbai police, including the crime and protection branches, and along the way, they pass through the hands of several top-ranking officers. The requests are then forwarded to the additional chief secretary's office, which in turn presents them to the home minister.

Home Minister Gopinath Munde, a BJP stalwart, was also the deputy chief minister of the BJP–Shiv Sena coalition, and he ruled his ministry with an iron fist. Despite the fact that the Sena was the senior partner in the coalition, Munde believed that he represented the aspect of the party that was concerned with a national image. He also believed that the Sena lacked serious orientation on macro issues in politics. He literally threw Gawli's file out of the door, lambasting his officers for letting it reach his table in the first place. He demanded an explanation: how had such an audacious application passed through so many departments without being rejected at the initial stage itself? The officers and bureaucrats could only mumble that they had acted on the recommendations of the Sena leaders. But Munde was clear that no man with a criminal record would get state security cover, even if the recommendation came from the highest quarters.

When a disappointed Gawli got in touch with Matoshree, he was told that his request had been turned down by Munde. Gawli then decided to seek the intervention of a relative, a BJP MLA from Madhya Pradesh. Munde was cornered by this leader from a neighbouring state and he did not know how to wriggle out of the situation. So he tried another approach. He convinced the MLA that Gawli's protection had been refused on the direct orders of the Sena supremo. This was blatant subterfuge, but Gawli was gullible enough to believe it, and was enraged by the Sena's duplicity.

Munde then asked his police machinery to ensure that Gawli was thrown behind bars, under some pretext or the other. Munde knew the don belonged in jail, and it was also a place where he would remain safe. Before Gawli could confront the Sena leaders and what he believed was their duplicity, he was picked up in March 1996 and lodged at the Harsul jail in Aurangabad.

Gawli began to notice a subtle shift in the state government's attitude towards him. While Ashwin Naik was given bail on medical grounds, facilitating his escape from the country, Gawli was reduced to being a sitting duck for Dawood in jail. He had been arrested on flimsy grounds and hauled off to a high-security prison.

While in jail, more events conspired to effect Gawli's final divorce from the Shiv Sena. Gawli held regular durbars for his men and met them frequently to issue directions to his gang members. His intelligence network remained well-oiled, including his moles and spies in rival gangs. One such person was Lalit Shah, who remained his confidante and lookout for more than fifteen years.

Gawli trusted Shah. He was a business partner of Amar Naik and they ran a video library together in Matunga. Though Shah was close to both ganglords, he owed allegiance to Gawli. He was in direct touch with him and thought him to be the more powerful and wealthy don, so he remained loyal to him.

Gawli valued Shah's advice, and was willing to risk large sums of money on his recommendation. When Shah advised him to invest Rs 30 lakh in Raghuvanshi Mills, which was owned by Vallabh Thakkar – Thakkar had promised that the amount would be doubled in a year's time – Gawli blindly asked Sada Pawle to deliver the money to the mill owner.

Lalit Shah frequently met Gawli at Harsul jail. On one such trip, Shah tipped him off to the fact that the Sena government was planning to shift him to Amravati jail, which was a 690-km or fourteen-hour journey from Mumbai. Gawli was comfortably settled in Harsul jail in Aurangabad, which was just twelve hours from Mumbai. It takes a long time to make the atmosphere in a jail conducive to one's stay, and as he had no base in Amravati, Gawli was averse to the idea of being shifted there. It is a long process: to buy jail officials, threaten them, intimidate other jail inmates and tame the government machinery to do your bidding. Gawli was also not sure about the motive behind the move. He asked Lalit Shah to use his connections in the Mantralaya to stop the transfer, and Shah assured him that he would pull all strings to do so.

On his next visit, however, Shah dropped a bombshell. He said the transfer to Amravati jail could not be stopped because the orders had come directly from Jayant Jadhav, who was like a godson or Manasputra to Bal Thackeray. Gawli failed to understand what Jadhav's role could be in this. He did not even know Jadhav. But Shah seemed to have inside information on the whole game plan.

He told Gawli that Jadhav was a friend of Amar Naik, and it was at Naik's behest that the transfer was taking place. Naik's plan was to kill Gawli en route from Harsul to Amravati jail, Shah told him. Gawli was dumbstruck. Even under the Congress-I, they had never conspired to kill him in such a cold-blooded manner. Yet, here was the Shiv Sena, which was run by his own godfather, baying for his blood. He decided to bump off Jadhav. (In the underworld, there is little sympathy for those caught in the crosshairs in a situation that has nothing to do with them. In an extreme example, two girls had been shot at while they were standing at a bus-stop because they had been laughing and a gangster, Dilip Bua, did not like it.)

On 30 April 1996, Jadhav was shot dead near his residence in Kamdar Park, Dadar. For the police, media and political analysts, it was a baffling case. They were not willing to believe that Gawli had the temerity to take on the might of the ruling Shiv Sena so blatantly. Killing Thackeray's godson was like an attack on the Sena chief himself. Seven people were arrested by the police and Gawli, too, was booked for the killing.

The police filed a report with the home department about Gawli being too comfortable in the jail – so much so that he had even plotted and executed a high-profile killing. They recommended his transfer to another jail immediately. The government decided to send him to Yerawada jail in Pune.

Gawli was furious. Though Yerawada jail was like a second home to him, the only thing he could think of these days was revenge against the Shiv Sena. He had launched his first attack on the Sena, but he was not satisfied; he wanted to go full throttle against the party that had promised to support him but had then back-stabbed and betrayed him in the most treacherous manner.

One day, Shah brought a surprise visitor to Yerawada jail: Jitendra Dabholkar, an office-bearer in the Kamgar Sena, the labour wing of the Shiv Sena. His fiefdom was the Hotel Oberoi, where workers obeyed his union's word without question. Dabholkar knew how a political party functioned and was well-versed in its management and promotion. Gawli and he joined hands to form a new political party. Dabholkar opened an office in Lalbaug, the heart of the mill land area, and began working on a plan.

Within a few months, Gawli had managed to secure bail in the Jayant Jadhav murder case and returned to Dagdi Chawl. Soon Dabholkar floated the new party that he called the Akhil Bharatiya Sena (ABS). Gawli was designated as its president, while Dabholkar became the secretary. Gawli's wife, Asha, was the head of the women's wing of the party. Dabholkar managed to woo Bharat Mhatre, a close confidante of Chhagan Bhujbal, to ABS. Mhatre became the vice-president of the party. ABS also managed to induct a few disgruntled Shiv Sena workers. The number of ABS members and ex-Sainiks joining the party increased steadily.

Gawli's rebellion baffled the Sena leaders. They had no notion that he had been manipulated into taking on his erstwhile supporters. They did not know that Gawli's reason for launching a political party was the Shiv Sena's support for Amar and Ashwin Naik. By now, Gawli had begun talking against the Sena and its flawed policies openly.

Thackeray, never one to mince words, made his own position amply clear. 'We had relations. Gawli went to prison under the Congress regime and now he is fighting against me. But he should remember that if he is alive today, it is because of Bal Thackeray.' He concluded, 'Gawli deserted me a few months ago.'

THIRTY

The Face-off

The small room in Nagpada police station, in the heart of south Mumbai, was crammed with press reporters and news hounds. They had come for a first-hand account of the chase that had landed gangster Amar Naik in a body bag. Never before in the history of the Mumbai mafia had a top don been felled by the police. The man who had managed the feat, Assistant Police Inspector Vijay Salaskar, was the cynosure of all eyes.

The press reporters, who outnumbered the television reporters, were restless and wanted Salaskar to start the press briefing immediately. It was an informal gathering. Everybody had assembled by word of mouth. When the clamour for him to speak got too much, Salaskar raised a hand for silence and stood up, unsmiling as usual. His eyes had still not learned to trust, and you couldn't help thinking he had been born with a scowl on his face.

In typical police jargon, he began to describe the hunt for the most elusive outlaw of Mumbai, and how he had vanquished him.

'We had received prior information that Amar Naik was expected to visit the Madanpura area after midnight. My team and I laid a trap for him and began the long wait. None of us knew what he looked like. Then, we saw a white Fiat car slowly approaching the spot. A man stepped out of the car. As there was no way we could identify him, we had to use the clichéd approach of surprising a criminal. One of my officers nodded at me and stepped out from his position. He called out to Amar, showing utmost familiarity:

'"Kaiy re Amar, tu ithe?" (Hey Amar, what are you doing here?)

'The man was startled, and he turned towards the plainclothes officer without thinking. One look at the man and Amar sized him up as a cop. In a quick reflex movement, which seemed blurred owing to the speed, Amar whipped out his Glock and fired at him. The cop showed presence of mind and dashed behind a vehicle, saving himself from the bullet, but injuring his shoulder.

'Amar began running. I lost no time and got into the vehicle and began chasing him, at the same time calling out to him. "Amar Thaamb… Amarrrr!"… But he did not stop. It was the dead of night and the whole of the Madanpura–Agripada stretch, which buzzed with activity during the day, was quiet. Everybody was fast asleep at that hour.

'He passed the Salvation Army building and I kept chasing him. He had become aware of my presence, and the trap. Then he turned onto the road leading to the YMCA and my car, which had climbed onto the pavement, came to a halt.

'I jumped out. Suddenly, he turned and fired. I ducked and knelt down on the pavement. I was wearing a bullet-proof jacket; the bullets grazed past my vest. I took aim on his leg and fired. The bullet hit him in the back. He doubled up with pain and tried to run, but pain slowed his reflexes.

'I rose and kept the gun pointed at him. Suddenly, I saw that he had turned again and a flash of light fell on his face. I will never forget that face. He was gritting his teeth, his eyes full of fury – it was the face of a resolute man, who seemed to know that if he was not quick enough to shoot me, he would die.

'All my life, encounters have been split-second decisions. I knew that this was the moment of truth. It was either him or me. I refused to die. I raised my gun and before he could shower me with bullets, I fired at him, more to save myself than to kill him. I was relieved to see him crash to the ground. My team members had by then caught up with me. I went closer to him, and disarmed him. He had another gun tucked in his pocket. He was lying flat on the ground, blood oozing from several wounds. His eyes were glazed, his jaw was still clenched. I asked my team to rush him to Nair Hospital at Bombay Central. But we could not save him.'

Salaskar was gesticulating with his hands as he animatedly described the encounter.

When he finished, the questions began. The *Indian Express* reporter was the first. 'How is it possible that Amar Naik, who was using a Glock, could not even injure you or any of your team members, while you with an ordinary revolver could kill him and escape unhurt?'

There was a deafening silence in the room. Everyone thought the reporter had cornered him. Salaskar was, however, cool personified. He ruptured the silence with a disdainful laugh. 'I am a police officer with thirteen years of experience behind me. I am a trained cop, part of a special squad of police. I am a veteran of fifty encounters. I have been in gunfights with hardened criminals. Criminals are desperadoes. They are not trained shooters. At times they cannot even shoot straight. It is not important to have an automatic weapon. What counts is the man behind the weapon. How many men had Amar killed in his life? He delegated the killings to his people. I work in the field and go through such near-death experiences every day. I am not a coward to send my men to get gangsters. I lead from the front.'

The horde of reporters was hushed. 'But why did you not target his leg or arm, which would have meant capturing him alive and not killing him?' ventured a reporter who worked with a Marathi daily.

'You know, Shrikant, we were not in a peaceful business negotiation across the table, with time and space to think, plan and react to propositions. We were in a duel. Both of us had guns. He would not have hesitated before pumping the bullets into us if we had not pre-empted it. We don't always want to kill, but it happens.'

The motley group of reporters seemed satisfied. Some of them congratulated Salaskar and then dispersed. They had already published the first story on 11 August 1996, when the Amar Naik encounter had made it to the headlines on the front page of most newspapers, or at least second lead. The killing of Amar Naik was like the jewel in the crown of the Mumbai police. It was their biggest trophy. Amar Naik was a gangster, a druglord, and the ringleader of a gang that had in its ranks several educated youth. If he had lived a little longer, there is no doubt that he would have rewritten the history of the Mumbai mafia.

At the informal press gathering, while Salaskar got all the accolades, the other policemen involved in the encounter were somehow sidelined. This included Police Inspector Ajit Wagh, Sub-inspector Satish Mayekar and Sub-inspector Dinesh Ahir, who had reportedly recognized Amar Naik and called out to him.

At the briefing, Salaskar revealed that Amar Naik had given them the slip several times in the past, just when they thought they had got him. When they did get him, he was carrying a pager, Rs 10,000 in cash, a card from a Thailand hotel and other documents from Bangkok. This was the first time that the police had heard of a Mumbai criminal with contacts in the Thai capital. Amar had been carrying two pistols – an Austrian-make Glock and a Chinese .9mm star pistol. His fondness for weapons was known to the police, just as it was known in the mafia circles. Salaskar apparently afraid that Amar would also be carrying an Uzi submachine gun. Naik had always believed that plenty of firepower would give him an edge over his rivals and cops. But his end was tame, too tame for a don who was such an illusionist, a master of disguises. His guns seemed to have failed him. Naik, the police said, had fired six rounds while the police team fired seventeen.

The press drew a parallel with the encounter killing of Colombian druglord Pablo Escobar, who had been worth US$227 billion. They say Escobar was hunted and killed in December 1993 by Search Bloc, a special squad of 200 policemen created only to get him. There were also claims that Escobar had committed suicide – his capture seemed so unbelievable. Similarly, that Naik, known for his Houdini acts, was killed by a handful of police officers seemed a bit difficult to swallow. He was nowhere in the league of Escobar in terms of wealth and notoriety. However, a few common factors made the press draw the comparison. Both men were druglords, and had influence with the ruling government. So much so that finally the government itself resolved to put an end to the menace. In Amar's case, it was the Shiv Sena–BJP combine.

While most of the press fraternity hailed Salaskar as a hero, two reporters from Mumbai thought differently. An *Indian Express* reporter and Prem Shukla, chief reporter of the Hindi tabloid *Dopahar ka Saamna*, had their own take on the Amar Naik encounter. Shukla did a series of stories on Naik's death. The *Indian Express* reporter, too, pursued the story and found a different version from the official one.

It went something like this: Drug baron Nari Khan, who had been acquitted by the specially designated NDPS court, was released from Arthur Road jail on 9 August. Nari left the jail premises empty-handed. He had even donated his comfortable mattress to his long-time cell mate, Askandar Shah. Not a single person was waiting outside the jail to receive the billionaire druglord. The woman he loved had duped him and he was a shattered man. He walked out of the jail, and in a little while reached a signal adjacent to 144 Tenements, the headquarters of the Amar Naik gang. A boy passed by and gave him a message, asking him to meet someone at Shabri Bar at Vile Parle. Unaware that he was being tailed, Nari whiled away the entire day doing nothing and reached the bar in the evening.

The police team saw Nari rendezvous with Naik, and watched as the two men spoke at length before leaving the bar together. The next instant, the police team swooped down and detained them. As Amar Naik had undergone facial reconstruction, they did not recognize him until Nari broke down and admitted who his companion had been. The cops had finally tracked down Naik but they realized that it would not be wise to leave an eyewitness like Nari Khan alive. They first killed Amar in an encounter, and kept Nari at an undisclosed location for two days. Subsequently, Nari Khan was killed in an encounter at Vikhroli while he was 'carrying one kilo of heroin'.

There was another explanation for why Nari was tailed and pursued by officers from the anti-narcotics cell of the crime branch. Ayesha still had a hold over her cop boyfriend, who was obsessed with her.

He had managed to put her current boyfriend behind bars and was afraid that Nari Khan, who had sworn revenge, would seek him out, so he orchestrated the whole operation. Salaskar had done a stint at the anti-narcotics cell, and now Naik was offered to him as a prize as long as he agreed to kill both men.

There were other stories that emerged, about how Salaskar was given the green light by none other than a senior minister in the Shiv Sena–BJP government. There was a report that days before the encounter, Amar had managed to sneak into the Mantralaya and had gone straight up to the sixth floor and barged into the office of his friend. The minister had begun sweating at the sight of him, not because he was afraid of Amar Naik, but because he was afraid of the media discovering the don in his cabin.

Naik had apparently come to blackmail him and make an unreasonable demand in person. His unhindered access to the minister's cabin indicated their close proximity, which was most damning. The senior politician from Mumbai was left with no option but to call him home the next day. He also invited Salaskar, a known Sena loyalist. Salaskar picked up Naik from the minister's house and then killed him in an encounter at Byculla.

Prem Shukla, the Hindi journalist, followed a highly controversial line of investigation while pursuing the trail of the sensational Naik encounter. His paper carried the following story on its front page.

Soon after Amar Naik had killed mill owner Sunit Khatau, panic had gripped the business community. A group of businessmen, including relatives of Khatau, had formed an informal action group and a corpus had been created which allowed for a reward of Rs 10 crore to whoever was willing to kill Naik. Initially, they approached Chandrakant Khopde, the boss of Babya Khopdya of the Golden Gang, who had been Naik's first rival. Despite the promise of big money, Babya admitted his inability to accept the offer; he did not have the wherewithal to track down a slippery target like Naik, leave alone kill him.

But he made a valuable suggestion. He said that Naik could be tracked and killed by a resourceful encounter specialist. The Hindi tabloid reported that the supari was then offered to several encounter specialists in the city, and that Salaskar had accepted the challenge.

The many versions of this story blur. However, the most credible is the one that has the police tracing Naik through Nari. Nari had lowered his guard and unwittingly led the police team to Naik's hideout, resulting in the encounter. This was the story detailed in the *Indian Express*, and it was later picked up by other papers too.

The shopkeepers and business establishments in Delisle Road, Chinchpokli, Mahalaxmi and Parel areas observed a bandh for a few days after Naik's death. But his gang members shied away from being seen near his house or at his final rites. Naik's funeral was attended by barely fifteen to twenty people from the Chinchpokli-Byculla area. However, one notable person attended the funeral and stayed till the end: Shiv Sena MP Mohan Rawle. Rawle was also vociferously critical of the police version of the encounter.

But Nari Khan's death was far more pathetic. His body lay unclaimed for over 10 days in the morgue of J.J. Hospital. No one came forward to give it proper burial according to Islamic customs. Finally the police approached Pakhtoon Jirgae Hind, the official organization of the Pathan migrants settled in India. Pakhtoon had been formed by Khan Abdul Ghaffar Khan, also known to Indians as the Frontier Gandhi. However, Pakhtoon office-bearers sternly turned down the police request to accept Nari's body for final rites on the grounds that he was a criminal and a drug peddler. There was no way that the organization would accord him respect by performing his final rites.

Nari Khan, once a millionaire with assets worth Rs 400 crore, died a pauper's death.

THIRTY-ONE

Carte Blanche

It is not every day that a police inspector is summoned by a top minister in the ruling government. Assistant Police Inspector Vijay Salaskar was nervous, anxious, uncertain.

API Salaskar, who normally had his .38 service revolver in his bag and three mobile phones in his pockets, was carrying nothing with him today. He had been to the bungalow just once before. After a brief wait, he was called in. Salaskar walked into the huge room that seemed to reek of power.

The minister was sitting on a sofa.

'Ya, Vijay, ya,' he said in Marathi, welcoming him into the room.

Salaskar saluted, then folded his hands in a cordial gesture. 'Namaskar, sir.'

The minister waved him into a chair next to him.

Salaskar saw that he was the only one in the room. This was unlike his meetings with other senior ministers, who were always surrounded by a host of people.

The minister began with small talk. The conversation veered from the police department to postings and law-and-order problems in the city. The minister then surprised him by applauding Salaskar's consistently good work since his days in the narcotics cell of the crime branch after which he had moved to the Nagpada police station. Salaskar smiled a thank you.

'I want you to continue the good work,' the minister said.

Salaskar looked at him. This did not seem like the usual encouragement. The minister was not smiling. He was looking directly into Salaskar's eyes. The hardened cop, who had locked eyes with many a tough criminal in his life, was unable to decipher the shifting expressions of the droopy-eyed minister. This unsettled him and he filled the silence with a quick 'Ho sir.'

'I want you to go after the Gawli gang with full force,' the minister announced.

'Ho sir,' came the reply.

'The way you got Amar Naik?'

It was a question or a command, or both. But Salaskar understood.

'Yes sir, I will try my best,' he said.

'We will give you full support in whatever way you need.'

'Ho sir.'

'I will ask Pradeep Sharma to go after Chhota Rajan and the Dawood gang.'

Salaskar nodded.

The minister indicated that the meeting was over.

Salaskar rose, saluted again and slowly walked out of the door. He wasn't sure if he should celebrate, laugh or share this strange meeting with his colleagues. For the moment, though, he felt happy that a minister had shown such trust in him that instead of talking to his seniors or his bosses, he had called him directly and personally given him instructions.

Salaskar was one of the most successful officers of the Mumbai police. He had an enviable track record of major hits against the Mumbai underworld: he had killed more than thirty gangsters so far and had also been involved in major drug seizures during his tenure in the anti-narcotics cell of the crime branch.

The minister's carte blanche was incredibly significant, and Salaskar decided to capitalize on it.

Salaskar knew that Gawli and the Naiks had forced the minister's hand. They had crossed the Lakshman Rekha, the proverbial last line of permissible limits. The ruling Shiv Sena was convinced that Gawli in particular deserved to be punished for his belligerence towards the powers that be.

Matoshree had barely finished mourning for Jayant Jadhav when Gawli threw another googly its way by launching his political party that posed a direct challenge to the Shiv Sena. The ruling party was willing to overlook Gawli's political ambitions, but what got its goat was Gawli's strong-arm tactics during the Mumbai municipal corporation elections.

Gawli had fielded ABS candidates in the Dadar, Parel and Byculla areas. He began threatening and intimidating Sena candidates in these constituencies. When this did not work, Gawli's men resorted to violence and began thrashing Sena workers. There was deep fear in all the constituencies. Gawli's men began bullying voters even in the constituency of Chief Minister Manohar Joshi. When the election results for Dadar were declared, ABS candidate Meenakshi Tandel, wife of Gawli's notorious sharpshooter Vijay Tandel, had come second to Shiv Sena candidate Vishakha Raut; the Congress candidate, who had been a strong contender, lagged behind, as a distant third.

The police acted swiftly and detained Arun Gawli under the National Security Act (NSA). But it seemed that Gawli still had his sympathizers among the top Sena leaders. Mohan Rawle perceived the arrest as an act of gross injustice. He protested against the detention of Arun Gawli by the Mumbai police and sat on a hunger strike at the Agripada police station. After eight days, Rawle broke his fast when Gawli's mother gave him a glass of juice.

Meanwhile, Gawli was well prepared for the government's retaliation. Asha Gawli filed a writ petition with the Nagpur bench of the Bombay High Court challenging her husband's detention under NSA. Arvind Bobde, ex-advocate general of Maharashtra, appeared on behalf of Gawli. The high court not only found the detention unjustified and set it aside, but it also imposed a fine of Rs 25,000 on the police commissioner of Mumbai and the additional chief secretary of the state, both of whom were signatories to the detention order. Such strong strictures and the levying of fines on such senior administrators and the police chief were unprecedented. They left the government reeling in embarrassment.

An emboldened Gawli returned to Dagdi Chawl with great pomp and began working on the promotion of ABS with renewed vigour and intensity. This time, he wanted to expand beyond Dadar to the Byculla belt and eventually to the entire state.

On 18 July 1997, Gawli threw an open challenge to the state government when he organized a morcha and led a large number of people to Hutatma Chowk, condemning the government for police firing on Dalit demonstrators at Ghatkopar East. The media reported that more than two lakh people participated in the morcha, and that Gawli had turned the tide against his 'sympathizer party'. He was being hailed as a renegade politician, a harbinger of change.

Political analysts were shocked at the media's glorification of a criminal and his moves against the government. According to a Special Branch report, Gawli spent more than Rs 1.5 crore to organize the morcha and make it a grand success.

The media reports, changing public opinion and the lack of support from the judiciary stifled the government's campaign against Gawli. There was a feeling that there were too many watchdogs and they had better play it by the ear.

But exactly a month after the Hutatma Chowk rally, on 18 August 1997, while the government was still smarting from the public humiliation, Gawli had top builder Natwarlal Desai killed in the middle of the day in Mumbai's elite business district of Nariman Point. It was the first high-profile killing in the area, and the movers and shakers of south Mumbai were very upset. Nariman Point was a place where most multinational companies and foreign brands had their offices, and the killing was regarded as a blot on the reputation of the state as well as the central government. The furore was heard in Parliament as well.

As if the government had been waiting for just such a slip-up, the next day the police prepared the essential warrants and launched an offensive. On 20 August, the cops were knocking on the huge iron gates of Dagdi Chawl, led by Deputy Commissioner Param Bir

Singh of Zone II. They turned the whole place upside down; every nook and cranny was searched.

Their fastidiousness paid off. The killers of Natwarlal Desai were found hiding inside the house: in special cavities under the kitchen sink, which was blocked by an LPG gas cylinder; in a crevice in the prayer room; and in a hole under the bathroom. They also discovered a tunnel that led to a passage outside Dagdi Chawl. It was as if they had stumbled into a nest of snakes!

DCP Singh's team confronted Desai's killers, including Vijay Muchwa, Vijay Shirodkar and Pankaj Pandey. All three were later gunned down by the police in an 'encounter'.

Importantly, the cops also found the kingpin during their search. When they dismantled one of the box beds, they found Gawli hiding inside it, a carbine lying next to him. Fortunately, Gawli did not make any attempt to touch the gun.

The police received more intelligence and raided another safe house at Kabutar Khana on N.M. Joshi Marg, Byculla. They found two trunkloads of court papers and affidavits, some with names and others with blank spaces for names. Gawli had employed Suresh Bhaskar to look after court matters for the gang; they kept such documents ready to meet any eventuality.

Gawli strongly contested every case against him. He had realized that the judiciary was a good weapon against the state and the police. He filed writ petitions in the high court when the government made any move against him. He and his wife also made applications to the National Human Rights Commission (NHRC) and high-ranking officials in the government as well as judges of high courts.

After the raid on Dagdi Chawl, the government unleashed special police squads to go at the Gawli gang hammer and tongs. It seemed the state had declared an unofficial war against the gang.

On the same night, the crime branch killed gangster Jeetu Mane in an encounter at Trombay. But these gangsters of Gawli were small fry; their killings did not make much of a dent in the gang's arsenal. The real decimation of the gang began with Vijay Salaskar. With three sharpshooters on his side, he took them down one after another.

Barely three days after the Desai killing at Nariman Point, Salaskar killed Ganesh Bhosale alias Vakil at Kurla East. Bhosale's killing came as a shock to the Gawli gang – he had been a crucial part of their machinery. Even before they could recover from the shock, Salaskar struck again.

On 26 September, he killed Gawli's top shooters, Sada Pawle and Vijay Tandel, in another encounter at Ghatkopar East. Pawle was found with an AK-47 in his jeep when Salaskar confronted him on a busy, crowded road. This almost broke the back of the gang.

Gawli was shaken by Pawle and Tandel's killings. He now lived in mortal fear of being killed by Salaskar. He had even arranged for his lawyers to prepare briefs urging the courts to intervene. To make matters worse, the government was using the Salaskar card against him all the time. They erected a special police chowki right in front of Dagdi Chawl and posted Salaskar in that chowki. It is said that Gawli never stepped out of the iron gates of Dagdi Chawl when Salaskar was on the prowl.

THIRTY-TWO

The Bullet Raj

The crime conference of the Mumbai police was in full swing. All the DCPs of the different zones of Mumbai were present. Most of them hated these long-winded meetings; they were boring and rarely produced results.

On that particular Wednesday in 1995, Ram Dev Tyagi, the police commissioner, brought the somnolent IPS officers out of their reveries when he declared that each zone should kill at least ten criminals in encounters. 'Why should encounters only be the prerogative of the crime branch? Even zones should participate,' he declared.

An officer tried to interject. 'It is not always possible to eliminate criminals in encounters.' Tyagi gave him a dirty look and shot off his famous quotable quote, which was later repeated and mimicked by various DCPs. 'Don't teach your father to fuck,' he said. This silenced the whole room.

Ram Dev Tyagi was known as the boldest and perhaps the most controversial police commissioner of Mumbai. He came from an army background. He never minced words and was blunt to the point of being brutal. When a spate of robberies in south Mumbai's jewellery shops rocked the city's business community, Tyagi came up with an instant solution. He organized a public meeting near Zaveri Bazaar and addressed the business community in a manner that people would never forget.

'I urge all of you to keep a hockey stick in your shops and when the robbers come, defend yourself with the stick. Beat them black and blue. If the robber dies, the police will support you, I promise,' he said.

The hockey stick remark, reproduced in the *Indian Express*, set off a debate and people mocked him. He was perceived as a commissioner who exhorted people to take the law into their own hands and kill people.

His past preceded him. Ram Dev Tyagi had become a police commissioner after serving as a bureaucrat in Mantralaya, the seat of state administration. Prior to his stint at Mantralaya, Tyagi had served as joint commissioner, crime. During the communal riots of 1993, he had ordered his men to storm a masjid situated above the Suleman Bakery, resulting in the killing of nine unarmed Muslims.

Perhaps it was his in-your-face approach that appealed to Bal Thackeray. Tyagi was a favourite of his but was disliked intensely by Home Minister Gopinath Munde.

Tyagi had taken charge at a time when gang wars had escalated and Mumbai was fast turning from financial capital to crime capital.

By now, the city was willing to pay to get rid of this mafia that had spread its tentacles to real estate, Bollywood, and almost everywhere it could smell money. In the nineties, few flaunted their wealth for fear of being spotted by the mafia, which lost no time in making that give-or-die call: 'Pay or else.' Tyagi believed that gangsters and robbers only understood the language of violence; you could not be diplomatic with them. Perhaps it was his army background that made him believe in the credo, 'eye for an eye'.

Tyagi wanted to instil the fear of death into the minds of criminals. He reintroduced an old weapon from the police arsenal – encounters. Already, after 1993, soon after the communal riots in Mumbai, encounters or extra-judicial killings by the police had become commonplace. But it was Tyagi who officially greenlighted the era of police encounters.

Once the police commissioner gave his blessings, the zonal DCPs lost no time in forming their own special squads. The men in these special squads formed an elite group with their own offices and working at their own pace. They could trail and stake out a quarry for days or even months.

The DCPs now began vying with each other to get the best men for the job.

Satyapal Singh, who was DCP Zone VII – the area ranges from Bandra to Andheri – formed a special squad and made Pradeep Sharma its head. DCP Param Bir Singh, Zone II – which spanned almost half of south Mumbai – formed two special squads led by Praful Bhosale and Vijay Salaskar.

These three officers belonged to the 1983 batch of the Maharashtra police service. There was something about the officers of that batch. They had no qualms about killing and were utterly fearless daredevils. Almost all the encounter specialists came from this batch.

According to orders from above, in Zone II, Salaskar and Bhosale went after Arun Gawli and his men while Sharma took on the Shakeel gang. Between the three of them, they eliminated more than 300 gangsters. Sharma alone took out 110 gangsters, including three LeT terrorists. Bhosale killed more than ninety gangsters from both the Gawli and Rajan gangs. Salaskar managed only sixty, but these were important hits: he managed to destroy the prime muscle power of the Gawli gang.

In ten years, between 1993 and 2003, some 600 criminals were killed in Mumbai. Every time the bell tolled for a gangster, it was the cop who walked away with the good press. The only time the cops were overshadowed by the victim was when the quarry was a big fish like Amar Naik, Sada Pawle or Suresh Manchekar.

At last, Tyagi, who had never bowed to the home minister, was shunted out of the police commissionerate unceremoniously. His strategic positioning as a Bal Thackeray-approved officer did not help.

Subhash Malhotra succeeded Tyagi as the police chief. Malhotra did not have a proven track record either in the crime branch or in the zones, but because he had seen Tyagi's strategy of 'shoot first, talk later' work, he allowed the encounters to continue. The police believed that these encounters worked as deterrents for the mafia, as they instilled fear into the minds of the otherwise reckless gangsters. Also, a section of the press glorified the encounter cops, who were portrayed as heroes.

The media loved to write about Daya Nayak in particular. His story had all the elements of a fairytale: the little boy from a blink-and-you-miss-it village called Yennehole in Mangalore, who came to work as menial help in a Udupi hotel, swabbing the floor and scrubbing the dishes, and studying in a night school before joining the police force. Nayak was hailed as a hero both in Mumbai and his hometown in Mangalore, where he built a multi-million-rupee school that was inaugurated by none other than Amitabh Bachchan.

Then there was Vijay Salaskar, who seemed fearless as he knocked off the big fish. Salaskar was not media savvy, but he got his fair share of good press.

Salaskar and Daya Nayak's stories inspired several policemen. They all wanted to be famous and they all wanted to be encounter specialists. So the killings continued, with more trigger-happy policemen added to the list of encounter specialists. They were now posing with their guns, strutting like peacocks, a la Dirty Harry. Alex Perry, the bureau chief of the Indian subcontinent for *Time* magazine, did a full-page article on the encounters of the Mumbai police, in which he called the officers 'urban cowboys'.

The press notes from the police on the early encounters were the same. 'That the police received information that the fellow was about to commit such and such crime and we laid a trap. The criminal arrived in a white Maruti 800 and we saw the car from a distance. We identified the criminal and called out his name. But he opened fire with his AK-47 and we had to resort to firing in self-defence. The criminal was injured in the melee and we took him to the nearest hospital but he succumbed to his injuries and was declared dead on arrival.'

Initially, the public, happy to see the city rid of criminals, was very supportive. They were happy that a motley bunch of uniformed men had changed the character of Mumbai from a mafia city to a moderately safe city. Trouble started when the encounter specialists went out of control. Their methods had now become a short-cut to fame. Some unscrupulous officers began attributing unsolved cases to their encounter victims and claiming that the cases had been detected and solved.

Human rights agencies were watching this trend. They had remained mute spectators in the beginning, but when they saw that the encounters had become the norm rather than the exception, they cried foul.

In an interview to the *Telegraph*, P. Sebastian, of the Committee for Protection of Democratic Rights (CPDR), said that when they were investigating the encounter deaths for a writ petition, they found that the criminals were always shot in the head and the chest, which indicated that the cops meant to kill and not injure their targets. Sebastian, who investigated 137 deaths and filed a writ petition stating that the deaths be treated as culpable homicide, was stonewalled by the courts, which threw out the petition. But he believes that 'the story that the dead criminal was armed with an AK-47 is the most outrageous. An AK-47 is a battle weapon and can mow down a crowd. It can fire ten bullets in a second and 600 in a minute. But, invariably, the policeman at the receiving end of the AK-47 would come out of the whole episode smelling of roses and without a scratch, and the criminal would be dead as a dodo.'

Also, the cops' thirst for blood was becoming like that of the mythical demon Bakasura. It showed no sign of abating. The good thing was that for the first time, young men who may have been lured into a life of crime were rethinking their choices. They didn't want to end up in body bags, adding to the count of the encounter specialists.

Meanwhile, television highlighted the killings, the blood and the gore, and it was all very unsavoury. Soon, the press notes stopped making any difference: every time somebody got killed, people wondered about the motive.

Tracing the trail of disrepute, Rakesh Maria, Joint Commissioner, Crime, said in an interview, 'Initially the encounter cops targeted the top rung of the mafia, the ones who were in power. Then they started off with the third and the fourth rungs, then it was the turn of the robbers. And then the public didn't know who was being shot and everybody was suspicious. And soon there were too many watchdogs – the electronic medium, the press, society, the human rights activists.'

It was the murder of music magnate Gulshan Kumar on 12 August 1997 and the subsequent encounter which put the spotlight on police excesses. After Gulshan Kumar's killing, Joint Commissioner of Police, Crime, Ranjit Singh Sharma, found it difficult to handle the intense media glare. His daily schedule was so hectic that even those eyeing his position were pleased that they were not in his shoes. He had to constantly field phone calls from several ministers, including the chief minister and the home minister. Each time a heavyweight telephoned Sharma, he offered explanations and provided reasons for not being able to make a breakthrough.

The police had barely recovered from the backlash of the Gulshan Kumar murder when the mafia struck again and gunned down builder Natwarlal Desai at Nariman Point on 18 August 1997, in front of Tulsiani Chambers, opposite Mantralaya. The newspapers the next day screamed: 'Murder under the nose of Mantralaya!'

Joshi and Munde were under fire from the media and the business community. They felt that the police machinery was failing them, and that there had to be a change of guard. Munde felt that Subhash Malhotra was incompetent to lead a police team and so, two weeks after the killing, he was unceremoniously shunted to the nondescript posting of police commissioner, housing and welfare. His name would go down in the annals of Mumbai police history as the first chief to have suffered the ignominy of a transfer because of one high-profile killing. On 28 August, Ronald Hyacinth Mendonca was appointed police commissioner of Mumbai.

On the same day that Mendonca became the commissioner, there was a controversial encounter that killed a man called Javed Fawda, at Ballad Pier. Assistant Police Inspector Vasant Dhoble headed this encounter, and his men cleverly leaked news of it to some of their friends in the print media. 'Gulshan Kumar's shooter killed in an encounter', 'Crime branch hits back in style, guns down Gulshan Kumar's killer' read the headlines.

The press, especially the Marathi press, applauded Dhoble's courage. However, the mood was far from celebratory at the crime branch headquarters. In underworld parlance, the man who pulls the trigger on his victim is the main shooter, while the man who gives him cover is merely a sidekick and is known as the second shooter. That the cops were quiet over the role Fawda had played in Gulshan Kumar's murder meant the case came under a cloud.

Javed Fawda turned out to be the crime branch's nemesis. Abu Sayama Abu Talib Shaikh, also known as Javed, had earned the nickname 'Fawda' because of his bucktooth. Unfortunately, the man Dhoble had killed wasn't the real Javed Fawda, the gangster, but Abu Sayama, a peanut vendor.

His sister Rubina, who lived in a Bandra slum, kicked up a storm. She cried that her brother had sold peanuts outside the masjid near Bandra railway station and had been missing since 26 August, following which she had lodged a missing person complaint. On 29 August, she was summoned to identify her brother's badly mutilated body. The autopsy revealed that Javed had been riddled with bullets at close range. He had also been run over by a vehicle, his ribs crushed under the impact of the wheels.

The Samajwadi Party, which was trying to project itself as the messiah of the Muslim community, raised a massive stink about the killing of an innocent Muslim. Abu Asim Azmi, the man at the helm of the party in Mumbai, went after the police administration with zeal. This put the police in a difficult spot. DCP K.L. Prasad and his chief R.S. Sharma desperately tried to explain to the media and human rights watchers that they had killed a criminal and not a harmless peanut vendor.

Three days after the encounter, the crime branch chief hoped that his sensational disclosure about ganglord Abu Salem's musical extravaganza in Dubai, attended by Nadeem–Shravan and other Bollywood biggies and business rivals of Gulshan Kumar, would distract the press. The conspiracy to kill Gulshan Kumar had been hatched at that particular party, the police said. Following the press conference, the police commissionerate was besieged by fans; they sought to catch a glimpse of their favourite stars, who all came in to to give their statements.

The press forgot Fawda – but Sharma didn't. For a long while after that, there were no encounters.

A series of Public Interest Litigations petitioning the Bombay High Court to stop the encounters had also kickstarted. The petitions insisted that the encounters were actually murders in cold blood, and that victims were handed the death penalty on the spot, without a trial. The high court came down heavily on the police, forcing them to consign their guns to their holsters. The petitions around the Fawda encounter, and subsequently around the Sada Pawle encounter, put the brakes on the Mumbai police's extra-judicial killings – and when a division bench of the Bombay High Court was appointed in 1997–98 to probe the veracity of the controversial encounters, the cops were caught on the back foot.

Sessions court judge Aloysius Stanislaus Aguiar was the head of the probe committee. After several months of investigation, he filed a 223-page report and declared that the police encounters of Javed Fawda and Sada Pawle were fake and did not match the version cops had given during the proceedings.

Mendonca, known for his integrity, did not believe in the methods practised during such encounters. For months, he tried to experiment with more punitive laws like the Maharashtra Prevention of Dangerous People's Act, which did not allow for easy bail.

With this cessation of encounters after more than a decade of living in fear, criminals heaved a sigh of relief and went into celebration mode – by launching a spree of killings. The year 1998 recorded the highest number of shootouts: more than 100 people were either killed or badly injured in firing by underworld operatives. In police parlance, the word 'shootout' means an incident where a gunman opens fire on the victim with the intention to kill; sometimes, if a victim is fortunate, he may survive. The police registered a shootout every third day. The crime branch was constantly on the alert, and the morale of the police force was at an all-time low. Arguments over the genuineness of the encounters raged on in the Bombay High Court.

The cops realized that they had been pushed to the wall and had to retaliate. They could not allow gangsters to run amok, for every mafia shootout was a mockery of their presence and Mendonca's three-decade-long career. Ministers from Mantralaya had begun pressing the panic button at the sight of so much lawlessness.

Then the unexpected happened and the proverbial Red Sea parted for the cops. A division bench of the high court rejected the Aguiar report and declared that the encounters were not fake.

Mendonca decided to shed his mild manners for good. He roped in Colonel (retired) Mahendra Pratap Choudhary of special operations in the Indian Army to train cops for gun battles with the underworld. He organized a press conference and announced his 'bullet for bullet' strategy against the mafia. There were two aspects to the plan: psychological warfare and covert operations.

The encounter cops were back in business. After a hiatus of a year or so, the specialists began shooting to kill again. Even Bollywood decided to pay tribute to them. Film-makers like N. Chandra, who made *Kagaar*, and Ram Gopal Verma in *Ab Tak Chhappan*, made encounter specialists their main protagonists.

THIRTY-THREE

Death of a Doctor

A new year had dawned, but trade union leader Dr Datta Samant was not happy. The continuing mill strike was weighing him down. In two days, it would be exactly fifteen years since he first called for the strike on 18 January 1982.

'I think I am the only foolish trade union leader fighting for the workers' rights and I know I am going to die an unsung hero,' he had said in a rare public display of emotion, a couple of days earlier. He was being driven in his jeep from his residence in Powai to his office at Saki Naka. Though he had a house in Ghatkopar East, he lived in a one-storey house in Powai.

As Samant's driver Bhim Rao took a sharp turn on Padmavati Road near IIT Powai, a rickshaw appeared out of nowhere and headed towards the jeep. Samant was used to being accosted en route to his office by mill workers, party workers, or activists, or workers in engineering and other companies who sought his intervention in some matter or the other. Samant usually met them briefly and went onward. At any time, there was a motley group around him, of four to 40 people. These gatherings always ended in loud chants of 'Doctor Datta Samant zindabad'.

That particular day, on 16 January 1997, when Samant saw the four men who had intercepted his jeep, he didn't think there was anything out of the ordinary. As was his habit, he asked his driver to halt. The men came up to the jeep and took their target by surprise, riddling him with seventeen bullets.

Samant succumbed to his injuries while his driver Bhim Rao survived. The case, initially registered by the Saki Naka police station, was later taken over by the crime branch. It was one of the most complex cases that the crime branch had handled, and Inspector Teja Chavan managed to only partially uncover the conspiracy behind the murder.

Dr Dattatray Narayan Samant, originally from Sindhudurg in Konkan, Maharashtra, had become one of the most popular and powerful trade union activists in the world in a short span of less than twenty years. Samant had stumbled onto the plight of his patients, most of whom were quarry workers in the Thane–Dombivli belt, and taken up the battle against the injustice and hardships inflicted upon them by powerful industrialists.

At a time when trade unionism was in the grip of communists, the management-pliant Shiv Sena and the Congress, Samant's fresh and practical approach to labour disputes had made him a darling of the workers. Though he had kickstarted his political innings with the Congress when he contested the state assembly elections in 1972 from Mulund and won, he could not live with the Congress hegemony and struck out on his own. During the Emergency, while the Shiv Sena almost sang paeans to Indira Gandhi, Samant found himself behind bars for being too militant and vocal about his opinions. In the Lok Sabha elections of 1984, post Indira Gandhi's assassination, there was a huge sympathy wave for the Congress – the joke was that if a dog or a donkey had contested the elections on a Congress ticket that year, the animal would have won hands down. But the Congress, which swept Mumbai, lost one seat, and that was to Samant. The victory wave had humiliated all the anti-Congress parties, including the BJP, which could manage only two seats in the entire country and the CPI(M), which was routed in its home turf of West Bengal.

Most of the strikes called by Doctor Saheb had wound to their logical end but the textile mill strike was never officially called off. It petered out gradually and Samant began to lose his grip over the trade union movement in the city. As a result, he also got a sound thrashing in politics. He had launched the Kamghar Aghadi Party, but he lost all three assembly elections he contested from the same working-class mill pockets of south-central Mumbai.

The Congress had a hand in undermining Samant's clout; the Indian National Trade Union Congress (INTUC) and RMMS had revived their stranglehold on the dying textile mills once again, turning into stooges of the management.

When Sunit Khatau of Khatau Mills joined hands with Sachin Ahir of RMMS to sell the surplus mill land and make his fortune, they came into bitter conflict with Samant. Though the state government stalled the sale of surplus land after the killing of Khatau in May 1994, the hostility continued between the two unions. Soon, Ahir toppled Samant from Modistone's Sewri unit and anointed his own man as the president. He also systematically began ousting Samant from all the major unions in the city where he had clout.

When Samant was upstaged during the Premier Automobiles Limited (PAL) lockout in 1996, fingers were pointed at Ahir's clever manipulations. Samant's union in PAL and the Shiv Sena called for a strike, but the INTUC union continued working. PAL had two plants, one in Kurla and another in Dombivli. Clever politics resulted in the defection of two of Samant's aides, Eknath Angre in Kurla and Ratan Patil in Dombivli, who were known as the right and left hand of Samant. Consequently, Samant lost his hold over both the plants of PAL. This gave rise to bad blood and intense animosity among the various union leaders.

The police dossier on the Samant killing is revealing. 'During investigation, it was revealed that Datta Samant had hired the services of underworld gangsters to eliminate those who defected from his union and the leader of the opposite union. Having learnt about the plan, Ramesh Patil, son of Ratan Patil, spoke to Chhota Rajan through Bharat Nepali, a gangster from the Chhota Rajan group.'

The crime branch had questioned several hundred people in the case, including Sachin Ahir, who was repeatedly interrogated for several hours. After eleven months of investigation, the police managed to arrest three shooters and six others for conspiracy, including a couple of union leaders. However, only three shooters were convicted and the conspirators were acquitted for lack of evidence. Mystery surrounded the killing of Samant; his murder was likened to the assassination of Shankar Guha Niyogi, an activist who was killed in Bhilai in 1991. Analysts tried to draw parallels between the killings and even pointed accusatory fingers at the ruling BJP government, as both union leaders had been killed during BJP rule.

There were various conspiracy theories. Some said it was the miffed managements, some said it was the Shiv Sena, yet others blamed RMMS and some Congress bigwigs, and of course, the cogs in the wheel of the Chhota Rajan gang.

Despite the arrest of sixteen people and the conviction of three, Dr Datta Samant's killing has remained an unsolved case. The real conspiracy and the truth behind the killing will probably never be known. But it did expose Chhota Rajan's hollow claims of being a patriotic don and a messiah of the underdogs, for Dr Samant was most certainly a man who represented the masses.

Thousands of workers participated in Samant's funeral, shouting 'Doctor Datta Samant zindabad' and 'Joshi–Munde aaj ke gunde' (Joshi and Munde are today's goons). The Saki Naka intersection, in the north-western suburbs, which witnesses some of the worst traffic snarls in the city, has become a memorial to Samant. It is now called the Kamgar Aghadi Chowk. The emblem of a closed fist rising above the roofs of mills immortalizes Samant and his endless struggle.

Samant's killing cleared the path for mill land redevelopment under the aegis of Sachin Ahir. Parel became upmarket and upper Worli – Currey Road, Chinchpokli, Byculla and Sewri, where the chimneys towered over a labouring population – boasts the highest number of towers.

Tragically, the textile mills strike has had a ripple effect on all industrial and manufacturing sectors in Mumbai. The workers are now a marginalized lot. There are no real trade unions that look after their interests. Those that exist are management-appointed. History will remember Dr Datta Samant for leading the last big battle of workers against industry in India. It will also remember him for changing the dynamics, geography and profile of the south-central mill pockets of Mumbai.

THIRTY-FOUR

Shakeel Stuns the Sena

After Bal Thackeray adopted 'amchi muley', 'our boys', from the mill heartlands and other pockets of Mumbai and called the Dawood gang Pakistanis and Muslims (Thackeray always equated Indian Muslims with Pakistanis), the mafia too got segregated along religious lines.

The Karachi-based gangsters of the D-Company chafed at the accusations and wanted to hurt the Sena. The D-Company, however, was already fraying at the edges; things were never the same after the serial blasts in Mumbai in 1993. The absence of Chhota Rajan, who had held together all the disparate groups within the gang, was keenly felt. Sautya had been mowed down in Dubai, and Subhash Singh Thakur, the late bloomer in the gang who had managed to inveigle his way to the boss's heart, had been arrested (and is now comfortably ensconced in Gujarat's Sabarmati jail). Dawood had had to relocate to the safe houses of Karachi and had his hands full trying to cope with being a yes-man to the ISI. It was in these circumstances that Shakeel Baubumiya Shaikh, alias Chhota Shakeel – who had started off as a local ruffian and became part of the inner circle of Dawood Ibrahim – took centre stage.

Dawood's men looked up to Chhota Shakeel and took instructions from him because they knew that he had virtually become the Chief Executioning Officer of the company.

The gang wanted to respond and retaliate to Thackeray's 'our boys' rhetoric at the party's annual Dussehra rally. Elaborate plans were drawn up, strategies were discussed and, after many brainstorming sessions, they decided to hit the Shiv Sena as a party. They spoke about many possible scenarios and some improbable ones.

They all agreed that liquidating Bal Thackeray or his family members might prove counterproductive for Muslims, who were still reeling from the communal flare-up and the resultant backlash in 1992–93. Finally, after toying with the idea of bumping off different Shiv Sena leaders, they came to the conclusion that they would target those Sena leaders who had been at the forefront of the communal riots of 1992–93.

However, the dossier on Dawood prepared by the Mumbai police attributed a larger cross-border conspiracy to the attack on the Shiv Sena. 'The Inter-Services Intelligence (ISI) wanted to instigate communal unrest in the country so, along with Dawood Ibrahim and Chhota Shakeel, the ISI hatched a conspiracy and masterminded a plan to attack the office-bearers of the Shiv Sena. Chhota Shakeel instructed his gangsters to go after the office-bearers of the Shiv Sena and kill them. He was so desperate that he ordered his gangsters to even kill Shiv Sainiks of any other part of Maharashtra if the gangsters were unable to liquidate the Shiv Sainiks of Mumbai. Chhota Shakeel arranged for the delivery of weapons and money to the shooters. This resulted in a number of attacks and killings of office bearers of the Shiv Sena in and around the city.' ('Organized Crime', Dawood Ibrahim files, p. 43.)

The police version notwithstanding, one thing was certain. The D-gang was not going to sit back and listen to Bal Thackeray rant against its proud members. They were tired of Thackeray usurping the garb of patriotism by virtue of being a Hindu. They were sick of his constant haranguing and unforgiving of his role in the riots.

The first Shiv Sena leader that Shakeel's men targeted was former Mumbai mayor Milind Vaidya. Vaidya had been indicted by the Justice B.N. Srikrishna Commission inquiring into the communal riots for inciting violence against Muslims in the Mahim area. On 17 December 1998, Vaidya was travelling in his Tata Safari. As the vehicle passed through Bandra, six men from the Dawood gang fired at him through the windscreen, injuring him. However, he survived the assault. Shakeel was furious at the botched attempt, and immediately issued orders to target Vaidya again.

Within three months, a nine-member team was put together. This time, the weapons were upgraded and the assailants were given AK-56s. The plan was to shower Vaidya with enough bullets to leave no room for survival. On 4 March 1999, Vaidya was sitting on the porch of his Mori Road residence in Mahim with his friends when the assailants drove up in a Maruti 800. They fired indiscriminately at Vaidya and his friends and fled the spot. All the injured were rushed to the nearby Hinduja Hospital. Vaidya was blessed with the proverbial nine lives; although three of his friends died and six were injured, he lived to tell the tale.

ACP Pradip Sawant investigated the case and arrested all the assailants. He recovered the AK-56s and automatic pistols used in the crime. This haul resulted in the conviction of all the nine men by the special MCOCA court. Later, Sawant was awarded the Deepak Jog trophy for best detection.

Even as the trial in the Vaidya case was continuing in the special court, Shakeel dispatched seven men to carry out a hit on a Shiv Sena shakha pramukh, or branch head, Vivek Kelkar. Kelkar was also a local cable operator. The man had his brains blown out on 9 December 1999 when he was sitting in his office at MIDC Andheri (East).

Within months of the Kelkar killing, Shakeel's men killed another shakha pramukh, forty-year-old Shivaji Chavan, at a suburban railway station in Goregaon, on 19 April 2000. Chavan was an employee of the Reserve Bank of India (RBI). He was involved in several controversial land deals which he had executed with the help of the Shiv Sena–BJP government when they were in power in the state. His job took him away from the city often and he was also known to spend long hours at the party office. He was shot dead at point-blank range shortly after he had parked his scooter outside the Goregaon railway station. Chavan's killing, however, remained unsolved.

The killings had the desired effect. Shiv Sena leaders now lived in mortal fear of being targeted by Shakeel's men. There was widespread panic and fear among the Sena shakha pramukhs across the city. None of them ventured out alone after dark. Some hired private security and ensured there were people around them to deter any attack.

It had turned into a small cottage industry. The remuneration for the hit squad was much higher than for other mafia-related murders. This spurred a lot of young men to volunteer for these assignments.

Mujahid Shaikh, popularly known as Raju Plumber, was an immigrant from Assam who struggled to make a living from his assignments as a plumber at his stall in the Dadar TT area. When he heard that Shakeel's men were scouting for shooters to kill the Shiv Sena men, he offered to moonlight as a hitman.

While newspapers and the media were still reporting on Chavan's killing, the next day, Shakeel's men struck again. Baban Atmaram Surve, a shakha pramukh in the Malvani Malad area, was known to intimidate local Muslim residents. People were so scared of him that he had become a law unto himself. Surve had the habit of inviting friends for drinking sessions in the open grounds in front of his house. His neighbours deeply resented this nuisance, but they were helpless to stop him.

On 21 April, while Surve was in the midst of one of his boisterous boozing sessions with his friend Bajaj, Raju Plumber zoomed up on his bike and opened fire on them. He did not leave until he was sure Surve had breathed his last. This proved costly, however, as Raju was identified and apprehended, and through him, other co-conspirators were arrested. He was finally convicted for the murder.

On 24 September 2000, Vivek Kamble of the Shakeel gang killed another Shiv Sainik, Ramakant Hadkar. The police reaction to the killing was particularly swift. When the first Shiv Sena murders happened, they had started by booking the gangsters under the draconian – and non-bailable (except under special circumstances) – MCOCA, but when they realized that even this was not proving to be a deterrent, they fell back on their favourite method of policing: extra-judicial killings.

Crime branch officers tracked down Vivek Kamble and snuffed him out on 29 September, four days after he had killed Hadkar. This halted the spate of killings of Shiv Sena men.

Several months passed peacefully and the Sena men finally relaxed. But just when they had let their guard down, thinking the worst was over, on 11 April 2001, Ram Agale, a shakha pramukh from Saki Naka area, was shot dead while he was on his way to a chemist's with his young daughter. A special squad led by Inspector Praful Bhosale hunted down the killers and, the very next day after his killing, even before his funeral, they had killed both the shooters of Agale in Mulund.

The determination of the police to hunt down and kill the shooters spooked Shakeel's men and the juggernaut finally stopped.

Mumbai, however, took a long time to come to terms with the killings of the Sena leaders. The cycle of vendetta deaths had made the metropolis unsafe for ordinary people. Before Shakeel, it had been Chhota Rajan, who had started the so-called reprisal killings, bumping off at least six of the accused – almost all of them Muslims – in the 1993 serial blasts.

Later, in an interview to the media, Chhota Shakeel claimed that if Chhota Rajan could anoint himself as a Hindu don, there was no reason why he, Chhota Shakeel, should not avenge the Muslims who were butchered during the communal riots. Since the Sainiks had been actively involved in the communal riots, he would target them.

Barring the attack on Vaidya, most of the other killings were inexplicable. Old-time police hands who knew Shakeel well claimed that he killed only if the victim was openly hostile to the company and could inflict some harm on it. Shakeel had been in Dubai since 1987, but there was no official record of his participation in the serial blasts of 1993.

Bal Thackeray alleged that the killings were happening at the behest of the Congress–NCP alliance. Narayan Rane, who was with the Shiv Sena at the time, also made the same allegation. He said the Democratic Front government headed by the Congress–NCP was behind the killings. But Chhota Shakeel had set the wheels of revenge in motion even while the Shiv Sena–BJP was in power in the state. Six Shiv Sena workers had been killed then.

City-based Dawood loyalists give another explanation for this killing spree. After Gawli had formed the ABS in 1996, his political party had begun to grow rapidly. The growth was so swift that even the ruling coalition of the BJP and the Shiv Sena had become jittery.

Gawli had managed to establish over 650 branches of the party in 31 districts of Maharashtra, of which 109 were in Mumbai. In the initial stages, the party had contested the corporation elections and performed well in them. Their next target was the assembly elections.

A joint commissioner of police of the crime branch, in one of his speeches at the Indo-American Society in Mumbai, said that the way the party was growing, Gawli might well end up in the home minister's chair. The state administration and police machinery were feeling increasingly insecure and frustrated. Despair was writ large in the corridors of power.

It was in this atmosphere that Shakeel opened a front against the ABS office-bearers. He fired the first salvo by targeting the founder secretary of ABS, Jitendra Dabholkar.

Shakeel unleashed two of his most dreaded shooters to eliminate Dabholkar. The shooter duo included Munna Jhingada and Sadiq Kalia. Jhingada means prawn-like, and the nickname had stuck because of his rather scrunched-up appearance. But Jhingada was a dangerous man and such a dependable shooter that he had been assigned the task of killing Rajan in Bangkok – he was no little prawn to be dismissed. Kalia had earlier served as a hitman of the Gawli gang, but Shakeel had managed to lure him over and he became a Shakeel loyalist. It was because of Kalia's recce and network that they managed to trail Dabholkar for a week.

Finally, on 4 October 1997, Shakeel's team intercepted Dabholkar's car near Khar subway and killed him. An innocent bystander was caught in the crossfire. Dabholkar's killing was a major setback to ABS. He was the founder, and there was a perception that the party might wind up as, in his absence, Gawli would not be able to sustain it. But Gawli, who had been witness to such setbacks earlier when all his ace gunmen had been killed, refused to buckle under pressure. Like in the mafia world, where he rose time and again even after being battered by rival gangs and the police, he rose like a phoenix in politics too.

For six months after Dabholkar's death, ABS floundered for lack of a leader. Finally, Gawli got his act together and asked Dabholkar's second-in-command, Bharat Mhatre, who was the party secretary, to take over the reins. Mhatre had earlier been close to the former Shiv Sena leader Chhagan Bhujbal, and he was conversant with the functioning of a political party. He was an ambitious man and had been waiting in the wings for some time; he jumped at the offer.

But this marked his doom. The moment Mhatre was announced as Dabholkar's successor, Shakeel pounced once again. Mhatre had just begun to draw up plans for the party when Shakeel's team of six shooters struck and shot him dead on 18 May 1998, at Nagpada.

Within a month, on 9 June, Shakeel's men killed another ABS leader, Dharmadas Solanki, in Goregaon. Police records indicate that this time Shakeel might have received assistance from the Ashwin Naik gang.

On 16 December, Sudhakar Lone, also of the ABS, was killed by Shakeel's gunmen in Byculla. Within weeks of this, they killed Prakash Mayekar in Agripada on 27 January 1999. The Mumbai police then swung into action and killed both shooters in an encounter.

But by then, the ABS workers were paralysed by fear. The party administration was in a shambles. Shakeel had managed to achieve what he had set out to do – nip Gawli's political aspirations in the bud.

While Shakeel was systematically mowing down ABS men, a rumour began doing the rounds in political circles, at beer bars, gatherings and closed-door meetings: did Shakeel's sudden interest in the decimation of ABS emanate from mafia rivalry alone? He should have been killing Gawli's aides, why target political functionaries? There was speculation that some political party had outsourced the contract to Shakeel.

As both the police and the political parties of the country are known to operate within and outside the formal apparatus of the state, both these narratives seem plausible.

THIRTY-FIVE

Ashwin at the Helm

When the landline buzzed, Ashwin Naik was sitting in his expensive Los Angeles apartment, sipping his daily poison. He wheeled his chair towards the phone to check the number. Calls from Chinchpokli were not just welcome, they were the only reason for his heart to continue beating. But for some strange reason, this time, he felt an icy clamp grip his chest even as he reached for the phone.

Amar's wife Anjali was on the line and she was weeping. 'They finished him. He is gone. The police killed him last night!'

Strange, Ashwin thought, as he felt his heart thump in his chest. His trusted aides, Amit Mukherjee and Kishore Rajput, were looking at him, aghast. Was he having a heart attack? What was wrong?

Ashwin turned around and told them, 'They have killed Dada.' Then he wept like a man who had lost his last lifeline. 'Dada, mala sodoon gele? (Brother, where did you go abandoning me?)' he cried plaintively through the day.

Later that night, he spoke to the two friends who had been his only anchors during his most trying times. 'Though Salaskar killed him, I bet Gawli is behind this. I can't understand how Dada was caught unawares. He was so careful.' Ashwin looked down at his useless limbs and felt a burning rage engulf him. First, Gawli had paralysed him and now he had managed to kill his brother. He had destroyed the peace and happiness of the Naik clan.

'I'll kill you, Gawli, even if it's the last thing I do in my life!' he swore and began weeping again. He felt orphaned. His brother had continued to shield him even after he had become paralysed; Amar had smuggled him out of India on a forged passport and flown him to Canada and the US to get him the best medical treatment. He was hoping to get his brother to walk, but the doctors had pronounced the unfortunate verdict that he would have to spend the rest of his life in a wheelchair.

'In the history of the Mumbai mafia, there has been no one like Dada. The police could never lay their hands on him; he was slippery as wet soap. Dada never kept in touch with any friends and even his wife and children would never know when he sneaked in for a visit,' Ashwin said as he kept talking about his brother that night.

In the interview with us, Ashwin spoke about his brother's death. 'The police claim it was an encounter, but everyone knows how much Arun Gawli paid to get my brother killed. He [Amar] did a lot for me. I cannot let his death go unavenged. Besides, the boys from the gang had to be looked after. The show must go on.'

In bed, sleep eluded him. 'It's a cold-blooded slaying,' his mind was telling him. He kept thinking about the turn of events that had turned him into a fugitive and robbed him of the right to perform the last rites of his slain brother. 'I should have been next to my dada, holding him and cradling his head. Instead, here I am, stuck in this strange, foreign land with no family and no shoulder to cry on.'

How he missed his beloved Dada and 144 Tenements, back in Chinchpokli. He missed everything about his country and wished he could take the next flight back and lead a normal life. Of course, if he took the next flight back, he would land not in the arms of his family but of the Mumbai police. Not for the first time in his life, he rued the day local goons had disrupted their peaceful middle-class existence at the Dadar vegetable market and turned their lives upside down.

If they hadn't intervened, he would probably have been at the crease with bowler Balwinder Sandhu and batsman Chandrakant Pandit, both of whom had practised at the nets with him at Shivaji Park under the tutelage of the great Ramakant Achrekar, who had chiselled Sachin Tendulkar into a master batsman. Dada had been very keen that Ashwin pursue cricket but there was no question of chasing the ball in the face of bullets.

The morning after news of his brother's death reached him, Ashwin was red-eyed. The glamour of living in the US suddenly began to pall. He looked around his bolthole. It was a warm and cosy place, and safe. It had been home for two long years; he had come straight here from Canada, after jumping bail in December 1995. In the beginning, Neeta had managed to meet him somewhere midway. But that too had stopped.

Something else was niggling at him. Neeta, his beloved wife and now a Shiv Sena corporator, had been giving him the cold shoulder for a while now. Even the death of his brother had not made her sensitive to his feelings. She had said not a single encouraging or soothing word to him.

Ashwin knew he had to take charge of the family and the business – or they would lose out in the race for survival and supremacy. In the last few years, Amar had established a crime syndicate that spanned the Afghani drug cartels and Sri Lankan Tamil groups like the LTTE and the People's Liberation of Tamil Eelam (PLOTE).

With Ashwin's help, Amar Naik had become the most resourceful don in Mumbai. None of the other gangsters – except Dawood and Chhota Rajan – had his chutzpah, and very early on in the business, he had realized where the big bucks lay: drugs, weapons and, of course, real estate.

Amar possessed immense charm and power too; he had managed to crack the inscrutable Pathans who rarely dealt with non-Muslims. After Dawood, Amar became the only don to have penetrated the drug cartels of the Pathan syndicate, spread out between Kabul in Afghanistan, Peshawar in Pakistan and Ahmedabad in Gujarat.

Amar was also in cahoots with Abdul Latif Khan in Gujarat, Nari Khan of Mumbai and the international drug trafficker, Naved Khan. Then there was his fascination with guns. He had never personally killed anyone, but he loved the sense of power that came with a gun. He was the first to smuggle an Austrian Glock to India. It was while getting an Israeli Uzi sub and other weapons for his gang that he had realized that he could use his network to supply weapons to those who needed it. He became inexorably drawn to gun running, which is a corollary to narco-terrorism.

Amar's connection with Krishna Pillai and his son Kumar Pillai paid off. The Pillais put him on to LTTE operatives, and he managed to strike up a rapport with the top bosses. For the LTTE, Amar Naik was an obvious choice; everybody in the know of weapons-smuggling was talking about his arsenal and his network. For any other gangster, to deal with the Pathans and the LTTE would have been like running with the hare and hunting with the hounds. But Amar Naik pulled it off. He also introduced his brother to the top commanders of both the outfits – this was to lead to Ashwin's downfall.

It was late evening in early 1997 and the sun had just set when Ashwin Naik arrived in India, via the porous town of Raxaul in the East Champaran district of Bihar. For an exit, he preferred North 24 Parganas in West Bengal. (At that point, Raxaul and North 24 Parganas were the chosen gateways for those who wanted to cross the border while giving the police the slip – North 24 Parganas was mainly used by Bangladeshi immigrants who came to India looking for a better life.)

Once back on Indian soil, Ashwin weighed his options. The Mumbai police were not to be trusted. They had become trigger-happy, and had killed Amar even though Neeta held an important position in the civic body and was known to be close to Bal Thackeray. Ashwin realized that his immobility would make him an easy target. Mumbai was off limits for him for some time.

He decided to stay in New Delhi. This would help him remain close to the gang as well as his family, and he would also be off the radar of the Mumbai police. Neeta could always travel to New Delhi without arousing any suspicion.

Ashwin managed to buy some property in Delhi, which included a palatial bungalow and a couple of farmhouses. The properties were under the control of Neeta. Since she was part of the state government, nobody would raise an eyebrow at her wealth.

Back in Delhi, Ashwin settled down in his flat in Geetanjali

Enclave in posh south Delhi. He thought that, like in the US, where he had managed to remain incognito, nobody would know about his whereabouts in Delhi. For two years, he remained undercover and, if he had not been exposed by a strange turn of events, he would have probably accomplished his dream of liquidating Gawli and his empire.

But old sins cast long shadows. Trouble came from the most unexpected quarter.

On 7 June 1999, LTTE commando Sriram alias Lamboo was gunned down and his aide Shiv Raman injured in the Nangloi area in west Delhi, by unidentified assailants. During investigations, the Delhi police recovered some fifteen kilos of drugs from their hideout. Subsequent investigations led to the arrest of drug baroness Hemlata Mankoo, and the seizure of heroin worth over Rs 80 crore. Hemlata was Delhi's top woman drug peddler, with connections to the LTTE. Some of the documents seized during the raids contained phone numbers which led the Delhi police to Chennai and from there to the training camps of the LTTE and PLOTE. The Delhi police were flummoxed when they found that the LTTE had joined hands with Pakistani and Mumbai drug traffickers to finance their proxy war and that Ashwin was their main conduit.

Sriram's killing proved to be a double whammy for Ashwin. Sriram had been planning to kill Gawli and avenge Amar's killing. His arrest not only put paid to the plan of avenging Amar, it landed his boss in the Delhi police net.

It transpired that Ashwin used to procure drugs from his Pakistani contacts and give them to the LTTE, who sold them in return for a supply of sophisticated weapons from their allies in West Asia, including Israel. Once the drugs reached Delhi through the Rajasthan border, they were sent to Chennai, packed into concealed spaces built into folding tables, through Sriram and Shivraman. From there, they went to Rameshwaram and were transported on boats to Sri Lanka. Ashwin was the channel between the Pathans and the LTTE, and the Delhi police realized that if he had managed to juggle two such dreaded groups, sitting right in the heart of the national capital, he was an exceedingly shrewd player.

Unlike the Mumbai police, who were known for their knee-jerk reactions, the Delhi police took their time. They were yet to be initiated into extra-judicial killings, and they decided to take it step by step. First, they found out where Ashwin Naik lived, then they tapped his phone. When they learned about his plans to escape from the country, they closed in. They arrested him and two of his aides, Amit Mukherjee and Kishore Rajput, while they were trying to cross the West Bengal border.

Ashwin's arrest on 6 August 1999 exposed the negligence of the Mumbai police. They had received intelligence that Ashwin Naik had returned to India two years ago, but something or somebody had obviously prevented them from doing their job.

In an interview with *The Week*, Ashwin regretted his bad timing. 'If I had managed to get out that day, I would never have come back.'

Ashwin Naik was charged with 16 cases of murder, extortion and criminal assault. After the cosy confines of his luxurious flat, he found himself in a cold cell in Tihar jail.

THIRTY-SIX

Murder of a Mafia Queen

It was exactly 12.15 p.m. In the area around 144 Tenements, mostly residential buildings with a working-class population, people went about their business of daily living.

A chilli-and-spices mill hummed with activity. Children were walking to school and there were a few passers-by, who barely noticed a car drawing up near an apartment called Shubhashis. A few minutes later, a woman stepped out of a taxi and walked towards the building. She was alone.

Neeta Naik was returning from Nagpur after attending a Shiv Sena rally. As she strode forward, three men who were watching her from the top of the building took a deep breath. One of them gave an almost imperceptible nod to the others, signalling the job at hand.

As she approached her second-floor flat, they came down the narrow flight of stairs till they too arrived at No 12. The woman saw one of the men, but ignored him and kept climbing the stairs. He gazed at her for a long time, his eyes filled with awe as he drew out his gun. She was a statuesque woman who wore her clothes – mostly expensive saris – beautifully. The woman looked at him and gave him a look of scorn. Guns did not frighten her. She was married to the mob after all. She thought this was another trick, a ploy to make her do their bidding. Then she saw the other two men, all part of her own gang. A question formed in her mind but before she could voice it, the first man pointed the gun at her head and fired two rounds. She did not even have the time to scream, as bits of her skull and brains splattered the walls and the stairs. Neeta Naik collapsed in a heap.

The man who had pulled the trigger was Sunil Jadhav alias Ekka. Ekka was a hardened killer. This was not his first assignment. He was immune to blood and gore, a human killing machine who executed his job with little emotion. He was trained to think that the victim deserved to die for his or her misdeeds. But when Neeta Naik tumbled down the stairs like a limp doll, he could not control himself.

He ran up to her and hugged her. 'Vahini mala maaf kara, vahini mala maaf kara! (Forgive me, my brother's wife, please forgive me),' he exclaimed, and burst into tears holding her lifeless body.

The other killers who had come with him, Santosh Bhalekar and Manoj Pagarkar, had to tear him away from Neeta's blood-soaked body. The wailing had alerted curious neighbours, who were opening their doors to check on the commotion.

They discovered its source soon enough. Neeta Naik was rushed to King Edward Memorial Hospital but was pronounced dead on arrival.

Bhalekar and Pagarkar had not known how to react when they were first assigned the job. They venerated Neeta Naik, and to kill a woman who meant so much to them was beyond their imagination. Ekka then showed them the photograph. Neeta with Ashwin on their wedding day, juxtaposed with Neeta with Constable Lakshman Ziman, her bodyguard, who had been assigned by the Mumbai police to protect her. The intimacy between the two people in the second picture outraged the middle-class sensibilities of Bhalekar and Pagarkar. Ekka also showed them a handwritten letter apparently written by Ashwin, asking everyone to follow his instructions and obey him.

Ekka told them about Neeta's betrayal of Ashwin Naik, the man whom she had professed to love from the core of her being at one point.

Soon after he fled India in a wheelchair, Ashwin Naik's life and love had taken a nosedive. Neeta was left on her own. In the initial years, she pined for him and was his compliant wife, waiting to do his bidding. As her stature and position in society as a civic corporator grew, however, she developed a different kind of world view. This was a miserable period for her, trying to fit her aspirations and potential into an inherited title and a life she did not want. Initially, she was very clear about her goals when she opted for politics. 'I am tired of the midnight knocks of the policemen who barge into our homes and disturb our children. If I get into politics, I can save my family from such harassment. We want peaceful nights,' she had said in her first interview to the *Afternoon Dispatch & Courier*, explaining to the reporter why she wanted to become a corporator.

Both she and Anjali (Amar Naik's wife) had contested the civic elections but Neeta Naik's effervescence had won her the seat. Anjali, who was more subdued, lost the election.

In the early days, Neeta was like a little girl who had just discovered she had wings. She bought a car and learned to drive, and she drove very fast. 'I went zip, zap, zoom from my Chinchpokli residence to the BMC building at Kemps Corner,' she would say. She was straightforward and honest, and tried her best to be a good politician. The Shiv Sena was happy with her because she was very different from the staid, boring women who usually got elected to the corporation. They could not have asked for a better public relations officer for the party: she was intelligent, good-looking, and possessed of great oratorical skills and leadership qualities. She fared better than all the other male and female corporators put together. She was even elected as the standing committee chairperson, which is a very important post in the civic body, for two terms.

Despite the glamour of the job, however, she was lonely. Though she was very popular, people were scared to be friends with her; you never knew when you would end up with a bullet in your head in an alley near 144 Tenements. At one point, when Ashwin was in the US, she was desolate and told a female reporter, 'I am like this dog, very lonely,' pointing to her dog, who was chained in the house.

While Ashwin remained in Mumbai and before the shooting that made him a paralytic, she had been the docile wife. She stood by her husband and never failed to turn up in the TADA courts for his hearing. But after he left for the US, his enforced absence and her rising political stature changed the dynamics of their marriage. She was left holding the baby, literally and metaphorically; she had to handle their children, her high-profile job and, of course, the gang.

Once he returned to Delhi, Ashwin and Neeta were in touch, but after his arrest, she started avoiding him and Ashwin sensed a gradual change in her demeanour towards him.

They had been very close once upon a time, which is why Ashwin was quick to figure out the meaning of her detachment. He realized that Neeta did not care for him any more. Was she interested in another man?

Maybe she felt lonely and needed a companion, a shoulder to cry on. But he would have expected her to be direct and honest. This gradual drifting away was excruciatingly painful.

Finally, Ashwin heard of Neeta's torrid affair with her bodyguard, Ziman. Ziman had been a commando constable with the Special Operation Squad (SOS) unit of the crime branch. He had resigned from the police force in 1994 and began serving Chief Minister Narayan Rane as his private bodyguard. Neeta met him when she visited Rane on work, as she frequently did. After 1997, Neeta and Ziman abandoned any pretence at discretion and began to spend time with each other freely, even publicly.

The news of her betrayal was broken to Ashwin by none other than Neeta's brother, Hitesh Jethwa. Ashwin was aghast. He expressed his helplessness to Hitesh, who told him to give her a warning. Even before Ashwin could come to terms with the betrayal, he realized that everyone knew about Neeta's affair. He wished she had at least been discreet.

When Neeta and his children visited him in jail in June 2000, an anguished Ashwin asked her not to tarnish the image of the family. Neeta did not pay heed to his admonition. As the months passed, Ashwin became increasingly frustrated by her insolence. One day, when the children visited Ashwin with their governess, Padmini Naidu, Ashwin went so far as to ask his daughter to talk to her mother about leaving her boyfriend.

After the initial shock, Ashwin wanted to kill Lakshman Ziman. He kept thinking of ways of getting rid of him. The man had violated the body that he was supposed to guard, he fumed. He asked his trusted aide Hemant Dhuri to bump off Lakshman.

Meanwhile, gang members like Ekka, Dhuri and Lali began visiting Ashwin in jail and demanding money from him. Ashwin realized then that Neeta managed the extortion rackets and dictated terms of payments but failed to remunerate his men, pocketing the spoils of the game instead. Ashwin suspected that Ziman was responsible for this. As a result of Neeta's financial mismanagement, there was growing unrest and disgruntlement within the gang.

Ashwin began writing letters to Neeta, expressing his anger and warning her of dire consequences. He even wrote to her that if she did not mend her ways and repent, he would be forced to kill her and the children too. But Neeta only laughed off the threats.

She stopped visiting Ashwin in jail though his daughter Winky and her governess continued to visit him. His old father Maruti, his sister Alka and her husband Suresh all found time to see him in jail; the only one who remained too busy to meet him was Neeta. Ashwin could not come to terms with his wife's apparent heartlessness.

At the same time, the gang members seemed to be on the verge of rebellion; they were financially constrained, and Ekka and Lali were furious with Neeta Naik. They had been the main shooters in the Sunit Khatau killing and had quite a reputation in the underworld, but Neeta defied even them because she was assured of her cop boyfriend's protection.

Ashwin was desperate to meet Neeta and talk to her. But the only way he could think of enticing her to Delhi to meet him was under the pretext of philanthropy. He asked his driver Nilesh Mukherjee, whose brother Amit had been arrested along with Ashwin at the West Bengal border, to tell Neeta that she should distribute clothes to the Tihar jail staff as an act of charity. When Nilesh conveyed this message to Neeta, she refused point blank, saying she had no time or money for such niceties.

By this time, news had trickled out that Ashwin was likely to distribute clothes in Tihar. The situation was quickly turning into an embarrassment for him. When Nilesh conveyed Neeta's refusal, Ashwin asked him to request her to sell the Delhi property to raise money. But when Nilesh approached Neeta again, she told him off, exclaiming, 'I will not give a paisa to Ashwin!' Her furious rant was overheard by other gang members who were present at the time.

The mafia was afraid of Neeta's reach and clout. She had direct access to Matoshree — so much so that she was considered to be a high-risk individual and was provided round-the-clock security. That Ziman — who had been assigned to her — belonged to Narayan Rane's security detail demonstrated her importance and stature in the party hierarchy.

Neeta refused to fear Ashwin's threats or the menace of his gang members. She was arrogant with them and even chided them publicly. Some of the boys had grown up in front of her. They had seen her enter her house as a coy bride, in that very building. They had looked up to her as the matriarch of the gang, and she was addressed as 'vahini', the respectful title given to a brother's wife. She had responded to them with equal affection and compassion.

But she was not the same Neeta vahini any more.

On 14 November 2000, Neeta Naik, the feisty woman who had entered the limelight only to save her husband from the wrath of the Mumbai police, finally met a gruesome end. Neeta's daylight murder was shocking for many reasons. She was an influential Shiv Sena corporator and the wife of Ashwin Naik. The cops could not imagine a rival gang bumping off Ashwin Naik's wife and getting away with it, and their suspicions were heightened by the eyewitness accounts of the neighbours. They immediately went to Tihar to question Ashwin, who flatly denied his involvement in her murder, though he expressed his doubts regarding Lali and Ekka.

Several months later, the police were yet to make a breakthrough in the case. Finally, after five months, they managed to arrest Bhalekar in Lalbaug, on 4 April 2001. Nilesh Mukherjee was arrested in Faridabad, Haryana, on 24 May. They managed to arrest the main shooter, Ekka, on 10 September, in Parel.

The crime branch booked all of them under MCOCA and also charged Ashwin Naik with conspiracy in the case. However, the Delhi judge refused to hand him over to the Mumbai police as he was undergoing trial in a narcotics case. His trial was separated from the rest of the accused and the Mumbai police had to wait for his custody until the Delhi police had finished with him.

In a statement given to the Mumbai police in December 2000, Ashwin had candidly expressed his resentment over Neeta's affair, though he claimed he never wanted to kill her, only her boyfriend Ziman. Despite his denials, he was booked for conspiracy in the case.

Before Dawood Ibrahim came into the picture, there was a tacit understanding in the mafia that women were not to be killed. When Dawood's men brutally stabbed Sapna Didi, a spunky woman who had decided to avenge her husband Mehmood Kalia's killing by Dawood, they rewrote the rules. In the new order of things, the mafia became debased and savage with women. The only women who managed to avoid drawing attention to themselves were those who were perceived to be silent and unseeing. Among the Maharashtrian gangsters, the first instance of a gangster killing his wife was reported in 1995 when Dubai-based gangster and Dawood's aide Anil Parab got his wife, Neha Patharia, killed by his shooters in Mumbai.

Parab, in his confessional statement to the Mumbai police after his deportation from Dubai in April 2003, explained the motive for killing his wife.

A Maharashtrian, Parab had married Neha, a Kutchi Gujarati, against the wishes of her father Premji Patharia, who lived in Ghatkopar, in 1989. They did not have a house of their own, and Parab lived in a Juhu flat given to him by Chhota Rajan. This flat was also shared by other gangsters. Unhappy in the relationship, in the very first year of their marriage, Neha picked up her husband's .9mm pistol and shot herself in the chest. Parab was in absolute shock – and panic. He could foresee spending his entire life in prison for a crime he had not committed. The police would have no qualms about nailing him. In desperation, he contacted his mentor Rajan in Dubai, who suggested taking Neha to a nursing home near Shreyas Talkies in Ghatkopar. The doctors at the nursing home treated her without informing the police about the incident. Parab immediately left for Dubai. Later, when Neha had recovered fully, her parents packed her off to Dubai. The couple resumed their intermittent squabbling there.

In three years, Neha gave birth to three daughters. According to Parab's statement, Neha used the children as bait and began punishing the daughters when the couple fought. She would brand the young girls with a hot iron or leave them in a tub full of hot water. He managed to rescue them each time at the last minute but he had to maintain vigil at all hours to save his children from her psychotic behaviour. He decided to send her back to Mumbai.

She returned in March 1995 – for her last rites. It is alleged that two of Parab's henchmen, Rajan Kabkoti and Dilip Jadhav, received Neha at the airport and took her to an office in Vakola. There, she was asked to make a call to her husband in Dubai. While she was on the phone, Parab informed her casually that she had timed out her life. Even before a startled Neha could register what Parab was saying, Kabkoti hit her on the head with a heavy object. Parab could hear Neha screaming. She was killed and her body was dumped near the Kalina university campus in Santacruz.

The Marathi daily *Saamna* could not resist adding a twist to the story. It suggested yet another angle, of a love triangle. The paper speculated that Parab, who had married Neha for love, had killed her because he suspected that she was having an affair with Dawood's brother Noora. But Parab, in his confessional statement to the police, staunchly denied the *Saamna* story and claimed that Neha was killed only because of her cruelty to her daughters.

Within a year of his deportation to India, Anil Parab managed to get himself acquitted by the sessions court in 2004. The court said the police evidence was weak and also acquitted four others who were charged with the murder.

Parab was subsequently convicted in the 1984 Hansraj Shah attempt-to-murder case: he had slipped into the metropolitan courtroom in a rickshaw driver's garb and tried to open fire. He was sentenced to life imprisonment. For more than a decade now, he has been part of the growing tribe of men who have made Maharashtra's prisons their home.

THIRTY-SEVEN

Rajan's Revenge

Rajan was incarcerated in his hospital bed. His abdomen was heavily bandaged, and a saline drip was connected to a vein in his arm. The oxygen mask had been removed after the doctors found that he could breathe normally. His gaze was fixed on the ceiling; despite his body being immobile and confined to the hospital bed, his mind was racing.

It had been a couple of weeks since the near fatal attack on his life at his residence, Charan Court, in Sukhumvit Soi, Bangkok. The date, 15 September 2000, was etched in his memory. It was the day he was reborn. Four men had stormed into his supposedly secure flat and sprayed bullets at him indiscriminately. The eight men, two of whom were Thai nationals, were dressed in jet black suits and leather jackets. They were carrying a large cake and had pushed past the Thai security guard after knocking him down.

Rajan's aide, Rohit Verma, answered the doorbell – and froze with fear. Even for a man who had snuffed out several lives in one decade with his trademark hammer and a long-barrelled .45 pistol, staring at death at such close and striking range must have been terrifying. But he didn't have time to register anything else, as a volley of bullets almost threw him across the room with their force. Verma's wife Sangeeta, standing nearby, was also injured in the firing. Rajan, who was in the bedroom, lost no time in figuring out the reason for the commotion. He locked himself in the room while men fired at the latch lock, trying to break the door open. They didn't succeed but a stray bullet managed to penetrate the door at last, and pierced Rajan's abdomen.

Rajan realized that if he remained holed up in the room, he would be a sitting duck. Sooner or later, the assailants would break down the door and liquidate him. He took a calculated risk and jumped out of the window of the first floor. He landed hard on his feet, fracturing his ankle, and bleeding and injured, he dove behind some bushes and hid himself.

The shooters eventually managed to break down the door but did not find Rajan. There were bloodstains in the room and on the window, which led them to believe that he had escaped, but by then, enough shots had been fired to draw the attention of the Thai police. The assailants gave up the search and escaped.

This attack on Rajan was part of the ongoing tussle with Dawood Ibrahim, initiated by Shakeel. They had parted ways seven years ago, but the friends-turned-foes were still after each other's blood.

Rajan could not get over the fact that Shakeel's men had managed to trace him to Bangkok, zero in on Rohit's home and breach the security so easily. It was divine decree that he had survived, despite coming so close to death. Now he wanted revenge. He wanted to kill Dawood, Shakeel and whoever had squealed on his whereabouts.

Rajan called his most trusted aide, Santosh Shetty, to the hospital.

'I want him dead,' he told him.

Santosh was one of the smartest minds in Mumbai's gangland. Well-built, handsome and fluent in English, Santosh could have been mistaken for the head honcho of a blue-chip company, if not a film star. But here he was, playing Man Friday to Rajan. He had been associated with Rajan for more than a decade now, and had major connections in Dubai. There were several cases of drugs, extortion and complicity in major crimes pending against him.

At the time of the attack, Santosh's priority was to extricate Rajan from the clutches of the Thai and Indian police. As Rajan was severely wounded and immobile, this was quite an arduous task.

However, Rajan was insistent on setting the wheels of vengeance in motion at once, before he left the hospital. He wanted his enemies to know that he was capable of taking revenge even if he was not hundred per cent fit.

'We will locate him,' Santosh assured Rajan. He found out that barely half a dozen people knew about Rajan's location – and this core group included himself and Rajan's family. The only other person was Rajan's Mumbai-based hotelier friend, Vinod Shetty, who owned Paris Bar in Goregaon, in partnership with Satish Hegde.

But Santosh did not want to punish Shetty merely on suspicion. Santosh himself belonged to the Bunt community of the Shettys, and he knew that the community network extended far and wide – any false move could prove counter-productive. He first had to establish Shetty's treason. After quietly working on the man's circle of friends and connections, Santosh stumbled onto some shocking information.

The hotelier had shifted loyalties from Rajan to his friend Sharad (Anna) Shetty in Dubai. Santosh could not discover what Vinod got in return for selling out Rajan to Sharad Anna, who had been harbouring a grudge against Rajan for more than a decade now. Sharad had in turn passed on the information to Shakeel in Pakistan, who moved in for the kill and organized the attack within a few weeks.

Rajan was enraged at this betrayal by his old friend whom he had trusted implicitly. He could barely stand because of his abdominal injury, but he was so angry that he actually got up from his bed and ordered a hit on Vinod Shetty.

Ironically, the man who was to lure Vinod was also a Shetty. Right from the beginning, the Shettys of Mumbai, who ran restaurants and beer bars where women danced through the night, had been close to Chhota Rajan. Fakira Shetty had been with Rajan for more than a decade. He had started his career as a dacoit and was famous for looting unheard of amounts from bank vans with the help of his friend D.K. Rao.

Jaggu Fakira Shetty telephoned Vinod and told him that Rajan had called and given him instructions about transferring funds to a particular account and also about handing over cash to some people in Mumbai. Could they meet at a safe place outside Mumbai? They decided to rendezvous at a beer bar in Panvel.

Vinod had absolutely no clue that he had been exposed. He continued to believe that he was in the good books of Rajan, and he thought he should continue to do his bidding for some time longer – until Shakeel got lucky the next time.

On 2 November 2000, barely a month and a half after the attempt on Rajan's life, Vinod Shetty, along with his partner Satish Hegde and a business associate, Shankar Iyer, left for Panvel. They were driven by Shaikh Shakeel. Vinod and his friends met Fakira Shetty and his two friends at Titan bar in Panvel. They all got drunk to the gills. Then Fakira got into his car and asked Vinod to follow him. Vinod did as he was told, a little anxious, but keen to not antagonize Rajan's messenger.

Fakira reached an intersection near Uran-Panvel Road and halted his car near Chinchpada village. Vinod was becoming increasingly nervous. He refused to step out of his car alone. His partner Hegde then walked with him to the spot where Fakira was standing with his back towards them. As they came closer, Fakira turned and opened fire. Hegde leapt for safety and dived into a gutter, while Vinod was riddled with bullets.

Shankar Iyer and Vinod's driver were also shot dead. Their bodies were later recovered by the Kalamboli police from an isolated spot. Hegde survived to tell the tale, hiding in the chaos, but the police failed to arrest the shooters for years after the incident.

The triple murder shocked the mafia, but they were quick to see Rajan's hand in the killings.

Rajan now wanted to kill Sharad Shetty. But Santosh managed to convince him that killing someone in Dubai was a far more complex task than in Mumbai. And first, Rajan needed to get out of the clutches of the Thai and Indian police.

The Mumbai police wanted to get Rajan extradited to Mumbai for his involvement in the Panvel triple murder. But Rajan decided to pay heed to Santosh's advice: escape from Bangkok.

On 24 November, Rajan was found missing from his hospital bed. Two ropes, along with mountaineering accessories, were found hanging from the window. Who had helped Rajan escape? Was the rope simply a ruse? The Thai police felt that it would have been virtually impossible for an injured and overweight Rajan to climb down the ropes, even with professional help.

Several years after the incident, after Santosh Shetty had been extradited from Thailand, he revealed the details of Rajan's escape and his role in it.

In his statement to the crime branch, which he also discussed with the media later, he said that the Thai military had aided Rajan's escape from Bangkok. Santosh and his aide, Bharat Nepali, got the Thai police team and the hospital watchman sozzled and, for good measure, also spiked their drinks with sedatives. Then came the master stroke. They managed to get Rajan into a military vehicle with some army officers in it. The military personnel then transported Rajan to the Cambodian border. From the Cambodian border, Rajan was airlifted in a chopper by a governor of Cambodia, who took him to a safe hideout in Siem Reap. His connections in high places had certainly paid off.

After the initial furore in the media had subsided, Rajan flew to the Iranian capital with a new identity. In Tehran, Santosh got the don a caretaker who happened to be a Muslim widow.

One room in the flat they shared was occupied by Bunty Pandey, Bharat Nepali and Santosh, and the other was left to Rajan and the nurse. The woman nursed Rajan and took care of him and somewhere along the way, he fell in love with her. Santosh claimed in his statement that she had become pregnant and delivered a boy. (Rajan is said to have gifted a flat to the woman sometime later.)

When Rajan was well again, he decided to take on the mastermind behind his attempted murder: Sharad Shetty.

After his split from Dawood, Rajan had tried to woo Shetty to his side. He had a good hold in the cricket-betting syndicates and he felt he could bolster his fortunes with Shetty on his side. But Sharad Shetty, also known as Sharad Anna, had never liked Rajan. Whenever

Rajan made overtures to him to join the gang, Sharad snubbed him, and as soon as an opportunity came to help eliminate Rajan, he had acted. Rajan was, however, mystified by the attempt on his life. There was no direct enmity between them, just cold vibes. But now that Shetty had came close to killing him, he was not to be spared.

Rajan, along with Santosh, managed to send four of his men to Dubai and ensured that they got weapons. The four shooters were Karan Singh, Manoj Kotian, Vimal Kumar and a Nepali called Amar Bam.

They conducted a methodical recce of Sharad Shetty's movements and trailed him for a week. Shetty was an astute businessman. He had been with Dawood Ibrahim in Dubai for several years and had invested wisely in a chain of hotels and restaurants, including the Rami group of hotels. He was often spotted lounging at the elite India Club in Oud Metha.

The team of stalkers found that Shetty was most vulnerable while he was at this posh club. Manoj Kotian was from Bangalore and could speak Kannada, so he became the one to meet and befriend Shetty casually in the club, posing as an Indian businessman.

On 19 January 2003, when Shetty emerged from the club, chatting with Kotian, two men opened fire at him. Shetty collapsed on the ground. The shooters then fired at his head at point-blank range. According to the Dubai Shurta, 20 bullets were fired; Shetty was declared dead on the spot.

Lt General Dahi Khalfan was reminded of the killing of Sautya in 1995. He tracked the shooters down with a vengeance. It took the Dubai police five days to arrest them, just as they were planning to board a ship back to India.

Khalfan expressed his anger against the Indian gangs operating in Dubai in interviews he gave to the Dubai press. Investigations by his team proved that Vimal Kumar had helped Karan Singh, Manoj and Bam get visas to enter Dubai. Kumar then armed them with 0.38 pistols and trained them in using the pistols at a shooting club until they excelled at marksmanship. He also helped them get guest memberships at the India Club, the venue of the murder. The prosecution alleged that he had helped the three suspects study Sharad's movements and timings, before providing them with the hit-and-run plan.

One man who got trapped in all this was the Nepali driver, Bam, who repeatedly pleaded his innocence. Bam said he had not known about the murder or the plan to murder anyone. He had been recruited in India to work as a driver in Dubai, and had no knowledge that his employers had criminal intentions.

When men from his village near Kathmandu visited him in prison, Bam accused the Dubai police of using torture to make him confess to the crime. He also complained that the language barrier (he did not speak English or Arabic) prevented him from understanding the case and the charges against him.

Dubai prosecutors dismissed a petition from Karan Singh and Kotian which stated that Bam had not participated in the murder in any way, and that he had driven the getaway car without knowing anything about it. Bam's wife had to mortgage her jewellery to pay for his defence.

Khalfan wanted everyone involved to pay, regardless of their role in the crime. Within nine months, all four had been executed by the UAE authorities. Karan Singh was thirty years old, Manoj Kotian, thirty-two and Vimal Kumar Ram, twenty-six.

Shetty was dead, and Rajan was satisfied. He now felt heavily indebted to Santosh, and opened his coffers to him, offering to help him in any business venture.

Santosh took advantage of Rajan's offer and borrowed two million US dollars to immediately open a plant for the production of Mandrax in Bottam, Indonesia. There, he manufactured a drug called Quaalude, a 'downer' drug sold extensively in South Africa, from which he made a neat profit.

Apart from the drug business, Santosh dealt in counterfeit; chiefly, printing American dollar bills. 'I got fake notes from China and Indonesia and sold them in Singapore. The profit out of this business was routed to buying a restaurant in Jakarta, which I named after my Chinese girlfriend Nayatali,' Santosh said in an interview. (His time in Indonesia bore many fruits. Santosh's good looks drew a Chinese girl, Nayatali, towards him; she worked for him in Jakarta. The girl gave him a son who was named Suraj.)

However, his business suffered huge losses when one of his consignments worth around 1.2 billion dollars was intercepted by the police in Singapore.

In his confessional statement to the Mumbai crime branch, Santosh Shetty gave details of Rajan's personal and business intrigues across several countries, in which Santosh by his own admission had played a major role.

THIRTY-EIGHT

Mumbai Gangsters in Bangkok

Santosh Shetty, one of the most suave and dangerous gangsters in the records of the Mumbai police, was deported from Bangkok on 12 August 2011. Unlike other gangsters who started off in the lap of want and poverty, Shetty was born and bred in the upmarket Warden Road area of Mumbai.

Shetty harboured ambitions of killing his one-time mentor and boss Chhota Rajan ever since they split in 2005 over a monetary dispute. His deportation from Bangkok, which was a joint operation of the Indian Intelligence Bureau and the Thai police, reinforced the belief of the Mumbai police that Bangkok was to Hindu gangsters what Dubai was to the Muslim mafia – a safe haven.

It is tough to be rootless, a wandering gypsy moving from shore to shore, country to country, looking for refuge. When the Mumbai mafia decided to physically shift out of the city and remote-control events from foreign shores, Dubai was the initial choice. When their business expanded exponentially, they travelled using fake passports to most of the countries they did business with. It was an era when you could get a fake passport easily enough and you could even bypass Interpol notices. 9/11 was yet to take place and there not much scrutiny done of dubious characters. In the nineties, you could get a visa on arrival in Bangkok on a payment of fifty dollars or so.

Chhota Rajan liked Dubai but felt stifled there after he ran foul of Dawood in 1992–93. He had been travelling in other countries like Malaysia, Cambodia and Bangkok. Bangkok emerged as the frontrunner because Dawood was so firmly entrenched in Dubai that it was impossible for the fleeing Chhota Rajan to hide in any corner of Dubai or any other Emirate without being scooped dead out of his burrow.

At one point of time, Chhota Rajan even thought of Nepal as an option, but during that period Mirza Dilshad Baig, Dawood-aide and one-time politician, held sway there. Eventually, Rajan had Mirza Dilshad Baig killed. But Nepal was very close to India and Rajan was terrified that the Indian enforcement agencies might make a play for him.

Unlike other organized countries in the east such as Singapore or even Malaysia, Bangkok is a little like Mumbai. The reputation of the Thai police is not very different from that of the Mumbai cops and the Thai attitude has shades of the Indian. Besides, Thailand is not an Islamic state, and this was a big draw for Chhota Rajan. This is not to deride the Thais or the Bangkok police, but it is a fact that from the mid-1990s to 2010, the Mumbai mafia had a free run in Bangkok. They killed and maimed and ran the drug trade without much interference.

Among other advantages, the city was much cheaper to live in when compared to other exotic destinations. The fact that Thailand thrived on tourism and Thais were friendly towards Indians helped.

According to intelligence officers, most Indian gangsters used to rent a one-bedroom flat and lived in anonymity among other Indians, albeit under a different name. They only needed a television that aired Indian channels and a telephone to call India to issue threats. Santosh Shetty was Nicholas Madan Sharma, while Chhota Rajan was Vijay Daman.

Long before Chhota Rajan found refuge in Bangkok, it was Amar Naik who discovered the city as the ideal mafia destination. He waltzed through Bangkok as easily as he did through Byculla, without calling any attention to himself. After he was killed, a slew of contacts and Bangkok addresses were found in his wallet.

Chhota Rajan, who lived there for five years after he split with Dawood, found it an ideal place for getting lost in. It was also perfect for conducting his anti-Dawood campaign and, of course, running the Mumbai crime syndicate. Soon after Rajan split from Dawood in 1994, his men lured Dawood's narco-man, Philoo Khan alias Bakhtiyar Ahmed Khan, to a hotel room in Bangkok and tortured him to death.

After Rajan fled Bangkok, the internecine gang war continued on the streets of the city despite his absence from the scene. In May 2003, Ijaz Lakdawala was attacked by members of Chhota Shakeel's gang. The killers sprayed him with bullets fired at close range while he was on his way to dinner at a restaurant. Ijaz was associated with both Dawood and Chhota Rajan.

Rajan's one-time Man Friday, Santosh Shetty, also established his base in Bangkok and grew to be a formidable gangster.

After Chhota Rajan disappeared from Bangkok, the Shettys were his stand-ins for a while. Santosh Shetty called the shots from Bangkok, and a couple of murders in Mumbai including that of Rajan henchman Farid Tanasha and the activist-lawyer Shahid Azmi, were spearheaded from Bangkok.

Bharat Nepali, who is reported to have killed Shahid Azmi, then had a fallout with Santosh Shetty. Apparently, Chhota Rajan got in touch with Nepali to kill his one-time friend. When Santosh heard about the plan, he lured Nepali to a Bangkok hotel, got him drunk and killed him in October 2010.

The law finally caught up with Santosh Shetty and he was arrested in Bangkok in 2011. He broke the golden rule of the mafia: never draw attention to oneself. One night, he got into a brawl at a bar with a few businessmen. When the police sought his passport, he gave them a fake one. Later, they fished out his real passport from his residence and realized that he was listed by Interpol as a wanted man. By August of that year, Santosh Shetty found himself on a flight to Mumbai, extradited. He is now cooling his heels in prison.

The quick extradition of Santosh Shetty made the Bangkok police realize the gravity of the battles that were being fought on their land. They don't have a determined police in-charge like Dubai's Dahi Khalfan, to uproot the mafia from their city. As a result, other Shettys and Mumbai mafiosi are still holed up in Bangkok and operating surreptitiously from there.

THIRTY-NINE

Manhunt for Maharaj

The two snipers were in place, the long barrels of their rifles pointing at the entrance to the portico of the three-star hotel in Dadar East, a south-central suburb of Mumbai. Their fingers were on the trigger, and they were itching to shoot.

The team of fifteen crime branch officers was ready to erupt into action, only waiting for a signal from the boss. Some of the officers were pretending to read newspapers in the foyer, and some others chatted with each other – only their eyes were on the revolving door of the hotel.

Another policeman, dressed as a concierge, remained attentive. The bulge in his trousers had nothing to do with the blood coursing through his manhood.

'Alertness is like an erection, it cannot remain for 24 hours,' says an IPS officer who is a top surveillance expert. 'You keep losing it and then stimulate it to stay in the game.'

Outside the hotel, there were others, equally alert. Two men at the bus stop, one at the tea shop, and one getting his shoes polished. The whole set-up was a well-prepared police dragnet – a police stakeout with zero room for error.

The waiting can take its toll. Some of the cops lit a cigarette, others gulped down cups of coffee. They were fagged out.

They had been waiting for hours, some longer than the others.

Assistant Police Inspector Ravindra Angre had been waiting for this moment for the past two years.

Suresh Manchekar was Angre's big ticket. The cop aspired to join the league of famous encounter cops that included Pradeep Sharma and Vijay Salaskar. The police in Thane do not receive as much media attention as the Mumbai cops do. Angre, who was from Thane district, was desperate for glory through the medium of encounters. He was so obsessed with Manchekar that he had even planted two of his men in Manchekar's gang. He shelled out a tidy sum to the moles and often complained about their starry tantrums. One day, the moles finally threw a few nuggets at him. They told him that their boss was addressed as Maharaj. 'M for Manchekar and M for Maharaj, which means the king.'

After he was externed from the mill heartlands of Mumbai, Manchekar, with the help of his mother and sister, had managed to carve out a career for himself by terrorizing the citizens of Thane, Dombivli and Kalyan. The brutal killing of Sudesh Khamkar and Dr Dipak Shetty had caused panic among the businessmen as also the medical fraternity in the fast developing townships that abutted Mumbai. The Thane police had launched a crackdown on the gang and killed more than twenty-five gangsters in 'encounters' but they never made any headway on the whereabouts of Manchekar.

Angre had decided to get him at any cost. So, when his snitches in the gang told him that Maharaj would be coming to a Dadar hotel to collect extortion money, Angre violated the turf issues that the police are very particular about; he got his men to keep a watch on the hotel without the rest of the Mumbai police managing to get a whiff of their operations.

The interminable wait seemed almost over. Suddenly, Angre noticed a white Premier Fiat NE 118 swerving in the direction of the hotel. It matched the description he had. Angre stubbed out his cigarette and crushed it under his shoe, signalling for his men to be alert.

'He is here, now it begins, now,' he thought, smiling to himself. The next moment a young woman, her face bearing layers of pancake-like foundation and dark lipstick and dressed in a white salwar kameez, emerged from the car. She was wearing a tight dress that highlighted her curves, particularly her bustline. Angre was aghast. Even in this form, it was an unexpected anti-climax!

He saw the woman walk up to the extortion victim and collect a bag. She opened it and scanned the contents, then shut the bag, rose from the sofa – her bosom heaving – and walked towards the exit.

Angre overcame his frustration. He asked his men to follow the vehicle. The officers got into an unmarked car, and within ten minutes they stopped at a building in Parel and left the car to follow the woman. A woman cop tailed her inside the building. She went into a flat on the third floor, and disappeared.

The police team began thinking of how to raid the flat: the men and the weapons to be used, and whether they should ask the local police to accompany them. What if Manchekar alias Maharaj was not there? He would be alerted and the only clue that they had managed to get after two years of painstaking investigations and intelligence from their embedded informants would be rendered meaningless. The cops decided to fall back on their old trick of penetrating a civilian hideaway.

Next day, the flat occupied by the couple was visited by two men posing as linemen from Mahanagar Telephone Nigam Limited (MTNL), responding to the complaint of a neighbour. The pretext was clichéd; they needed to check if the whole circuit had to be changed or just one faulty line.

They were quite pleased to be greeted by the well-endowed woman. During the twenty-two minutes that they lingered in the room, setting up the electronic surveillance, the desi Pamela Anderson seemed intent on distracting them.

The only other person in the flat was a young man who seemed to be in his mid-twenties; Manchekar, they knew, was in his forties. The young fellow's name was Santosh Naik.

Two of Angre's men began listening to Naik's calls and monitoring them round the clock. For a long while, they didn't make any breakthrough. There were calls ordering food from takeaways, medicines from the chemist, porn from the video parlour. They sniggered when they did some homework on the list of tablets the young man had ordered. He seemed too young to be suffering from erectile dysfunction.

Through the sundry calls, one number of significance that emerged belonged to someone in a sleepy hamlet near Belgaum, in Karnataka. And so, Angre's men finally bid adieu to their favourite girl and trained their sights beyond the couple holed up in the Parel flat.

Belgaum is located on the Maharashtra-Karnataka border and has a population of both Marathi and Kannada speakers. Though it is in Karnataka, Maharashtra has staked a claim to it as the Peshwas had ruled it between 1707 and 1818, except for a brief hiatus when Haider Ali of Mysore overran it. It is just 50 km from the Goa state border and 500 km from Mumbai. The Belgaum airport is only 29 km from the Maharashtra border.

Once they zeroed in on the address given to them by the cellular service providers, Angre's men had second thoughts. It looked like somebody had played a trick on them – they were standing in the front yard of the palatial bungalow of an Alphonso-mango dealer. The two-storey villa was spread over seventy acres and contained twenty rooms. It was owned by Shashi Shinde, who lived like a king in his palace in the affluent Maharashtrian neighbourhood and apparently kept his distance from his less wealthy neighbours, in keeping with his exalted financial status.

The policemen decided to stay put and keep a discreet watch over Shinde's palace. For weeks, they did not notice anything out of the ordinary and felt that they had reached a dead end; there was no way that this rich man could be connected to Manchekar in any manner. They also felt it was futile hanging around in Belgaum, because the extortion calls were coming from Goa.

Angre and his men made more than twenty trips to Goa, but made no headway on Manchekar. By 2003, cellular phones had made it easy for calls to be tracked, and they kept hoping that they would zero in on Manchekar through Santosh Naik. One day, the little lead finally turned up something and they hit pay dirt.

Santosh Naik slipped up. He called a prospective victim from a prepaid number and claimed that he was Maharaj. Then he added that he would be transferring the call to Manchekar in a few minutes.

The cops realized that Maharaj was not Manchekar as they had surmised. And because calls could not be forwarded from prepaid numbers, it meant that Naik was with Manchekar. They began trailing Naik in earnest – and this eventually led them to Manchekar.

Subsequent investigations revealed that Manchekar was one of the shrewdest brains in the business. He had stonewalled the efforts of the police to locate him for several years by maintaining extreme secrecy. His mother and sister were his only confidantes; when he did trust a third partner, it cost him his life. And yes, he was a mango dealer from Belgaum, but he was a man with one identity in Maharashtra and another in Goa. On weekends, Manchekar drove his SUV, with its tinted glasses, to Goa, barely 50 km away. He checked in at five-star hotels which were very particular about protecting the privacy of their customers. He used to carry more than twenty-four SIM cards to make extortion calls to his victims. in Mumbai and Thane, and switched off the handset once he left the hotel.

The offices of most mobile service providers are closed on weekends. Even if the cops managed to trace a call to a Goa hotel, the earliest they could land up there was on Monday morning; by then, Manchekar was at his villa in Belgaum and his phone was switched off.

But the Thane police team that had made Manchekar their mission closed the case at last – through their favourite kind of encounter.

The official version, which was described in the police press release and subsequently published in all major dailies, was the standard one dished out after every encounter.

'On 15 August 2003, at around 2.30 a.m., a team of officers intercepted a Tata Sumo near Ujjwaldeep Hotel at Gandhi Nagar corner, near ST stand in Kolhapur. The team of officers was led by API Ravindranath Angre.

'When Manchekar alighted from the Tata Sumo, he was told to

surrender. But Manchekar, who had managed to evade the police dragnet for several years, stupidly fired two rounds from a .38 Smith and Wesson revolver at the police. In retaliation, and in self-defence, they had to fire at Manchekar, who was injured. They rushed him to the nearest government hospital, the Chhatrapati Pramila Raje Hospital, where he was declared dead before admission.'

Thane police chief Suprakash Chakravarty told media persons, 'Manchekar had managed to give the police the slip for the past several years, but this time we tracked him down in Kolhapur and his killing will cripple the activities of his gang.'

Nobody wondered why Manchekar had fired back at the police, knowing that he could get killed. Or about the fact that he was cornered, not in Belgaum but in Kolhapur, 110 km away.

Angre is a veteran of fifty-two encounters, but Manchekar was his biggest hit, wanted as he was in thirty cases of murder and extortion. Within a week of the encounter, the cops also picked up Santosh Naik alias Maharaj, who was the backbone of the Manchekar gang. He, however, managed to survive an 'encounter' with the police.

Maharaj's calls had terrorized his victims. Unlike other dons, who would start with khokhas, or crores, Maharaj was pragmatic. He used to call and say, 'Maharaj bol raha hoon, dus peti mere aadmi ko de dena.' (This is Maharaj calling. Arrange for 10 lakh. My boys will collect it from you.) If the victim cried or begged for sympathy, the amount was slashed by 50 per cent and reduced to Rs 5 lakh.

The police apparently spared Maharaj's wife, who was identified as Avantika; she was not even booked for complicity. But the specially designated MCOCA court sentenced Manchekar's seventy-two-year-old mother, Lakshmibai Manchekar, to life imprisonment in the Khanvilkar murder case – thus bringing down the curtains on the gang.

FORTY

The Encounter-proof Gangster

The mayhem continued as the executioners of the Mumbai police force took the law into their own hands. In twenty years, the Mumbai police had killed more than 1,500 gangsters in encounters. Nobody lived to tell the tale – save one.

D.K. Rao survived not just one but two police encounters. The first one was executed by a woman police officer; the second was especially shocking – he survived 19 bullets shot at him by one of the top encounter specialists.

Mumbai has been home to thousands of gangsters. It has been called Gangland and Mafia Nagar, the crime capital of the country. Amidst all the myths and the noir tales about the city (archived in the dossiers of the Mumbai police), D.K. Rao's story is the most bizarre for several reasons. Rao is less than five feet tall and unimpressive looking – no aura of menace about him. He has a balding head, a bandaged leg – and has never met his boss personally, yet he is Chhota Rajan's top aide in Mumbai.

Having been in jail very long, Rao is said to be well-versed with the law and can carry on an informed discussion with advocates. Rakesh Maria sums up his chances: 'He is no pushover. He is a survivor and he is a fox. He is a heavyweight in the mafia whom you have to watch out for. He is to Chhota Rajan what Chhota Shakeel is to Dawood Ibrahim.'

Ravi Mallesh Bora alias D.K. Rao started off as a chindi chor (a petty robber, with a poor standing in the criminal hierarchy). He hailed from a denotified tribe called the Baria; denotified tribes were branded as criminal tribes by the British for over seventy-five years, and they lived a life of hard labour for several generations. Originally from Gulbarga in Karnataka, Ravi Bora's parents had come to Mumbai to work in the mills. His father worked at Prakash Cotton Mills in Lower Parel.

When he was twenty years old, Ravi Bora was involved in a murder that, according to police records, 'happened on the spur of the moment'. A little street brawl that went awry, but one that set him apart forever. His name was etched in the police diary, a sign of things to come.

Khalsa College in Matunga–Wadala was the gangster's hangout. This is where he cobbled his first group of robbers together, in the early nineties, at just twenty. They may have been neophytes, but their loot was not less than Rs 25 lakh in the year 1996.

Ravi Bora was the Gabbar Singh among his gang of forty. He did all the meticulous planning and, together, they staked out targets for days. Most of the time, the target was a van on its way from a bank vault with money. In a short span of time, Ravi Bora turned out to be a big headache for the Mumbai police and he had cases registered against him at several police stations: from Khar, Mulund, Vile Parle and Bhandup to Dahisar.

With such a record, the law soon caught up with him. It was while he was incarcerated in Thane jail in the early nineties that Sunil Madgaonkar alias Matyabhai decided to induct the boy into the Chhota Rajan fold. Soon, he found himself in the company of thieves like Babbu Pandey alias Rohit Verma, Vinod Matkar and Jaggu Shetty alias Fakira, who was known to have pulled off a Rs 66-lakh robbery in 1994.

Once out of prison, Bora took to carrying the identity card of a person called D.K. Rao, who worked at a bank. It is not known whether he stole the identity. The name stuck because of an encounter with a policewoman. At the end of 1997, in Juhu, a police sub-inspector, Mridula Lad, had been informed about a robbery that was being planned in the area by Ravi Bora and a man called Aware.

When the duo reached the spot, they realized that the police were onto them. Aware fired a round at Lad, but she ducked. She fired back, and the bullet hit Ravi Bora on his leg. He has a limp to this day. Aware escaped and is still at large. Ravi Bora was nabbed, and based on the identity card he had on him, he was recorded in the police diary as D.K. Rao. The name sat well on him. Ravi Mallesh Bora was a chindi chor, but D.K. Rao grew larger than life to take on the responsibility for Chhota Rajan's vast crime syndicate in India.

Both Mumbai's cops and the mafia still tell the jaw-dropping story about the miraculous rising-from-the-dead of D.K. Rao. It happened on 11 November 1998, around the time when Chhota Rajan and Dawood Ibrahim were into reprisal killings. Chhota Rajan claimed that he wanted to eliminate everyone who had participated in the 1992 serial bomb blasts to prove his 'patriotism', while Dawood Ibrahim's gang was eliminating Chhota Rajan-associated businessmen and rivals. D.K. Rao was on one such mission to kill Shaikh Mohammed Ehtesham and Baba Moosa Chauhan, when he almost met with his maker.

Shaikh Mohammed Ehtesham and Baba Moosa Chauhan had already been sentenced by the special TADA court in Mumbai. Shaikh Mohammed Ehtesham was charged with having helped with the landing of arms and ammunition in Raigad, Maharashtra while Baba Moosa Chauhan was charged with being one of those who had gone to film star Sanjay Dutt's residence to deliver AK-56 rifles. Both Ehtesham and Chauhan had been sentenced to ten years' rigorous imprisonment and were in court for their hearing.

At the time, a senior inspector of the Mumbai crime branch, Ambadas Pote, known for his loyalty to his job and his great daring, intercepted Ramesh Pujari, Raje Gore, Jairam Shetty, Vipin Khanderao and D.K. Rao in Dadar. The spot was Sayani Road, near Khed Gully, just below the Zandu Pharmaceuticals building. Rajesh Vithal Kamble, who was 18 years old then, recalls, 'The goons were in a Maruti Esteem and suddenly the cops came in a Maruti Gypsy van and intercepted them. They didn't give them any chance to open fire. They just riddled their bodies with bullets and put them in a police van.'

D.K. Rao matter-of-factly recounts the story of the day he came back from the dead. 'Raje and Vipin died on the spot but Jairam, Ramesh and I were still alive when Jairam, unable to bear the pain, called out "Amma!". That was it. The cops realized somebody was alive and fired more shots at us. Jairam slumped dead and so did Ramesh. I got the extra bullets in my feet. There were four bodies on top of me. I was conscious throughout. Once they took the police van to the morgue at the KEM Hospital in Parel, I got up and screamed that I was alive. I got nineteen bullets that day and lived to tell the tale. I don't know how I survived. People say that I know yoga and may have held my breath. But I will not tell you that because I really think it was my destiny to live.'

For ten years after his recovery from the bullet wounds, D.K. Rao found himself shut away from the world in prison cells across Maharashtra. Somewhere along the way, developments within the Chhota Rajan gang helped him climb the ladder.

Chhota Rajan's trusted aide, Sunil Madgaonkar alias Matyabhai, had been killed in a police encounter in 2000. Matya was a formidable gangster, and the one man Chhota Rajan could trust in Mumbai. Former Mumbai Police Commissioner Subhash Malhotra had given him the title 'Director of India Operations for Chhota Rajan' in 1997. He had executed three top hits for the gang: East-West Airline chief Thakiyuddin Wahid, businessman Mahesh Dholakia and Arun Gawli's ace sharpshooter, Ashok Joshi. After that, scores of gangsters from the Chhota Rajan group were locked up in jails under the dreaded MCOCA or killed by policemen – and Matya was one of them.

The day Matya died, Chhota Rajan was afraid he was done for, and fearful that his crime syndicate would collapse. It took more than a dozen of his trusted men to fill Matya's shoes. But he cobbled together a small group to manage affairs: O.P. Singh, Bharat Nepali, Ejaj Lakdawala, Rohit Verma, Balu Dokre, Farid Tanasha, Ravi Pujari, Santosh Shetty, Vicky Malhotra and, of course, D.K. Rao. Chhota Rajan would probably have laughed if anybody had told him that eventually D.K. Rao would be the one in charge of his entire network.

The attack on Rajan in Bangkok proved fatal for his gang. The wickets started falling one by one. Some were killed by Chhota Rajan himself when he felt that they had defected, others by Chhota Shakeel. O.P. Singh was killed in 2002; Ejaj Lakdawala left the gang and got shot in Bangkok in 2003 (some say he is still alive); Ravi Pujari left to form his own gang; Santosh Shetty also left to form his own gang and declared war on Chhota Rajan; Balu Dokre was butchered in Malaysia in 2005; Bharat Nepali, who left Chhota Rajan's syndicate to join Santosh Shetty, was shot in Bangkok in February 2011; and Farid Tanasha was killed in Mumbai in 2010. Vicky Malhotra manages the country's north-east operations for Chhota Rajan. And so, by a process of elimination, D.K. Rao remained the sole survivor in Mumbai from among the inner circle of Chhota Rajan's men.

In 1997, Matya had told an *Indian Express* reporter on one of his court visits that the gang easily made Rs 300 crore annually and that much of it was siphoned off to their boss through hawala channels. Rs 50 crore or so was kept with Matya, who disbursed the money among the gang members, both inside and outside jail, and also used it for procuring weapons. After D.K. Rao took on the mantle, it is anybody's guess how many zeroes have been added to the figure.

In the underworld, pedigree matters. A small-time robber can hardly expect to rise to the top. But D.K. Rao proved he could outlast all the other men in the gang. In the words of Rakesh Maria, chief of the Anti-Terrorism Squad, Maharashtra, 'At the Arthur Road jail, where Rao was lodged with rival gang members, he stood his ground and got a lot of respect.'

The way he killed his one-time colleague O.P. Singh, in 2002, is testimony to D.K. Rao's deadly skills – Rakesh Maria calls him 'the Black Mamba'. (The Black Mamba holds on to its smaller prey until there is no muscle movement, and against larger prey, it keeps striking repeatedly.)

When Balu Dokre filled Chhota Rajan's ears about O.P. Singh leaving the gang to either defect or start his own gang, Chhota Rajan wanted Singh to be liquidated. He squealed about his whereabouts to the Indian enforcement agencies, who picked him up from the New Delhi airport in 2001.

O.P. Singh got wind of Chhota Rajan's plans to finish him off and thought he was safer in jail, but he hadn't reckoned with Rao. Rao, who was lodged at the Arthur Road jail at the time, used his influence with the jail authorities to move to Nashik jail where Singh was doing time.

Rao knew he would need help to kill his target; he was a tall, big man, and smarter than him. So he also got a few of his cronies shifted to Nashik jail, where they lay in wait for the opportune moment.

O.P. Singh was the complete antithesis of Rao. While Rao had barely completed his tenth standard, Singh was a chemistry postgraduate from Mumbai University and he hadn't started off in crime. He was employed as a quality control officer at the Mazgaon docks when his elder brother Arun Singh, a professor at Jhunjhunwala College, was killed in the early nineties by the Amar and Ashwin Naik gang.

When Singh named them in his police complaint, he was targeted too. In 1995, during one of his frequent drinking sprees at a bar, he came in contact with some Chhota Rajan men, to whom he spilled his story. Rajan, who at the time was desperately looking for a brainy and educated strategist, thought Singh was a great find for the syndicate. He was quickly inducted into the gang. Though he started out with small robberies, he was 'fully absorbed' when he and his accomplices gunned down a security guard during an abduction attempt.

Soon Singh's crime graph soared; a number of cases were registered against him at Goregaon, Pydhonie, Khar and Malabar Hill in Mumbai. His meticulous planning and research impressed Rajan and Singh graduated to being his Man Friday in 1997.

Singh also initiated contacts with several policemen and politicians for Rajan, who was then based in Malaysia. Rajan then invited him to Kuala Lumpur and elevated Singh to the position of his advisor and planner. Singh managed to keep himself off the police radar for a long time and by the time they discovered him, he was holed up in Bangkok, from where he helped Rajan with his unfinished business: such as bumping off Mirza Dilshad Beg in Kathmandu in 1998.

Later, when there was a bid on Rajan's life on 15 September 2000 by Chhota Shakeel's men, Singh took charge of the gang and coordinated with Rajan's lawyers and the Thai media. It is said that Singh was instrumental in Rajan's escape from Smitivej Hospital in Bangkok. He also helped expand Rajan's network in the northern and western regions of India.

Why Singh decided to leave the gang and strike out on his own is not clear. Clearly, there was a lot of resentment directed against him from the Rajan cadre because he was educated and smart. On the other hand, it could be that there was some financial dispute that prompted Chhota Rajan's decision to bump him off. But to this day, the brutal killing of Singh at Chhota Rajan's behest, and at the hands of D.K. Rao, remains a spine-chilling story. There were no guns used and it all happened in the confines of a jail.

It was a Sunday and there was a cricket match on at Nashik Jail. D.K. Rao was playing, along with thirteen of his henchmen and O.P. Singh. It was a matter of minutes before Singh found himself kicked, beaten and strangled to death. The person who reportedly strangled him was Rao, using some jute rope at hand. The then Inspector General of Police (Prisons) U.D. Rajwade, while suspending jail officials and instituting a probe, admitted to the possible connivance of the staff in the killing. The Nashik Road police registered a case of murder and conspiracy under section 304 IPC against Rajan aides D.K. Rao, Sarfira Nepali, Bala Parab and ten others for the killing.

Most of the gang members involved in the killing of Singh were later killed in encounters with the police, including Sarfira Nepali and Bala Parab. Only Rao escaped.

Rao apparently managed to climb to the top of Rajan's crime syndicate because he was not only loyal (he once planned to travel to Dubai to kill Dawood Ibrahim during his daughter's wedding), he is said to have shared the loot with his network of men. It is said that Rao still recruits small-time robbers into the gang. These robbers eventually end up as contract killers, but Rao always takes care of his men. He arranges for their bail and provides for their families. It is said that he is the first gangster who actually took a smaller share of the loot for himself and disbursed the larger share among his men.

In 2006, when the crime branch was tapping Chhota Rajan's phones, they intercepted several conversations between him and Rao, then lodged at Arthur Road jail, which fuelled a major controversy. Rao had apparently asked for Rs 5 lakh from Rajan, which he needed pay Sitaram Mhetre for the reinstatement of 11 jail officials suspended in the O.P. Singh case. Mhetre at the time was a state minister in the home department. The conversation was placed in the MCOCA court and Mhetre had a tough time defending himself and protesting that he did not know Rao.

Rao was released from prison after 11 years of incarceration and made a posh home for himself in Dharavi. He calls himself president of the Anti-Corruption Forum and is teaching yoga on the terrace of his building. But the police are watching him closely; they keep slapping cases against him to try and keep him behind bars.

FORTY-ONE

Ashwin Atones

Ashwin Naik, who spent ten years in prison – five in Tihar Jail and five in Yerawada in Pune – was released on 1 May 2009, after he was acquitted of his wife Neeta Naik's murder and fifteen other cases including murder, drug peddling and extortion. He was given a rousing welcome by his neighbours and his two children at his home in Chinchpokli.

Ashwin had been brought to Yerawada from Tihar in 2005, to stand trial for Neeta's murder. On 31 January, the MCOCA court acquitted him. He now stays with his teenaged son and daughter in Chinchpokli.

In an interview to Velly Thevar in *The Telegraph* in 2012, Ashwin recounted his five-and-a-half-year stay at Tihar. 'Having done time at various prisons in Maharashtra, Tihar was the best. Kiran Bedi, the doughty IPS officer, transformed the prison into a veritable living space. At one point of time, she would not even allow the staff to walk in with a danda so as not to demoralize the prisoners. After all, there were undertrials lodged in the prison too.

'The prison was well organized and had a lot of facilities. There were several hospitals in all the jails that came under Tihar. The hospitals were manned by professional Keralite nurses and I was constantly spending time at the hospital because I was handicapped and needed attention. Sometimes, the nurses would even share their dabba with me and we sometimes flirted with them. There are several prisons in Tihar, extending right up to Rohini. At that point of time, there were six jails, now there are ten under Tihar. I was in Jail No. 3. The prisoners were clubbed together in alphabetical order.

'Though it is said that jail ki dosti phatak tak hai (friendships in prison last until the gate), I made friends with inmates and the guards that have stood the test of time. This, despite the fact that I was a highlight prisoner (that is the term they used for high-risk prisoners). Whenever a poor man came and told me that he could not afford a surety of Rs 2,000 as a precondition for being set free, I gave him the money.

'At Tihar, you could buy your own television (though it became prison property later); I sponsored around fifty television sets for those who wanted one but could not afford it. They also allowed transistors, watches, your gold chain, and you had access to visitors twice a week. In winters, we woke up at 6 a.m. or else the timing was 5.30. We had to store water for the day in buckets at 9 a.m. for our daily use.

'I was very stressed out when I landed in Tihar. I was framed in many cases and mere saath bahut bura ho gaya tha (life had treated me unfairly). Because of my name, mera frame ban gaya aur main picture ban gaya (my name brought notoriety to me and my picture began hanging on the walls of police stations as a wanted criminal). There was the fear of rival gangsters bumping me off and the fact that I was paralysed waist down did not make me too confident. The 9' x 12' cell was not overcrowded and I slowly found my bearings. Tihar is manned by Tamil Nadu State Police because the prisoners would not be able to speak to them, the Delhi jail police and the CISF. The guards change every three hours, though I think it is entirely possible to commit suicide if one wants to. We had several cases during my time and the guards had a tough time when the headcount showed a missing number. Sometimes the inmate would be plonked atop a tree or the water tank. There was a lot of dramabazi. We were locked up from 12 to 3 in the afternoon and between 6 p.m. and 6 a.m. at night.

'I went to Tihar in June '99 and when the Kargil war happened, we contributed a lot of money. I personally gave Rs 2 lakh. I also ran the canteen, not the regular food canteen but the one for the snacks. I had to dole out Rs 6,000 a day to run the canteen. We served bread pakodas and chai. Those who left for the court benefited a lot because they got breakfast. Out of the 3,000 prisoners in Jail No. 3, at least 400 went to court every day and they used their coupons to buy the bread pakodas. Actually, it was a no-profit thing some days, but then you could have access to the butter, vegetables and other food stuff, which is why I ran the canteen.

'Lack of sleep is a big problem in prison and often people said, Nitrovit (a sleeping tablet) lekar so gaya (he took a tablet and slept). There were instances of inmates being beaten up in jail; like our fingers, each guard had a different temperament.

'What I liked about the jail was that the system actually worked, though of course, everything is for sale like in all prisons. If you have money, you can avail of comforts. One Gandhi (a Rs 500 note) only got you seven pouches of tobacco. Kiran Bedi was so tired of seeing the tobacco stains and smoking that she tried her best to put a stop to it. Then she started meeting the relatives, asking them, wouldn't they like it if their near and dear ones stopped smoking or chewing tobacco inside the prison. So please don't bring it, she told them. She then adopted a carrot-and-stick policy with the prisoners, telling them that if they could forgo tobacco and smoking, she would ensure more facilities and better food. The inmates fell into the trap and thus tobacco and cigarettes disappeared. Though, of course, the guards took to blackmarketing of tobacco.'

Released from prison and home at last in Chinchpokli's 144 Tenements, Ashwin Naik has finally found peace. He was set up a company called Maruti Infrastructure, named after his father, which deals with real estate – the new bubble that the mafia and the politicians are latching on to. His daughter is slated to go to the US for further studies. This has unsettled him, he says, as he is close to his daughter and will miss her terribly.

Once in a while, there are reports that Ashwin has got on the wrong side of the law and the police pick him up on allegations of extortion. His past still haunts him and he is not happy that he is branded a criminal because it was not a calling of his choice. But no more shootouts, no more rival gangs. Ashwin is finally at rest.

FORTY-TWO

Amjad Khan's Sholay

Amjad Khan spoke just like his cinema icon, Amjad Khan. He strutted and strode just like the real Amjad Khan. Since he could not make it in Bollywood, he decided to become an Amjad Khan clone in real life. The menacing gaze, the half-crooked smile, the arching of his thick, bushy eyebrows, the sardonic glance, the mocking laughter, even the way he spoke – Amjad Khan was an uncertified copy of Amjad Khan in *Sholay*, even if he didn't resemble him physically. There was only one problem. Unlike other clones – for instance, of Amitabh Bachchan, Shatrughan Sinha or Anil Kapoor – there was no way that Amjad Khan could get a break in Hindi movies. He had been arrested for drug peddling by the Narcotics Control Bureau (NCB) and was being prosecuted for his involvement in the drug trade.

However, he belonged to the school that firmly believes that if life dishes out tomatoes, you should make sauce. He became an informant for the NCB, even as he waited for his trial to finish. He was sure that he would be acquitted in the end. Khan's intelligence network and tip-offs to the NCB sleuths had resulted in drug seizures across the country. The agency had never tasted such success, and it was this that made the NCB officers go soft on him.

At the same time, Amjad Khan ended up antagonizing the drug cartels, which had minted millions until Khan began squealing on them. Several big consignments were seized by the NCB, which left the drug mafia fuming. The ever increasing losses were causing a big dent in their annual turnover. A corrective measure was required, for which they put their heads together.

Finally, they decided to eliminate Amjad Khan. But who would bell the cat? Amjad Khan had one friend, the encounter specialist cop Pradeep Sharma. Khan publicized their friendship through his media interviews and open proclamations. Only a big neon sign outside his home and a placard on his car were missing. No shooter was willing to cross swords with Sharma, and this complicated things for the cabal that wanted Khan dead at any cost. The drug mafia kept upping the supari amount on Amjad Khan. Within a few months, what started as Rs 5 lakh went up to Rs 5 crore. But no one was willing to take up the job. Amjad Khan, meanwhile, was either clueless about the mounting bounty on his head or he had become delusional and complacent, for he continued inflicting losses on the drug cartel.

In sheer desperation, the cartel approached Chhota Rajan and offered a supari of Rs 20 crore. It was an amount unheard of for killing just one individual. In Mumbai, hit jobs were carried out for as meagre an amount as Rs 5,000. (Even the Lashkar-e-Taiba had spent a fraction of that amount – Rs 20 lakh – to execute 26/11.)

Rajan accepted the supari. After all, he had already thrown the gauntlet at Sharma once. So he did not fear his wrath. But who would identify Amjad Khan? Rajan had perfected the art of using the services of famed Mumbai cops for the execution of his work. In Amjad Khan's case, he asked an encounter specialist who had served with the Anti-Narcotics Cell of the crime branch to help him identify his target. The encounter specialist charged him Rs 5 crore and gave him his best man; a sub-inspector took the shooter in his Gypsy and pointed out Amjad.

On 16 October 2006, three men on a motorbike shot dead Amjad Khan and his friend Himanshu Choudhary, both of whom were on their way to the sessions court for the hearing of a big case of Mandrax seizure dating back to 2000. It was a shocking daylight murder that took place at one of the busiest traffic intersections of the city, opposite the sessions court and barely 200 m from the state police headquarters.

Khan's death left the NCB sleuths reeling. It also left a void for several crime reporters who had managed to beef up their stories with his encyclopaedic insights.

Police inspector Pradeep Sharma could not believe that Rajan had openly challenged him in this manner. Sharma was yet to recover from the death of O.P. Singh; Amjad Khan's death was unbearable. Khan was not just his informer but his friend, and Sharma mourned him.

Sharma's mole in the Rajan gang, O.P. Singh was widely alleged to have shared a lot of information with Khan, who passed on the intelligence to his contacts in the police. This had resulted in the arrest of several of Rajan's men and also encounters planned by Sharma's team. Rajan had trusted Singh far too much but when he realized that Singh was Sharma's man, he decided to get rid of him in a cunning way. Singh was based in a safe house in Greater Kailash-II in New Delhi, which was known only to Rajan and Sharma. Rajan called two encounter specialists of the New Delhi police, ACP Rajbir Singh and Inspector Mohan Chand Sharma, who worked for a special cell of the Delhi Police crime branch. Rajan tipped them off about the presence of his top aide in Delhi. Both of them immediately swooped down on Singh and arrested him. As Singh was not wanted in Delhi, he was sent to Mumbai. Soon he was transferred to Nashik jail, a sitting target for D.K. Rao and his men.

Through the killings of O.P. Singh and Amjad Khan, Rajan had clearly exposed the way he could use the police machinery to further his ends. Two well-known Delhi cops and one famous Mumbai encounter specialist kowtowed to him; in the killing of Singh in jail, it was established that eleven jail officials had shown their subservience to Rajan.

What Rajan had not reckoned with was the fact that Khan could prove more damaging for him in death than in life. Sharma decided to make Rajan pay for killing his friend. He decided to launch his own war against Khan's killers, and was determined to inflict serious losses on the gang and the ganglord.

Between 2006 and 2009, encounter specialists of the Mumbai police specifically chased down Rajan's men and more than thirty were killed. The fear psychosis that they unleashed was such that no new shooters were willing to join the gang, while those who already worked for Rajan refused assignments as they were tired of being harassed by the police.

Some of the gangsters even left Mumbai and shifted base to south India; others changed their phone numbers and their residences. 'We did not want to die in an encounter. Sharma can kill anyone,' disclosed an old crony of Rajan.

This sudden spurt in encounters and the exodus from the gang crippled Rajan; manpower and money power are the two main pillars of any gang. In the underworld, it was well known that the Dawood gang had more money and the Rajan gang had more men. But one cop, almost single-handedly, had managed to cut down Rajan's manpower.

Even before Rajan could recoup, the Mumbai police began hauling in the builders in the western suburbs who were loyal to Rajan and had earmarked a cut for him in their deals. They were told to cut off ties with Rajan – or they would be booked under MCOCA. This was a major blow to him.

The police also put scores of phones on surveillance and made a list of all those who were cutting deals in Rajan's name, using his clout. These men were hauled to police stations and asked to lay bare their business associations with the don.

In the two years after 2006, Rajan's business suffered losses of more than Rs 250 crore by a conservative estimate.

By the year 2010, Rajan had hardly any powerful lieutenants left in the gang, except D.K. Rao.

FORTY-THREE

Daddy Demolished

The court was teeming with Gawli's supporters, a battery of lawyers, the media, and hangers-on. Mumbai's city civil and sessions court in Kala Ghoda, south Mumbai, gets its fair share of crowd-pulling cases but on this day, even lawyers from other courts were milling about for a glimpse of Gawli and to know the outcome of a case that could change the course of life in Mumbai.

For four decades, Mumbai's resident don had been flitting between various jails in Maharashtra and Dagdi Chawl, his fortress in south Mumbai, as the Mumbai police ensured his incarceration in some case or the other. Not that Gawli was any less of a gangster during his captivity; he lorded over the jail and ran his operations even better in some ways.

In forty years of flirting with crime, he had accumulated forty-odd cases (one for each year!), most of which he had been acquitted of. However, today, 28 August 2012, his fate was to be decided once and for all.

Special public prosecutor Raja Thakre pointed at Gawli and roared, 'Kamlakar Jamsandekar was shot at point-blank range when he was watching TV, with his child doing his homework by his side and his niece in the kitchen. As an MLA, Gawli acted without any care for life.'

The prosecution sought the death penalty for Gawli and two others, Vijaykumar Giri and Pratap Godse. Despite the massive crowd, there was a hushed silence in the courtroom. Gawli had been accused of killing Jamsandekar, a Shiv Sena corporator, in 2007.

That day, the special MCOCA court judge convicted Gawli and eleven others for murder. However, the court adjourned the hearing on the exact punishment to be awarded to Gawli and his gang.

Gawli sought leniency, saying he was sixty years old and had to look after his wife, children and an aged mother. The prosecution maintained that these could not be mitigating circumstances. On 31 August, the special court sentenced Arun Gawli and the eleven others to life for the 2007 killing.

The sentence sealed the fate of Gawli. Already in his sixties, he was going to be incarcerated for life as a convict. With this move, Gawli was not just contained, he was almost finished.

The state government had been trying desperately to nail the gangster-turned-politician in some big case for the last two decades. But Gawli's battery of lawyers, his intimidatory tactics with witnesses and shrewd manipulations had ensured that he managed to walk free every time a case went to trial.

Over the years, the Mumbai police had made every effort in the book and beyond to ensure that Gawli stayed behind bars. Sometimes, they even sprang a surprise on Gawli's legal team and outsmarted them. When, for instance, on 24 July 1997, Gawli and his men had been given bail in the case of assault on a reporter, Anandita Ramaswamy, the police had been dismayed. They had not expected him to get bail so easily. But the media did not see any signs of disappointment or defeat on the faces of the police officers.

Public prosecutor P.R. Namjoshi had argued that Gawli's release could prevent witnesses from coming forward to identify the accused. 'His release could lead to more violence,' Namjoshi said.

And then the police had played their trump card. Even before an order could be passed, the prosecution told the court that another FIR had been registered against Gawli – relating to his involvement in evicting a woman from Dagdi Chawl in 1990. A seven-year-old case was raked up just to ensure that Gawli did not get a reprieve.

Gawli was supposed to be taken to the Arthur Road jail for judicial custody. But Gawli's men, who were following the police convoy, were shocked when they saw the police van in which Gawli was travelling suddenly break away from the convoy and head towards the crime branch headquarters. Gawli was remanded in police custody in the Gajare case.

Chandraprabha Gajare had complained in an FIR filed at the Agripada police station that she had been asked to vacate Room No. 12 at Dagdi Chawl. When she had refused to do so, she had been beaten up and thrown out by Arun Gawli and his goons. Gajare used to cook for Gawli's men, and she said that her problems started when she refused to surrender her house to Gawli, who was offering to pay Rs 50,000 for it. The house was worth well over Rs 3 lakh then. She also alleged that Gawli wanted to marry her daughter Sangita.

'I turned down his proposal. Gawli used to be always on the run. Besides, these gangsters used to abduct businessmen and beat them up... I did not want my daughter to marry a gangster,' she said.

Gajare said the complaint filed by journalist Ramaswamy had inspired her to stand up against Gawli.

The Gajare case ensured that Gawli spent three more years of his life in prison. But he managed to secure bail on 20 June 2000. According to the prosecution, he had managed to get the prime witness in the case, Manoj Birje, murdered through co-accused Sunil Ghate and Nagesh Mohite. Yet Gawli was given bail.

The police had tried to mount a case of extortion against him in 1990 too, but Gawli managed to extricate himself from this too. On 10 January 2007, he was discharged from the sixteen-year-old extortion case by the Bombay High Court. Gawli had a full-fledged legal team working for him and his men were ever ready to take on the powerful police and state machinery.

His unprecedented conviction in the Jamsandekar killing dealt a body blow to the gang. The life sentence meant curtains for the crime syndicate; their clout could not be all-pervasive any more, as it used to be prior to his conviction. A pall of gloom descended over Dagdi Chawl.

Once an impenetrable, well-guarded, three-storey building in

Byculla West, Dagdi Chawl is now relatively deserted. The huge iron gates had always stayed shut – opening only to welcome those who deified the don as a demigod. Some claim that Gawli made them feel so safe that they could sleep with the doors of their homes open – or approach him even at 3 a.m. in the night if they needed help. Even today, there are guards who keep a watchful eye on people entering and leaving; these include ABS workers and certain neighbours.

Once you enter, there is a small gate to the left which leads to Gawli's house, and to the right is a billboard advertising a gym. An avid gym enthusiast, Gawli had got this gym built and named it after his father – Gulabrao Ahir. He had spent more than Rs 40 lakh to make it a modern gym with sophisticated machines and the latest equipment. But few people have enrolled, perhaps understandably.

Gawli has also left land free inside the four walls for Durga Devi's pandal, for the annual pooja and celebrations. The residence, which used to be in bad shape, was transformed by him into a secure building with lifts and a security set-up. When Gawli was at home, no one could get to it without passing through several obstacles and hurdles – not even the cops.

The locals take pride in the fact that Dawood Ibrahim visited Dagdi Chawl on more than one occasion; a huge clash took place on his last visit and he never came after that day. They say the place is more secure then even Dawood Ibrahim's Musafirkhana, on Pakmodia Street in Dongri.

Further ahead is a small locked area, which was once a dispensary set up by ABS. Then, there is the ABS office in front of the temple. The kalash on top is made of pure gold, a symbol of Gawli's devotion. Next to the temple is a cowshed with three or four cows. The fascination with cows stems, of course, from the fact that he is a gawli, or milkman. Ironically, the dilapidated structure that has now been made into a cowshed once housed Gawli on the first floor.

Gawli would organize sabhas for people on his terrace. These meetings would go on till very late in the night and he would ensure that everyone was well fed, even if it was late. The sabha system partially continues because his daughter Geeta has taken over his mantle.

Gawli lost in the last assembly polls, leaving even his political career in a shambles, but his daughter Geeta and sister-in-law Vandana have been elected as corporators. Geeta is now trying to wipe out Gawli's past and hopes to make a new beginning. She projects her father as a Robin Hood and a messiah for the downtrodden and poor. She claims that she joined politics in 2007 to carry forward her father's legacy.

She thinks that Gawli has tremendous local support. 'In the first parliamentary election that Dad contested, he won a total of 94,000 votes alone while the Congress plus NCP together managed one lakh votes. Dad was new, yet he managed so many votes. Is this not a yardstick to judge his popularity by?' Geeta says, in fluent English.

When asked about Gawli's crimes and about his being a gangster, she quickly retorts, 'Everyone has a dirty past. We have to move on in life.'

Geeta meets Gawli regularly, whenever he comes to J.J. Hospital for a check-up. When she is asked why she, and not her other siblings, decided to take on the responsibility of the party, she explains, 'Well, Mahesh has his own restaurant business. Yogesh has finished his twelfth standard. He has also done a course in automobile engineering. Yogita has done her BA in political science and plans to join politics along with me. Asmita, the youngest, is currently in the eighth standard.'

Geeta plans to approach the high court to challenge her father's conviction. Until then, Arun Gawli will have to bide his time in jail.

EPILOGUE

The End of the Encounter Elite

VIJAY SALASKAR

Mrs Smita Salaskar is proud that her husband has become a hero of
sorts. He killed more than seventy dreaded gangsters in his career of
twenty-five years. However, on the fateful night of 26 November 2008,
when Mumbai faced its biggest terrorist attack ever, her husband left
the house abruptly and there was no time for goodbyes.

Salaskar, who was attached to the crime branch, had met Anti-
Terrorism Chief Hemant Karkare and Additional Commissioner
of Police Ashok Kamte near Victoria Terminus around midnight.
Reports suggested that the terrorists – Pakistanis Ajmal Kasab and
Abu Ismail – had gone towards Cama and Albless Hospital. Karkare,
Kamte and Salaskar immediately decided to head there. Salaskar took
the wheel and the others sat behind him.

As they crossed the Special Branch building and drew close to
Cama Hospital, Abu Ismail and Ajmal Kasab opened fire on the
police officers. Later, they pushed all three of them out of the car. Of
the three, Karkare and Kamte were the first to succumb. Salaskar was
still alive. One bullet had hurt him on the forearm and another had
grazed his abdomen.

Perhaps Salaskar knew that his injuries were not fatal and he
could survive if he got timely medical aid. He began screaming for
help as he lay on the steps of Cama Hospital. 'Mala vachwa goli

laagli aahe, mala vachwaaaa! Help!' But no one responded to his call for help.

There were people hiding in the Special Branch building. Salaskar's cry for help could be heard far and wide. He was bleeding continuously, but no one rushed to his aid for fear of the terrorists, who were still at large. (Unsubstantiated reports say that some of his team members preferred to hide rather than rush to his rescue.) Lying alone, writhing in agony, he screamed for help intermittently as he continued to lose blood.

Meanwhile, the police control room had heard of the ambush and a police party rushed to the spot. To their relief, Salaskar was still alive and breathing. He was rushed to the nearby G.T. Hospital. The doctors and para medics immediately began working on saving him. But forty-five minutes were far too long, even for an extremely fit officer like Salaskar. Eyewitnesses say that Salaskar was still in his senses at the hospital. Though blood had drained from his body, he still communicated with the doctors and others around him. Apparently, he complained of a thick bunch of keys in the pocket of his trousers which were hurting him. He signalled with his eyes for someone to remove the keys.

Despite best efforts, Salaskar died due to the heavy and excessive bleeding. Among all the martyrs of 26/11, he was perhaps the only one who could have survived if he had been rushed to the hospital sooner. The man who had relentlessly trailed and killed seventy people, including big fish like Amar Naik and Sada Pawle, finally died a pitiful death himself.

RAVINDRA ANGRE

Though Manchekar was a big-time don, the cop who finally sent him to his grave had his own reputation besmirched in an even more sensational way. Police Inspector Ravindra Angre was arrested on 22 February 2008 after a Thane businessman, Ganesh Wagh, lodged a complaint of extortion and attempt to usurp his property. Angre was imprisoned for fourteen months but managed to get an acquittal in the case in 2009.

Angre laughed at his misfortune when he was thrown into the Anda Cell, meant for hardened criminals, in Thane Central Prison. His cell mate was Sajid Chikna, who was only too happy to see Angre. 'Kya saab, pehchaana kya? Didn't you want to kill me in an encounter?' Chikna reminded Angre that he was on his hit-list, and that once, he had come very close to getting killed by Angre's bullets.

Chikna was a well-built gangster and had a dozen cases against him, while Angre was slim and in his late fifties. Chikna's disclosure so unsettled Angre that he could not sleep for fear of being strangled or smothered to death. The psychological stress of living with the constant fear of getting killed by someone who nursed a deep grudge against him deprived him of sleep and mental peace.

Angre eventually managed to get bail in the case from the Supreme Court on 9 May 2009.

PRADEEP SHARMA

The man who proved to be Chhota Rajan's nemesis, Police Inspector Pradeep Sharma, was arrested and found himself languishing in prison for three years. A veteran of 111 encounters, Sharma was arrested on 8 January 2010 for the fake encounter of Ram Narayan Gupta alias Lakhan Bhaiyya in November 2006. He was accused of the deed while he was serving at the D.N. Nagar police station. Apart from Sharma, twenty-one others were arrested, including eleven policemen.

After a three-year-long trial, Sharma was acquitted by a sessions court in Mumbai on 5 July 2013.

Acknowledgements

This book is the result of the selfless contributions of several friends and colleagues, who helped without any expectation of reward or remuneration.

I must thank V.K. Karthika, Chief Editor and Publisher of HarperCollins India, for her plate load of patience. She has been a great pillar of support. My thanks also go to Antony Thomas, Shantanu Ray Chaudhuri, Shuka Jain, Jojy Philip and Rajni George.

I should thank Sandra Almeida of *Hindustan Times* who first edited this book, making it error-proof. She had to forego her Christmas celebrations to meet the deadline.

While I got a lot of information from the Mumbai police dossiers, the gaps were filled by several people who came to my rescue and gave me so much of their valuable time.

The list kicks off with the go-to-man-for-all-seasons, Rakesh Maria, chief of the Anti-Terrorism Squad of the state police. I am grateful to Mr Maria, whose valuable insights from his days as the first deputy commissioner of police, detection, at the crime branch, paved the way for my understanding of the Mumbai underworld.

I am also indebted to Mr Maria's deputy at the Anti-Terrorism Squad, Pradip Sawant, who was a storehouse of information on the Maharashtrian mobsters.

Pradeep Sharma, veteran of 111 encounters, contributed to this book with his anecdotes and amazing inside stories.

Credit is also due to Sachin Waze, who generously shared several documents, statements and interrogation reports of various gangsters from the Gawli and Naik gangs.

My thanks to the Mumbai police officers would be incomplete if I did not mention the late Vijay Salaskar. Salaskar shared a lot of classified information with me but with a rider that I should withhold the information as long as he was in the service. He was very concerned about my reporting on the mafia and once gifted me a small two-foot-long axe. I laughed off the threat, but he was so insistent that I keep the axe that I agreed. Eventually, I flung it into the sea after his death.

Prem Shukla, currently the editor of *Dopahar Ka Saamna*, who reported on crime during my time at the *Indian Express*, analysed for me the political angle vis-à-vis the growth and decline of Maharashtrian mobsters.

The other journalist that I should mention is Vaibhav Purandare, author of *The Sena Story*. Vaibhav was my colleague at the *Indian Express*, *Mid Day* and *Mumbai Mirror* and helped me understand the Shiv Sena's follies and foibles.

Many thanks, too, to Sagnik Choudhary and Gautam Mengele at the *Indian Express* for helping me with clippings.

My appreciation and debt extend to a young team of students from St Xavier's College, Mumbai. Dedicated work was done by Yesha Kotak, Akash Jain, Foma Ramtekke and Herman Gomes, who pored over newspaper clippings, the state police journal, *Dakshata*, and interviewed Geeta Gawli, Smita Salaskar and Ashwin Naik. They also made several rounds of Dagdi Chawl in Byculla and 144 Tenements in Chinchpokli. Two of them, Yesha Kotak and Akash Jain, went out of their way to finish their assignments on time. Akash was on his toes even while running a very high temperature. Yesha got me some important pictures and co-ordinated with all the other students and helmed the research work. Yesha and Akash, kudos for your good work.

Bilal Siddiqui and Vaibhav Sorte were two others from St Xavier's and Raheja College respectively who helped me in compiling and assembling data from various police dossiers. They both spent several sleepless nights to ensure that I got the content in a consolidated lot. It was their tireless attitude and their inspiring dedication that kept me clacking away at the computer.

Kedar Nagrajan and Aashna Gopalkrishnan also chipped in by researching and scouring the Centre for Documentation at Colaba for details.

My grateful thanks to the renowned legal eagle, advocate Ayaz Khan. Khan, who has an encyclopaedic knowledge of the Mumbai underworld, sat with me for hours to help me understand the conspiracies behind various criminal cases.

My immeasurable thanks to my young friend Vikrant Joshi, who in his endless enthusiasm helped me set up meetings with several functionaries of the Shiv Sena. Vikrant also introduced me to senior journalist Bhau Torsekar, former editor of *Marmik*, who generously spent hours with me, tracing the early years of the Shiv Sena vis-à-vis the local gangsters.

My thanks also to Nadeem Inamdar of the *Pune Mirror*, who sent me some research material from Pune.

I would like to thank all the unnamed sources who were part of the events in the book but did not want to be identified.

No thanksgiving of mine can be complete without mentioning my friend, mentor, professor, guru, Vikram the great Chandra. Had it not been for his mentoring and hand holding, I would never have made it so far. Thank you, Vikram, for being my guiding light.

Talking about friends, I shall always remain indebted to my other teacher and mentor, Dr Shabeeb Rizvi, in whom I found a brother. Dr Rizvi showed indescribable courtesy when I visited Dubai for research and his far-reaching influence opened several inaccessible doors to me. He looked upon this book as a common enterprise and his whole family made me a part of them. His father Janab Yusuf Rizvi Sahab and his brother Ozair Rizvi magnanimously threw open their newly acquired house in Deira Dubai, where I was hosted while researching the book. Thank you, Yusuf uncle, for the generosity.

Dr Rizvi's two magnificent sons, Rayyan and Mohsin, have helped make this a better work. Rayyan Rizvi suspended his studies and office and drove me to various nooks and corners of Dubai, braving the maddening traffic. His younger brother, Mohsin Rizvi, took time off from his work to design a great cover for the book. I will always remain indebted to Shabeeb sir for all kindness and magnanimity. Thank you, Rayyan and Mohsin. I am deeply touched.

The most crucial contribution to this book comes from my better half, Velly Thevar. She painstakingly edited the book and enhanced the narrative. She became my confidante, my sounding board, my co-conspirator and my editor-in-chief in the enterprise. I humbly doff my hat to her, for being the marvellous woman and fine journalist that she is.

Narjis, with her many talents, became my assistant and secretary; she was available at all hours and kept me stress free. My profound affection for her.

My superhero sons sacrificed their outings to ensure that I could finish the book on time. Love you both, Ammar and Zain.

Sources

The primary sources for this book were essential government documents which include:

Police dossiers on various gangsters;

'The Growth of Gangsterism in Mumbai', a compilation by M. N. Singh, former joint commissioner, crime;

Charge sheets filed by Mumbai police in several courts, including Sessions and MCOCA;

Statements and interrogation reports of Ashwin Naik, Anil Parab, Bandya Mama, O.P. Singh, Arun Gawli and others.

I also culled a lot of information and insights into the lives of gangsters from personal interviews with several members of the Arun Gawli and Chhota Rajan gangs. I knew Ashwin Naik's wife Neeta Naik personally and she was a great raconteur.

Anti-Terrorism Squad chief Rakesh Maria, who was in the thick of action while he was DCP, Detection, in the crime branch between 1994 and 1998, was as usual very generous with his help.

Field officers like Pradip Sawant, Pradeep Sharma and the late Vijay Salaskar were immensely helpful with their inputs and perspectives.

The early history of Bombaim was sourced from *Greater Bombay District Gazetteer*, 1960.

My research on the mill lands owes a great deal to Dattaraya Karve or D. K. Karve, as he is known in Bhiwandi. He was the vice-president of the Bhiwandi Textile Manufacturers Association Ltd and still lives in an old wada. In his eighties now, he took time out to speak to Velly Thevar about the evolution of Girangaon in Mumbai.

Daryl D'Monte's pathbreaking investigative book *Ripping the Fabric: The Decline of Mumbai and Its Mills* was an amazing source of information on the unholy nexus of mill owners-government-gangsters.

Rajan's interview is extracted from an exclusive by Harinder Baweja, published in *India Today*, 31 January 1996.

Insights and perspectives on the politics of the Shiv Sena vis-à-vis gangsters like Arun Gawli and Amar Naik emerged through extensive interviews with Bhau Torsekar, the former editor of *Marmik*, the Shiv Sena weekly.

The late Bal Thackeray's decisive stance on Gawli was gathered from opinion columns by Varsha Bhosale, who quoted from a *Saamna* editorial: http://www.rediff.com/news/sep/12varsha.htm 'Swimming with the Sharks', commentary by Varsha Bhosale.

Ashwin Naik's interview, 'The Reluctant Gangster' by Somnath Batabyal, appeared in *The Week* magazine.

Information on Ashwin Naik and his life in jail was sourced from 'The Heart of Darkness', a story on Tihar jail in the Sunday edition of *The Telegraph*, 17 March 2013. Velly Thevar interviewed him for the story.

Many of the incidents in this book were witnessed and reported by me while I was on the crime beat for the *Indian Express* and *Mid Day*

I have also referred to other newspapers including the *Times of India*, the *Hindustan Times*, *Mumbai Mirror*, *DNA* and websites including Rediff.com.